New Dramaturgy

Katalin Trencsényi is a London-based dramaturg. She gained her PhD at the Eötvös Loránd University, Budapest, Hungary. As a freelance dramaturg, she has worked with the National Theatre, the Royal Court Theatre, Deafinitely Theatre, Corali Dance Company and Company of Angels among others. From 2010 to 2012 she served as president of the Dramaturgs' Network. For her research on contemporary dramaturgical practices, she was a recipient of the Literary Managers and Dramaturgs of the Americas' Dramaturg Driven Grant.

Bernadette Cochrane is a lecturer, dramaturg and director based in both Australia and the United Kingdom. She completed her PhD at the University of Queensland. As a freelance director and dramaturg she has worked for several independent companies in both Australia and the United Kingdom. She co-convenes the Translation, Adaptation and Dramaturgy Working Group of the International Federation of Theatre Research and edited a special issue of *Journal of Adaptation in Film and Performance* which focused on the work of the IFTR's Translation, Adaptation and Dramaturgy Working Group (2011, Vol. 4 No. 3).

This book was supported by:
dramaturgs'network

Also available from Bloomsbury Methuen Drama

Affective Performance and Cognitive Science
Edited by Nicola Shaughnessy

Postdramatic Theatre and the Political
Edited by Karen Jürs-Munby, Jerome Carroll and Steve Giles

Theatre in Pieces
Edited by Anna Furse

Theatre in the Expanded Field
Alan Read

New Dramaturgy

International Perspectives on
Theory and Practice

Edited by
Katalin Trencsényi and Bernadette Cochrane

Bloomsbury Methuen Drama
An imprint of Bloomsbury Publishing Plc

B L O O M S B U R Y
LONDON • NEW DELHI • NEW YORK • SYDNEY

Bloomsbury Methuen Drama
An imprint of Bloomsbury Publishing Plc

Imprint previously known as Methuen Drama

50 Bedford Square	1385 Broadway
London	New York
WC1B 3DP	NY 10018
UK	USA

www.bloomsbury.com

**BLOOMSBURY, METHUEN DRAMA and the Diana logo
are trademarks of Bloomsbury Publishing Plc**

First published 2014
Reprinted 2014

British Library Cataloguing-in-Publication Data
A catalogue record for this book is available from the British Library.

ISBN: HB: 978-1-4081-7709-9
PB: 978-1-4081-7708-2
ePDF: 978-1-4081-7711-2
ePUB: 978-1-4081-7710-5

Library of Congress Cataloging-in-Publication Data
A catalog record for this book is available from the Library of Congress.

Typeset by Deanta Global Publishing Services, Chennai, India
Printed and bound in Great Britain

To the memory of Marianne Van Kerkhoven (1946–2013)

Contents

List of Illustrations

Foreword

New dramaturgy: A post-mimetic, intercultural, process-conscious paradigm

Katalin Trencsényi and Bernadette Cochrane

The term *new dramaturgy* is deceptive in its auto-descriptive simplicity. New dramaturgy is suggestive of expansion and reinvigoration but, as a description, it lacks exactness. It implies a demarcation between and a differentiation from an 'old' (traditional) dramaturgy. The term suggests change but does not identify the nature of that change. In fact, 'new' could be easily replaced by words such as 'open',[1] 'expanded',[2] 'contemporary',[3] 'slow',[4] 'porous'[5] or even 'postdramatic'.[6] The adjectival accretions have been accompanied by the emergence of new terms such as dance dramaturgy, visual dramaturgy, new media dramaturgy and neologisms such as mediaturgy. These articulations signal the need for a vocabulary with which to express the fundamental shift in the dramaturgical landscape.

Dramaturgy, having been freed from its historical association with Aristotelian poetics or considered only as an attribute of a dramatic text and/or textual analysis, gradually reconfigured itself by the late twentieth century, and has become synonymous with the totality of the performance-making process. Dramaturgy is now considered to be the inner flow of a dynamic system. With new strands of dramaturgical work (devised theatre, dance, new-circus, performance art etc.) emerging, new material with which to work (gained from improvisation, chance, interdisciplinary stimuli or new media), and changing relationships with both space and audiences – the practice has not only expanded, but it has also been transformed.

The term *new dramaturgy* is a collective noun. New dramaturgy does not replace traditional dramaturgy; it incorporates it into a wider paradigm. The paradigm of new dramaturgy is not a stable one; it acknowledges the multitude of theories and aesthetics, and the diversity of practices (some sympathetic, others clashing) that coexist within our expanded contemporary theatre, dance and performance field. These ideas inform the way we think about theatre and the way we make theatre today – regardless of genre or location. They are in continuous dialogue and interaction with one another, and are in constant motion. The reason that these, sometimes contradictory, ideas and practices deserve a collective noun is that they share three characteristics: they are *post-mimetic*, they embrace *interculturalism* and they are *process-conscious*.

We understand by 'post-mimetic' that the work acknowledges and recognizes the decline of mimesis as the dominant dramatic model and, by extension, the decline of representational theatre culture. This acknowledgement doesn't necessarily mean refusal, or the absence of representation, nevertheless, it acknowledges a distancing (sometimes melancholic, sometimes ironic) from the mimetic theatre tradition.

By 'interculturalism' we understand that we no longer live in a monolithic culture, but are surrounded by multiple value systems and cultures which are often intertwined, and between which we negotiate; and this is reflected in the processes and the products of theatre-making. We include in our definition of interculturalism the increased hermeneutic negotiations between the cultures of various periods or genres. We consider interdisciplinarity as being part of interculturalism – as it is an exchange between different knowledge systems and the cultures of those self-same knowledge systems. Within the paradigm of new dramaturgy, the traditional hermeneutic action of understanding and interpreting a text has expanded to understanding, interpreting and negotiating between different cultural systems.

Finally, by being 'process-conscious' we understand that when creating a piece of theatre, the way it is made, the process's ethics, aesthetics, ecology etc., become dramaturgical concerns, as they inform and shape the materiality of the production.

These three characteristics of new dramaturgy affect the role of the dramaturg. The dramaturg is no longer a critic or a 'third eye' in these processes, brought in during the later stages of the work. The 'new dramaturg' is a curator and a facilitator who helps with respectful negotiating between different cultural values, and supports interweaving of various systems. In order to help develop the architecture and aesthetics of the work unique to the given production, the dramaturg brings to the company's attention the way(s) they've chosen to work by articulating, challenging, or, at times, disrupting the creative process(es).

The place where the dramaturg stands in relation to the performance process has changed too. Compared with traditional dramaturgical roles, the 'new dramaturg' is nearer to the centre of creation; sometimes so near that the role itself dissolves and is taken on by the company.

The term new dramaturgy was introduced by Marianne Van Kerkhoven, arising from the realization that in many countries a form of theatre is being produced which answers to paradigms other than the traditional (reflected significantly in the play's dramaturgy), and the realization that there was no terminology available to describe those new paradigms in all their aspects.[7]

Van Kerkhoven and her colleagues' first attempt at demarcating and describing this new realization at the 1993 Amsterdam conference[8] was followed by a special issue of *Theaterschrift*, entitled *On dramaturgy*.[9] The volume began to establish a new theoretical and critical discourse in its attempt to define, clarify and better understand this emerging paradigm of (post)modern theatre-making. The 'Encyclopaedia' section of the volume defined new dramaturgy thus: 'in the modern theatre dramaturgy revolves in a conceptual sphere between the aesthetic categories, social relations, and philosophical functions of the performance itself.'[10]

In Van Kerkhoven's understanding new dramaturgy is referred to as a process-oriented method of working, a 'quest for possible understanding', where:

> the meaning, the intentions, the form and the substance of a play arise during the working process. In this case dramaturgy is no longer a means of bringing out the structure of the meaning of the world in a

play, but (a quest for) a provisional or possible arrangement which the artist imposes on those elements he gathers from a reality that appears to him chaotic. In this kind of world picture, causality and linearity lose their value, storyline and psychologically explicable characters are put at risk, there is no longer a hierarchy amongst the artistic building blocks used...[11]

The discourse continued at laboratories, for instance, *SARMA* (established in 2000 by Myriam Van Imschoot and Jeroen Peters, in Brussels) and *The Dramaturgies Project* (co-founded by Peter Eckersall, Paul Monaghan and Melanie Beddie in Melbourne 2001). It was taken up at various conferences, for example, *Conversations on Choreography* (1999, an itinerant conference that took place in Amsterdam, Barcelona and Cork) discussing the role of the dance dramaturg; or *European Dramaturgy in the 21st Century* (2007, Frankfurt am Main) interrogating 'contemporary dramaturgy as an expanding field of tasks and skills, challenges and strategies'.[12] The subject was further explored at the *Australian Theatre Forum* (Melbourne, 2009) thinking about the changing attitudes to dramaturgical practice and the future of performance in Australia; *The International Seminar on New Dramaturgies* (Murcia, 2009), that discussed 'how the concept of dramaturgy is understood from other disciplines of knowledge';[13] *Dance Dramaturgy: Catalyst, Perspective, Memory* (York [CAN] and Toronto, 2011) that for the first time in North America, brought together 'an international body of scholars and artists to discuss the growing impact of the discipline, history and potential of dance dramaturgy'.[14] It was also debated at *The Birth of New Media Dramaturgy* (Berlin, 2013) investigating a 'new interwoven approach to understanding composition and representation in performance'.[15] New dramaturgy was also discussed in academic journals, including the *On Dramaturgy* issue of *Performance Research* (2009).[16]

Another milestone in the conversation was the Cathy Turner and Synne K. Behrndt edited special issue of *Contemporary Theatre Research*, entitled *New Dramaturgies*.[17] This volume acknowledged this 'increasingly significant field',[18] and investigated what 'new dramaturgies' may mean in a British context. The starting point of the volume was an understanding of dramaturgy 'as a critical engagement with the processes and architectonics of making and articulating performance'.[19] The plurality of the title suggests the editors' recognition of the phenomenon being broader and more complex than would fit comfortably within the remit of a single theory. Moreover, the issue argued that 'dramaturgy must also be capable of development and expansion'.[20] As the volume's main focus was the United Kingdom, it brought an element of freshness to the discourse, since the term has not yet been fully settled in the British theatrical vocabulary. It allowed, therefore, more room for both new perspectives and flexibilities.

New Dramaturgy: International Perspectives on Theory and Practice continues this conversation. The genesis of the book lies with the *d'n café*, which is an ongoing series of conversations organized by the *Dramaturgs' Network*. With no fixed address, the *d'n café* is a conceptual space for theatre practitioners to meet, talk and reflect on practice. Established by dramaturgs Emma Purvis and Katalin Trencsényi in 2010, the *d'n café* is driven by the desire of British practitioners to discuss the changes and expansion of the dramaturgical field in an open forum format.

Instead of documenting past *d'n cafés*, however, the editors of this volume have sought to widen the scope of the conversation again, and shift it from regional considerations to a more global perspective. The collection, drawing on contributors from four continents, offers diverse viewpoints on dramaturgical practices in the first decades of the twenty-first century. Embedded throughout this geopolitical variety are the notions of the post-mimetic, interculturalism and a consciousness of process.

This volume is divided into five sections, each surveying a different aspect of this new paradigm. The chapters of and the contributors to this book have been selected carefully in order to engage in a dialogue with one another; the resultant resonances, references and debates are the consequence of a (process-)conscious editorial approach.

In the first part of the book, entitled *Towards a New Theory*, we attempt to see what theories emerge to describe the phenomenon. This section does not attempt to give one answer to the question; in fact it embraces debates and controversy. In the first of three chapters, French theorist and dramaturg **Joseph Danan** discusses the 'crisis of representation'[21] and the dissolving role of the director, arguing that the twentieth century's paradigm of 'art in two steps' (whereby 'the author writes a play, the director "gets hold of it", and puts it on'[22]) has been replaced in the twenty-first century by the realisation of Artaud's utopia of the 'single Creator'. The study examines the attendant dramaturgical implications of this shift for writing, for the performance-maker and for the audience. The second, a collaborative article by **Peter Eckersall, Paul Monaghan** and **Melanie Beddie,** examines the development of dramaturgical practices in the Australian performing arts over the last decade through the case study of *The Dramaturgies Project*, 'that explored the themes of collaboration, diversity and pedagogy as a way of fostering an ecological model for dramaturgical practice in the new century'.[23] The final chapter, by British composer **Alan Lawrence**, somewhat controversially, suggests that the proliferation of terminology associated with new and extended dramaturgical thinking is unnecessary; instead, he introduces an alternative approach, identifying the commonalities of structure that attend all elements of theatre.

The following section, entitled *Text*, investigates an important question: how do we relate to the text-based theatre in postdramatic times? It explores how new dramaturgy has changed our approach to text-based work, including the areas of both new writing and production dramaturgy. In the first of three chapters, **Yolanda Ferrato** interviews Brian Quirt, the artistic director of *Nightswimming*, a 'dramaturgical' company that commissions, develops and workshops new Canadian performance. In its focus on the processes and materials of both performance-generation and story-telling, one again encounters notions of fragmentation, exploration, collaboration and porosity. In many ways, at the core of *Nightswimming* is a commitment to slow dramaturgy. The second contribution is a complex case study by **Duška**

Radosavljević, describing her work as dramaturg on *Imagining O* with the director of the production Richard Schechner. The chapter examines the cultural exchange between theatre studies and performance studies as it relates the role of the contemporary dramaturg in a globalized context. It describes how the dramaturg challenged and transformed the mundane task of research into 'performed dramaturgy' by making her 'live programme notes' part of the performance. The final chapter consists of theorist and dramaturg **Gad Kaynar** in conversation with Ruth Kanner, an Israeli creator of experimental theatre. The chapter discusses her company's work, which includes the re-examination of Israeli hegemonic narratives, performed through literary and documentary texts, with the aim of creating innovative storytelling theatre. It provides an insight into their search for a local theatrical language, interweaving storytelling, physical theatre and visual imagery, and employing disturbances and distortions in order to renew the language of contemporary storytelling.

Devising considers a particularly topical concern – the application of current dramaturgical thinking within devised practice. The section demonstrates how the imperatives of new dramaturgy are a key factor within, and intrinsic to the production of new work. It takes up some of the themes started in *Text*, thereby suggesting that the division between text-based and devised work is artificial. The first chapter, by British lecturer **Jackie Smart**, focuses on the dramaturgy of the devising process. By probing the notion of 'playful openness', it explores some of the 'implications of the interpersonal and interactive aspects of devising processes in the context of perspectives on the emotion-cognition relationship drawn from neuroscience and psychology.'[24] The 'fuzzy line' between dramaturgical research and free association emerges in **Ana Pais**'s interview with John Collins, artistic director and founder of the American company, *Elevator Repair Service*. Eclectic in their assemblage of materials, and utilizing the chaos of colliding ideas, Collins emphasizes the laboratory nature of the development process. The third chapter is a study by **Alex Mermikides**, which addresses the complementarity of science and art. Interestingly, the project, entitled

Bloodlines, which employed postdramatic and interdisciplinary devising strategies in the theatrical realization of biomedical science, sometimes resulted in dramaturgies more aligned to those of the so-called dramatic tradition.

The following section, *Dance*, investigates an emergent strand of new dramaturgy. Dance dramaturgy may be a new strand, but its contribution to contemporary dramaturgical articulations and understandings figures large in today's evolving dramaturgical field. Through three case studies, the section explores the ever-expanding, shape-shifting boundaries of the dramaturg's role in relation to dance. The first case study by **Rachael Swain** exposes some of the functions of dramaturgy in the work of *Marrugeku*, an intercultural dance theatre company working at the nexus of Indigenous and non-Indigenous experience in remote communities in the far north of Western Australia. While one again encounters the notion of slow dramaturgy, one also encounters the dramaturgy of loss. In the second case study, British dramaturg **Lou Cope** and Flemish choreographer **Koen Augustijnen** reflect on their production of A*u-delà* for *les ballets C de la B*. In this collaborative reflection, they offer insights into not just the relationship between dramaturg and choreographer, but also into the very nature of the various phases of the process of dance dramaturgy. The third chapter is also an act of remembering. Here Flemish dramaturg **Guy Cools** actively engages with the notion of subjective memory to discuss the dramaturg being both within the creative process and being an external observer of the creative process. Through this act of 're-membering' the creation of *zero degrees*, a collaboration between Akram Khan, Sidi Larbi Cherkaoui, Antony Gormley and Nitin Sawhney seven years after it took place, Cools reveals some of his 'insights and fundamental beliefs about dance dramaturgy as a creative practice'.[25]

Spectatorship examines the dialogues and relationships between the dramaturg and the spectator across a range of performance environments – this is another area that has undergone significant dramaturgical changes in recent decades. The section begins with a chapter on site-specificity by **Cathy Turner**, a British theoretician. It proposes and unpicks the metaphor of 'porous dramaturgy', then 'points to a number of dramaturgical concerns in relation to the ethical, political and spatial implications of site-specific work'.[26] The second contribution turns to the audience reception and the dramaturg. In his case study, director **Pedro Ilgenfritz**, conceives 'dramaturgical analysis as being a dialogue between author and audience'; modelling his approach on the work of Bertolt Brecht's dialectical theatre, the concept of perverted logic and the logic of clowns. Through consideration of the New Zealand-Brazilian production of *Alfonsina*, Ilgenfritz demonstrates how the audience reception shaped the development of the piece. In the final chapter of the collection, German theoretician **Peter M. Boenisch** introduces the notion of 'relational dramaturgy' in order to articulate the dramaturgic approach towards a crucial experiential gap involved in the activity of spectating a theatre performance. Applying a Lacanian psychoanalytic perspective, this uncanny double experience of 'the audience watching itself watching' is outlined, and explored in the context of three performance instances, the Toneelgroep's *Roman Tragedies*, Shunt's *Money* and Zecora Ura's *Hotel Medea*.

While the responses are notionally grouped under the rubrics of 'theory', 'text', 'devising', 'dance' and 'spectatorship', what becomes apparent is that these are flexible divisions. It is this provisionality, which gives rise to new dramaturgy as being both inherently interdisciplinary and intercultural. Singly or collectively, however, they are the key theatrical issues of our times.

If new dramaturgy can be characterized as being multi-perspectival, provisional, non-hierarchical and enquiring, then so too can *New Dramaturgy: International Perspectives on Theory and Practice*. The richness offered by both new dramaturgy and by the collection has been constructed around notions of enquiry. The collection questions what is understood by the term new dramaturgy, it asks what current practices are, and it queries the status of the dramaturgical shift across different countries. The responses to these questions come from those who do not accept a division between 'industry' and 'academy'. The contributors differ in age, background, approach and cultural orientation. Moreover, their responses are frequently at odds with each other. It is a diverse collection but it is one that instantiates the very notion of plurality that is at the core of new dramaturgy.

References

Eckersall, Peter. 'Towards an Expanded Dramaturgical Practice: A Report on The Dramaturgy and Cultural Intervention Project'. *Theatre Research International* 31.3 (2006), pp. 283–97.

Eckersall, Peter and Paterson, E. 'Slow Dramaturgy: Renegotiating Politics and Staging the Everyday'. *Australasian Drama Studies* 58 (2011), pp. 178–92.

Gritzner, Karoline, Primavesi, Patrick and Roms, Heike. 'On Dramaturgy. Editorial'. *Performance Research, On Dramaturgy* 14.3 (2009), pp. 1–2.

Lehmann, Hans-Thies. *Postdramatic Theatre*. Trans. Karen Jürs-Munby. Abingdon: Routledge, 2006.

Lehmann, Hans-Thies and Primavesi, Patrick. 'Dramaturgy on Shifting Grounds'. *Performance Research, On Dramaturgy* 14.3 (2009), pp. 3–6.

Staudohar, Irena. 'Encyclopaedia, "New dramaturgy"'. *Theaterschrift, On dramaturgy* 5–6 (1994), pp. 187–9.

Turner, Cathy. 'Porous Dramaturgy: "Togetherness" and Community in the Structure of the Artwork', 1 November 2012. http://expandeddramaturgies. com/porous - dramaturgy - togetherness – and community – in – the – structure – of – the – artwork (Accessed: 25 June 2013).

Turner, Cathy and Behrndt, Synne K., eds. 'Editorial'. *Contemporary Theatre Research, New Dramaturgies* 20.2 (2010), pp. 145–8.

Van Kerkhoven, Marianne. 'Le processus dramaturgique'. *Nouvelles de Danse, Dossier Danse et Dramaturgie*, nr. 31 (1997), pp. 18–25.

—'On dramaturgy'. *Theaterschrift, On dramaturgy* 5–6 (1994), pp. 8–34.

Acknowledgements

The editors would like to express their gratitude for the support, advice and dedication of colleagues and friends who helped their work immensely: *Ada Denise Baptista, Annie Birch, Peter M. Boenisch, Alyson Campbell, Matt Delbridge, Peter Eckersall, Hilary Emmett, Wieke Eringa, Veronica Kelly, DD Kugler, Elizabeth Langley, Mark Lord, Alex Mermikides, Andrea Pelegri Kristić, Maggie Philips, Emma Purvis, Brian Quirt, Kurt Taroff, Sarah Thomasson, Nick Tomalin, Joanne Tompkins, Cathy Turner, Carole-Anne Upton, Stuart Young and all the contributors.*

Part One

Towards a New Theory

Dramaturgy in 'Postdramatic' Times

Joseph Danan

*Translation by Ada Denise Bautista, Andrea Pelegri Kristić
and Carole-Anne Upton*

A change is taking place – a radical transformation of the theatre and our relationship with the stage; a phenomenon at least as important as the rise of the director at the end of the nineteenth century. Hans-Thies Lehmann named this phenomenon 'postdramatic theatre',[1] although the expression itself is debatable, since the emergent theatre forms that we are seeing do not necessarily dispense with drama; on the contrary, they give rise to new forms of dramaticity which need to be identified and named.

What is the nature of this radical change? There has been an explosion in theatre and it is certainly true that this explosion has caused a rupture with the dramatic. A good number of theatre productions nowadays are not based on any pre-existing dramatic work and therefore have no call for a director to *stage* the piece. There is a widespread preference for non-dramatic texts (prose texts and various kinds of material ranging from philosophical or scientific essays to postcards, from poems to newspaper articles or historical documents); for writing developed from the stage (whether authored by a single person or a group); for interdisciplinarity, bringing together different languages – of video, dance, live music, circus … – which reduce the text to just one element among others, and no longer the womblike origin of the whole show (by which I mean its capacity to *exist as the source* but also to engender an indefinite number of possible mise-en-scènes). More fundamentally the very nature of representation is transformed. In particular, the influence of performance art has shaken *mimesis*, the bedrock of western theatre from Aristotle onwards.

'Theatre is fake', says Marina Abramović, 'there is a black box, you pay for a ticket, and you sit in the dark and see somebody playing somebody else's life. The knife is not real, the blood is not real, and the emotions are not real. Performance is just the opposite: the knife is real, the blood is real, and the emotions are real. It's a very different concept. It's about true reality.'[2] Yet, the contemporary stage constantly brings this opposition into play, searching not for the 'effect of the real' (i.e. illusion) but for what I would call the 'real effect'. And so by opposition with representation we prefer *presentation*,[3] giving full weight and value to the present tense of the act of theatre, to presence. This means: a theatrical scene that exists in its own right, in the here and now of the representation (or of the presentation), without seeking to evoke an elsewhere (another time, another place). The actor is also now before us in his own right: a performer who, more and more frequently, erases the concept of character.

'These boards don't signify a world. They are part of the world. These boards exist for us to stand on. ... There is no mirage./This stage represents nothing. ... Here you are not experiencing a time that pretends to be another time.'[4] The 'non-illusionist theatre',[5] the theatre without *mimesis*, is where the contemporary creative approach to the stage today seems to be heading, ever since Peter Handke's manifesto play *Publikumsbeschimpfung* [*Offending the Audience*] (1966), in which, instead of characters, 'four actors', share out unattributed lines.

In a scene from Romeo Castellucci's *Inferno*,[6] I find the perfect example of this theatre. People who are certainly not characters and can hardly be called actors (dancers, children and many extras mix in with a small professional cast), one after the other, walk towards the audience to offer them their faces and their bodies. Pure theatre of presentation and of presence, where nothing is represented, nothing but this ray of humanity, presenting itself on the stage – and by metonymy, if you like, humanity.[7] For these theatre forms exclude neither symbol nor metaphor, but it is as if these things come later, like a second crop to be harvested by the spectator, who is captured above all by the power of the present moment.

It's not a 'deliberate' symbol, as Maeterlinck says, opposing it to a symbol which 'would take shape without the poet's knowledge ... and would almost always extend beyond the limits of his thought'. 'I do not believe', he goes on to say, 'that a viable work can ever be born from a symbol; but the symbol is always born from the work, if the latter is viable.'[8]

In another emblematic scene from *Inferno*, at the beginning of the show, Castellucci comes downstage and announces to the audience: 'My name is Romeo Castellucci.' He is then kitted out in full view with a protective harness, before facing an attack by angry dogs who force him to the ground. In the sequence that follows, an acrobat climbs up the facade of the Palais des Papes, in Avignon, for whose space (the Cour d'Honneur) the show was conceived. The attack by the dogs was real, Castellucci was not playing any character, and the climbing of the wall was a real action, carried out in real time, which could not be compressed. The density of the real in these two actions saturated the space-time of representation, to the point where nothing else could be perceived, while they were being carried out.

In the same show, children could be seen playing in a big glass cube, as if in a nursery, unaware of the audience watching them, and this was like a fragment lifted from the real world, and in the absence of any intermediary sign, set down on the stage just as it was, as in a collage.

The power of the moment. The power of crude reality. The power of the living, of 'the actor [who] does not repeat the same gestures twice'.[9] This is precisely Artaud's utopia, which seems to be striving for embodiment now, at the beginning of the twenty-first century, in productions like this.[10]

These theatre forms are dissolving the role of the director. In his relationship (constructive as well as conflictual) with that of the author (meaning the playwright), the director has stood as the cornerstone of the theatrical art of the twentieth century, which relied upon this duality, or this coupling: the author writes a play, the director, 'gets hold of it', and puts it on. It was the paradigm of the theatre as 'art in two steps'.[11] Craig and Artaud, those great 'reformers' of the theatre, had, since the early decades of the twentieth century, been calling for another figure, at that time still utopian, that of the 'single Creator' as Artaud calls it, to merge the 'old duality'.[12] It is this figure who is embodied today, in the guise either of total creator (Castellucci, credited on *Inferno* for 'mise-en-scène', scenography, lighting, costumes and, with Cindy Van Acker, choreography) or ensemble group (in France, companies like D'ores et déjà and Les Chiens de Navarre).

Dramaturgy is inevitably affected. Obviously in the original sense of the word, as 'the art of constructing a play' will need to be replaced by 'the art of constructing a show'. The meaning might easily dissolve into the later definition, since it is no longer a question, in this type of process of transferring to the stage a play that has been written in advance.[13]

In fact, the change is even more fundamental. Dramaturgy provided a framework through which the meaning of a piece could be played out. The theatrical art of the twentieth century was not only structured by the dyad of author-director, or, to make it less personal, by the relationship between a play and its mise-en-scène, but by a triad involving the play, the mise-en-scène and the dramaturgy. The collapse involves the equal and mutual dissolution of all three elements of the triad. And how could it be otherwise? Dramaturgy cannot be separated from playwriting or mise-en-scène, because it is the process which crosses between the one and the other, and connects them both.

In terms of 'organising the action', dramaturgy was linked to the story (*la fable*), which the twentieth century has seen gradually crumble away – in other words, to action in its mimetic dimension. This was the basis of dramaturgy. This culminated with Brecht, whose 'epic' theatre, far from constituting the opposite of the dramatic, was its ultimate realization. It was in the 1970s, with linguistics and humanities at their peak, that we took full measure of the theatre's semiologic dimension. Everything was a sign and a system of signs: the play itself and, even more so, the mise-en-scène. Dramaturgy became the agent of this system. Everything must signify something. The spectator was a decipherer of signs, a decoder.

This is perhaps the most radical change. The spectator is no longer someone who, by means of more or less active contemplation, seeks to understand the work. Torn away from the realm of meaning (which can be destabilizing), the spectator is invited to have an experience.

And the relationship in which he is to engage with the theatrical performance is not fundamentally different from how he experiences other events in his life. Is this not how we are to make sense of the face-to-face opening of *Inferno* mentioned previously? As a kind of encounter, in the full sense of the word, between stage and audience. The encounter as event, symbolized a little later in the show by a canopy being pulled from off the stage and spread over the heads of the entire audience. The whole show: a route through an experience. The more securely a theatrical performance can establish a strong relationship with the spectator, the greater the chance of it 'making sense' to him, but later on in his life, through the conscious and unconscious workings of his memory, just as an event he has lived through will eventually take its place in a chain of significance, charged with meaning – unstable, changing over the years. 'In the midway of this our mortal life,/I found me in a gloomy wood, astray':[14] these are the first words of Dante's *Divine Comedy*. Art takes on life.

*

So that is my description of the theatrical landscape, in broad outline. An archipelago of ever-shifting forms, criss-crossed by multiple currents, from which I see two questions emerge: What is happening to dramaturgy today, in relation to the staging of pre-existing playscripts? What is happening to dramatic writing? We suppose that in neither case can the transformations of the theatrical landscape leave the practice unaffected.

However different the practices are, they coexist within this landscape because they are of the same era. The borders between them are necessarily porous. In practical terms, a classical or contemporary play cannot be staged outside of the context I have just described. This has implications for the mise-en-scène. It will also have implications for dramaturgy, for in its absence, only the most superficial aspects of the new stage forms will take hold. Blind and uncontrolled practices, as Bernard Dort said.[15]

Not that dramaturgy has to provide a 'reading' of the play, as was expected in the 1970s. Such an interpretation would inevitably be reductive with regard to all the possibilities inherent in theatrical performance as lived experience. Once the meaning of events is prescribed for you, there can be no further possibility of personal experience. But somewhere between the transformation of a playscript into a 'raw material'[16] – setting aside any internal dramaturgy (in sense one) that might set it within its historical context – and providing a 'framework for interpretation', there should still be room for an open and sensitive dramaturgy, defining the forces at play in the work and creating *the conditions for the experience*.

The way is narrow. What's to be done with characters when we don't believe in character anymore and we want to see a performer accomplishing a series of actions that refer only to themselves, without *mimesis*? What's to be done with narration when the story is clearly no longer the priority for the person on stage, who seems to be improvising? Then we stop staging *Andromaque* or *Romeo and Juliet* or even *The Seagull*. But if we still want to put them on – and the least we can do is ask ourselves why – we must find in the plays that which will resonate in the language of the contemporary stage, and can take its place there. Strip away the character to reveal the actor as a human being, in his existential 'nakedness',[17] unconstructed. Don't search to create 'another world' but trust in this one, in the material presence of the stage. Indeed, these are questions for the director concerning mise-en-scène and acting, but it is for dramaturgy to establish what is at stake in the experience: first for the actors, who must live it on stage, so that others should have the chance to live the same experience in the auditorium. This was how, in 2004, I approached the dramaturgical work on *When We Dead Awaken* by Henrik Ibsen, staged by Alain Bézu.[18] Here is what I wrote at the time, in some dramaturgical notes intended for the director:

> We have to create a device for thought. This device includes the spectator. Faced with the experimental box, each spectator must decide upon the undecidable, as in the experiment with Schrödinger's cat –

whether the cat is dead or alive, which is not altogether unrelated to *When We Dead Awaken*. This is deliberate, it's a play which goes direct to the heart of what matters: life and death – are we dead or alive?

What this means, for the mise-en-scène, is that the signs, the meaning must be fixed as little as possible. Make people feel it. Jean-Luc Nancy speaks of the 'experience of the sense'. It's exactly that: for the actors (and everyone involved in the production) and for the audience alike.

What happens *when we dead awaken*? 'We', meaning all those participating in the experience: everyone alive, including the audience. We will feel it together, (each for himself, in solitude: there will be no communion, this is not a Mass), for as long as the experience lasts – or maybe, to be precise, over a series of experiences.

For this awakening doesn't occur in one go. The change of state keeps on happening, in every conceivable direction. Strangely it seems that there are more than two possible. In any case, this is not resurrection in the Christian sense (the very fact that the transition happens more than once should dispel any religious meaning).

...

The spectator (mentally) projects himself into the scene of the experience, because it is his own life, distilled to its most essential experience that he is asked to bring to bear. Is he dead, is he alive? Each spectator must decide for himself, if he can.

...

The least possible effect of characterisation. Because it's a play with the least possible drama and one which brings us closer to 'presentation' than 'representation'. Hence its modernity.

There is no drama between Rubek and Maja. Maja runs away and gets closer to Ufheim. Rubek lets her go. There is (almost) no drama between Rubek and Irene either. There is a series of movements which resolves itself in one big movement which brings them closer together and, leads them both closer to death.[19]

All four are at the closest point to life. To the experience (the feeling) of life. And to reflecting on their lives – but this is secondary to what they are actually experiencing in the moment.

This experience of life, this doubt (this *restlessness*) that permanently lingers is what makes the play more like a 'presentation'. For the actors, there is a sense of being as close as possible to this life, in the nakedness of the moment, sharing it with the audience.

Evidently, *When We Dead Awaken* belongs to the new paradigm of drama that Jean-Pierre Sarrazac calls the 'drama-of-life', as opposed to the 'drama-in-life': a kind of drama reduced to the essential, the drama of a whole life. Quoting Maeterlinck: 'It is no longer a violent, exceptional moment of life that passes before our eyes—it is life itself.'[20] However, the following year, when Alain Bézu and I started work on *L'Illusion comique* by Corneille, we were beset by similar questions:

Calling everything theatre does not resolve anything, for we could just as easily call everything real life. Everything appears to be real life and indeed it is, since these are living actors who are sharing time and space with us for the duration of the performance. It is a shared experience, in which Pridamant is both victim and beneficiary, guinea pig and privileged witness, with an enviable faith in everything he sees (a level of trust that we will never achieve ourselves).

The major challenge for the staging could very well be how to make the audience share (as far as possible) this same degree of faith.[21]

Even if in certain respects *L'Illusion comique* might be regarded as a 'drama-of-life' ahead of its time (the drama of Pridamant, searching for time as well as for his lost son), it also contains some fragments of a 'drama-in-life' (the play within a play) which date it historically and pose some difficulty for the dramaturg and for the director who must, by identifying its potential for '*presentation* before representation', find the spark in this play for the contemporary spectator, while acknowledging that the play was not written yesterday – and placing before his eyes an outdated and improbable fiction and characters, effectively creating a *mise en abyme* to reflect (and test) his own incredulity. *L'Illusion comique* is not a play written for the postdramatic stage. In fact it is quite the opposite. And unless the historical nature of the play (a reflection on drama and illusion) is held in tension with the nature of audiences at the beginning of the twenty-first century, from a very different theatre context, it will simply never work.

What I have just expressed with reference to the exemplary case of *L'Illusion comique* (exemplary because of the nature of the play), should, I think, apply to any dramaturgical process today. This has always been the case (since the invention of mise-en-scène), for delivering a play to spectators who are our contemporaries has always meant reading it for our times – except that the rupture created by the invention of mise-en-scène has since been followed by a greater one, as discussed above: more than a rupture, this is a fault line, opening up a wide gulf.

It seems that since about 2010, European productions of pre-scripted plays, and especially of the classics, have situated themselves within this great gulf. Let us recall for example how Thomas Ostermeier places us on a level with Ibsen's *Hedda Gabler*:[22] actualizing the very base of the play which builds on the rewrite provided by Marius von Mayenburg's translation. The dramaturgy here is inseparable from the mise-en-scène: in the direction of the actors who are not playing composed characters; the modern costume; the stage design revealing the wings by means of video surveillance; the brief utilization of filmed images at the beginning of each act to 'enter into this world' which turns out to be our own ... The most distinctive effect is the replacement of Løvborg's manuscript that Hedda throws into the flames with an eminently powerful *performative* act: the actual and complete destruction of a laptop with a hammer. An action so violent in its materiality and in its substance that it puts us, the audience, within the same experience without ignoring or denying the dramaturgical structure of the play.

*

The same problem of alignment with the contemporary stage is sharply felt by the playwright. Certainly he can, as before, delegate the problem to the 'second step' of the theatrical process, by passing it on to the director. Such a position is hardly viable nowadays, firstly because, as explained already, the theatre is less and less an art in a 'two steps' and secondly the pairing of playwright and director no longer occupies the dominant position that it held in the twentieth century.

Today's playwright is faced with an alternative. The first option is chosen by a growing number of writers, who direct their own work. Sometimes they do it by maintaining the traditional 'two-step process' (first they write a script without thinking necessarily of the staging; *then* they mount the play). Or they may do it by merging the two phases simultaneously, as does Joël Pommerat, who, in his practice dating back almost twenty-five years, has conceived his work as a playwright in no other way:

> I think that today, one can only truly become a theatremaker by binding the process of writing the text very tightly together with the process of the mise-en-scène. I think it's a mistake to think of these two stages as naturally separate from each other.[23]

This theoretical position (supported by a sustained critique by Pommerat of the power of the director throughout the twentieth century), though eliding quite different approaches, can be traced through the creative work of practitioners as diverse as Romeo Castellucci, Robert Lepage, François Tanguy, Angelica Liddell, Rodrigo Garcia and many others. For these authors, the text (often non-dramatic) is only one element (in a variable hierarchy) among all those that make up the theatrical score. Several of them are also visual artists by training, who are situated, explicitly or otherwise, in the lineage of the likes of Robert Wilson or Tadeusz Kantor. This bundle of phenomena (close proximity of writing and stage, non-separation of text and mise-en-scène, the importance of the visual aspect) must affect the nature of the texts that are produced, which *de facto* provides an answer to our question.[24]

The second option is taken by authors (I prefer to say 'theatre writers') who, by choice (sometimes), or of necessity (often), continue to write at a far remove from the stage, producing texts in isolation (many of these are still written, as attested by script reading committees) which then sit waiting to be mounted, and which will often and increasingly lie as texts in waiting, whose union with the stage, no matter how admirable they may be, risks never being consummated.

To conclude, the hypothesis I would like to propose is that these texts must also remain in step with the contemporary theatre, even when they start out as autonomous dramatic writing. We see only too well what no longer fits: stories (*fables*) that are too obvious, a dramatic structure that is too robust (the word 'plot' has practically disappeared from the vocabulary of dramaturgs and writers on contemporary theatre), characters with too much characterization. It is more difficult to pinpoint, not so much what still works (which may become obvious) but why it works. And so much the better: the point here is not to reinstate a norm that disappeared with the birth of modern mise-en-scène – especially since these pieces can be deployed in ways so different as to be considered contradictory, integrating the interdisciplinary aspect of the contemporary stage with the writing, in the service or not of a story (*fable*), and participating, to varying degrees, in the deconstruction of *mimesis*, possibly even to its quasi-eradication. We can see why the very foundations of dramatic art are shaken: if it is a question of creating first and foremost stage actions, which cannot be seen as representing other actions, and which only rarely (if ever) open onto another place, another time, then clearly what we are doing is inventing new forms of dramaticity.

The weakening of character in the course of the twentieth century has been a major symptom of the critique of *mimesis* – or what has been referred to as the 'crisis of representation'.[25] It leads, in a writer like Jon Fosse, to a sketched outline that can be compared, *mutatis mutandis*, (that is, considering that he is very obviously a writer of plays), to what we described earlier in relation to the face-to-face, stage-auditorium encounter in *Inferno*: 'featureless people' – you, me – in the absolutely minimal drama of anybody's life. Hardly a drama, hardly characters.

This weakening of character culminates in works which now seek to present, in the manner of the 'four actors' of *Offending the Audience*, only 'performers' with no identity but their own. No longer even 'figures', but instrumentalists. It is in these terms, for example, that Russian playwright Ivan Viripaev talks about interpreters of his play, *Delhi Dance*:[26] 'This text is not to be "played" but to be "interpreted" like a musical score.'[27] Galin Stoev, who directed it, is even more explicit: 'The actor is not to play the character, but "play upon the character" in the same manner as a musician "plays upon his instrument".[28] Is this purely a declaration of the author's intention (relayed by the director), recommending a way of performing his play? Certainly not: the structure of the piece is entirely defined by this choice, with the interpreters repeating a series of variations from one scene to the next, each one initiating action with a fresh throw of the dice from a given situation.[29]

Sometimes the use of one or more narrator figures (or a presenter, commentator or chorus) comes to replace represented action with the narration of the action in the present tense of the performance. From Daniel Danis[30] to Biljana Srbljanović,[31] there are plenty of examples in contemporary dramatic literature. And to move still further from the dramatic, in the 'plays' of Valère Novarina, behind the profusion of names of pseudo-characters, might we not see merely the presence of the actor-performer struggling with words?

Figure 1 *Sous l'écran silencieux* by Joseph Danan (théâtre des deux rives, Rouen, 2002, dir: Alain Bézu), with Marie Lounici and Frédéric Cherbœuf. Photography: Grégoire Alexandre.

More generally, *mimesis* is brought into question every time the dramaturgical structure of a play demands the completion of any real action on stage that represents only itself: a dance, a 'performance', playing a piece of music. In my play, *Sous l'écran silencieux*, [*Beneath the Silent Screen*]³² it is the act of taking photographs that functions this way, and the photographer's studio provides the scenic space as he shoots his model in the real time of the performance.

But we should also consider specific works such as Martin Crimp's *Attempts on Her Life* (for its systematic destruction of representation) or Sarah Kane's *4.48 Psychosis* (for bringing into play the author's personal life, to the limit), and many others which, in various ways and to varying degrees, might constitute some responses to the upheavals of the stage with which we began this chapter (or, even better, they might form part of those upheavals), testifying to the vitality of writing which still persists in seeking to create, perhaps not dramas, but drama of some kind.

References

Abirached, Robert. *La Crise du personnage dans le théâtre moderne*. Paris: Grasset, 1978.

Artaud, Antonin. *The Theatre and Its Double*. Trans. Victor Corti. Richmond: Oneworld Classics, 2010.

Ayres, Robert. "'The Knife is Real, the Blood is Real, And The Emotions Are Real.'" – Robert Ayres in Conversation with Marina Abramović'. *Sky Filled with Shooting Stars*. 2010. http://www.askyfilledwithshootingstars.com/wordpress/?p=1197 (Accessed: 26 February 2013).

Barbéris, Isabelle. *Théâtres contemporains. Mythes et idéologies*. Paris: PUF, 2010.

Biet, Christian and Frantz, Pierre, eds. 'Le théâtre sans l'illusion'. *Critique* n° 699–700 (août-septembre 2005), pp. 569–71.

Bougnioux, Daniel. *La Crise de la représentation*. Paris: La Découverte, 2006.

Chevallier, Jean-Frédéric. 'Le geste théâtral contemporain: entre présentation et symboles'. *L'Annuaire théâtral. Revue québécoise d'études théâtrales* n° 36 (automne 2004), pp. 27–40.

—'Le geste théâtral contemporain'. *Frictions* n° 10 (automne-hiver 2006), pp. 39–45.

Corneille, Pierre/Danan, Joseph, ed. *L'Illusion comique/Dramaturgies de l'illusion*. Rouen: Publications des Universités de Rouen et du Havre, 2006.

Cousin, Marion. *L'Auteur en scène: Analyse d'un geste théâtral et dramaturgie du texte né de la scène*, doctoral thesis directed by Jean-Pierre Ryngaert, Sorbonne Nouvelle - Paris 3, 2012.

Danan, Joseph. 'Du mouvement comme forme moderne de l'action dans deux pièces d'Ibsen'. *Etudes théâtrales* n° 15–16 (1999), pp. 211–18.

—*Sous l'écran silencieux*. Carnières-Morlanwelz (Belgique): Lansman, 2002.

—*Qu'est-ce que la dramaturgie?*. Paris: Actes Sud - Papiers, 'Apprendre', 2010.

—'Témoins d'une présence'. *Etudes théâtrales* n° 51–2 (2011), pp. 124–8.

—*Entre théâtre et performance: La question du texte*. Paris: Actes Sud - Papiers, 'Apprendre', 2013.

Danis, Daniel. *Terre océane. Roman-dit*. Paris: L'Arche, 2006.

Dante, Alighieri, 'Canto 1' *Divine Comedy, The Vision of Hell*. Trans. Rev. H. F. Cary. Project Gutenberg, 2004. http://www.gutenberg.org/files/8789/8789-h/8789-h.htm#link1 (Accessed: 27 July 2013).

Dort, Bernard. 'L'état d'esprit dramaturgique'. *Théâtre/Public*, n° 67 (janvier-févier 1986), pp. 8–12.

Gouhier, Henri. *Le Théâtre et les arts à deux temps*. Paris: Flammarion, 1989.

Handke, Peter. *Offending the Audience and Self Accusation*. Trans. Michael Roloff. *Plays 1*. London: Methuen & Co, 1971, pp. 8–39.

Huret, Jules. *Enquête sur l'évolution littéraire* (1891). Thot: Vanves, 1982.

Lehmann, Hans-Thies, *Postdramatic Theatre*. Trans. Jürs-Munby, Karen. Oxford and New York: Routledge, 2006.

Maeterlinck, Maurice. 'The Tragical in Daily Life'. *The Treasure of the Humble*. Trans. Alfred Sutro. London: George Allen, 1897, pp. 97–119 (108–9).

Nancy, Jean-Luc. *Le Sens du monde*. Paris: Galilée, 1993.

Pommerat, Joël. *Théâtres en présence*. Paris: Actes Sud - Papiers, 'Apprendre', 2007.

Sarrazac, Jean-Pierre. *Poétique du drame moderne. De Henrik Ibsen à Bernard-Marie Koltès*. Paris: Seuil, 'Poétique', 2012.

Srbljanović, Biljana. *Barbelo, à propos de chiens et d'enfants*. Trans. G. Keller. Paris: L'Arche, 2008.

Viripaev, Ivan. *Danse 'Delhi'*. Trans. T. Moguilevskaia et G. Morel. Paris: Les Solitaires intempestifs, 2010.

Dramaturgy as Ecology

A Report from The Dramaturgies Project

Peter Eckersall, Paul Monaghan and Melanie Beddie

At the inaugural Australian Theatre Forum in Melbourne in 2009, the question of the definition of dramaturgy was fiercely debated. The forum drew more than 200 people from across the spectrum of Australia's national performance scene. In one of the workshops, responses became heated; it was stated that everyone in the creative process contributes to dramaturgy, but not everyone is, or wanted to be known as, a dramaturg. The session broached some timely questions. Dramaturgy as a compositional frame was noted, but the question of who did dramaturgy was unresolved. Why was the collapsible disposition of the dramaturg occurring, and what could we discern about changing attitudes to dramaturgical practices amidst a large, multi-skilled gathering of theatre and performance professionals? The habitual unease about discursive practice broached by some in the forum, who could not see the point of talking about dramaturgy, was matched by a deeper interest in dramaturgical thinking. For some, the discussion risked breaking intuitive processes of creative production; a form of dramaturgy where theoretical arguments are elided in favour of empathic and intuitive processes was promoted. Others, however, defended the idea that dramaturgy as compositional *and* ideological was an essential starting point from which to think creatively around the future of performance in the Australian context. Notwithstanding the diverse tone of the debate, people agreed that dramaturgy has been largely accepted as a methodology in contemporary practice. In fact, one got the sense that *we are all dramaturgs now*; what that means in practical terms, however, is still being resolved.

The authors of this chapter have contributed extensively to these debates in the last decade, in particular through the activities of our workshop-research unit called *The Dramaturgies Project* ('*Dramaturgies*'). In this chapter, we aim to report on three of the most topical aspects of contemporary dramaturgical practice highlighted in the forum: the relative lack of *diversity* in Australian theatre, *collaboration* as dramaturgical practice, and the need to improve dramaturgical *pedagogy*. We explored these themes in our most recent event, 'New Dramaturgies for the Twenty-first Century', through targeted working groups, general discussions and guest presentations.[1] Here we report on that event, and frame the themes of diversity, collaboration and pedagogy within a specifically *ecological* model for dramaturgical practice in the new century.

Founded in 2001, *Dramaturgies* aims to promote dramaturgical awareness in contemporary theatre in Australia, to connect theatre to social and political life, and to broker dramaturgical research nationally and internationally. We define dramaturgical practice as: 'a confluence of literary, spatial, kinaesthetic, and technical practices, worked and woven in the matrix of aesthetic and ideological forces'.[2] Dramaturgy is multifaceted and requires attention to an imaginative complexity, much like what is needed in our everyday discourses and politics, and we believe many artists practise a range of dramaturgical processes as a framework for alternative creative thinking. Hence, rather than offer a single universalizing definition, we aim to discuss what Eckersall calls 'an expanded dramaturgy', a dramaturgy that is unrestricted and that makes connections between theatre and context.[3] To paraphrase a line from Dorothy Hewett's *Labyrinth* ('I must break the glass that reflects the single image'),[4] we need to break the glass that reflects a single image of dramaturgical practice. In this sense, we also agree with Cathy Turner whose recent writing on spatializing dramaturgy views the compositional frame of dramaturgy 'as critically creative, always working itself out, always being redefined by the dynamic connections and exchanges between internal elements and between these and their external contexts.[5] In this chapter we aim to show how these ideas can shape the development of dramaturgical practice in Australia in terms of not only an expanded dramaturgy that recognizes the ecologies of cultural production, but which also encourages and promotes a sustainable artistic practice.

Theatre-ecology: The conditions for performance in the new century?

In relating dramaturgy to architecture, Turner's essay explores how artistic practices deterritorialize public space and create awareness about the compositional dimensions of space in human, geographical and political terms.[6] Taking this idea further, we need to think about the nature of connectivity as it pertains to dramaturgy as a whole, to theorize dramaturgy as a deterritorializing factor in the connections that artistic production makes with social life. A deterritorializing dramaturgy sees these connections as potentially expanding, transcultural, and open-ended. In her concern to reimagine space, Turner's work fixes dramaturgy in precisely this way, and she wants to explore the connections between the theatrical encounter and the compositional-architectural environment. This awareness of the transformational moment of dramaturgy, considered with the powerful concept of deterritorialization, posits, for us, a connection to ecology.

To think of dramaturgy in terms of ecology foregrounds the crucial importance of connectivity, of relationships between people, objects, natural forces and their interaction in the human/natural environment. As Una Chaudhuri has shown, ecology furnishes powerful metaphors for theatre.[7] We see dramaturgy-as-ecology working not at the level of metaphor, however, nor at the level of theme and consciousness-raising, but *materially, that is, as an ecological practice* opening onto deterritorializing forms of connectivity. There is some history to this idea: at the turn of the new century Michael Hardt and Antonio Negri remarked how cultural and political forces were shifting in similar ways when they observed 'a *decentred* and *deterritorializing* apparatus of rule that progressively incorporates the entire global realm within its open, expanding frontiers'.[8] This means that culture and art must increasingly respond and adapt to contradictory and overlapping themes. Globalization distributes power in new and confusing ways and the new century has seen the world face great challenges, not least in the diaspora and refugee movement of peoples and renewed environmental awareness. While we certainly need to ask how theatre can engage with such important questions, we also need to make these themes intrinsic to the *practices* of theatre, so that they can influence creativity at the level of composition and dramaturgy. An awareness of dramaturgy as involving processes of connectivity – between 'materials, words, bodies, sounds, spaces, times, concepts, audiences, socio-political contexts, subjects objects, ideologies [and] aesthetics'[9] – but at the same time as a deterritorialization of the 'lines of force' between such elements, constitutes the complexity of a dramaturgical ecology, or an ecological dramaturgy.

It would be foolish to attempt to summarize theatre/performance over the last decade, but some things are clear. It is characterized by complexity and interdisciplinary practices to greater degrees than before; even the terms are often blurred. Contemporary performance is globalized and transformed by new forms of collaboration and by responding to new audiences. Digital technologies, intermingling texts with acting, dance, lighting, sound and design have radically transformed theatrical space and time. And as new trends have grown, older forms have also revived and there is new attention to dramatic realism, albeit of a new kind, a parallel focus on documentary and verbatim kinds of theatre, and reargued discussions of theatre writing. Over the decade performance has moved through staging extremes of corporeality and media towards investigating more ambient and everyday currents of life. Writing about the adaptation of classical texts in recent European theatre, Peter M. Boenisch argues that dramaturgy shows a process of texturing performance that 'above all revokes the unapt separation of "production" and "reception" aesthetics'.[10] The idea of texturing as a dramaturgical process that leads to the collapse of the separation between performance and audience can also be seen in ecological terms. The metaphor of texturing suggests a gradual shaping of forms, it suggests sculpting and tactile elements, rather than blunt rupturing aesthesis; it suggests more hands in the making.

The embodied nature of performance means that ecological models of dramaturgy are immediately interconnected with other aspects of life. And with a new ecology comes the need for 'new dramaturgy'; a term coined by veteran dramaturg Marianne Van Kerkhoven. She calls this: 'learning to handle complexity ... and feeding the ongoing conversation on the work, it is taking care of the reflexive potential as well as of the poetic force of the creation. Dramaturgy is ... is above all a constant movement'.[11] A constant movement – and so thinking back to Hardt and Negri, decentred and yet simultaneously integrating systems require a new attentiveness to complexity, to artistic ideas of ecology, to artistic practice as ecology.

Thinking about how *Dramaturgies* could extend our work, it was clear that we needed to foster a discussion about how dramaturgical practices could evolve to do this. Hence, the focus on collaboration, diversity and pedagogy, themes that formed the specific focus of the three working groups in our 2010 event, 'New Dramaturgies for the Twenty-first Century'.

Ecologies of collaboration

Baz Kershaw's *Theatre Ecology: Environments and Performance Events* is a recent study of how performance is connected to ecological themes.[12] The book explores the narrative functions of theatre in raising environmental questions. It also shows how systems of performance making and their sites of production are connected to ecological practices. This is relevant to consider in thinking about how a dramaturgy formulated by collaborative creative processes might work. Are there connections between performance dramaturgy, collaboration and contemporary expressions of deterritorialization that we have discussed above? We aimed in our working group to better understand how ecological practices might become evident in artists' processes, and in the cohering of diverse compositional ideas and forms.

Approaching this idea in a slightly less directional way, we also considered Judie Christie, Richard Gough and Daniel Watt's edited volume, *A Performance Cosmology: Testimony from the Future, Evidence of the Past.*[13] We were interested to explore how the discussions of performance in this book connect cultural histories with the possibilities of imagining a future ecology in ways that also promote ideas of fusion and multiplicity – both essential attributes in a collaborative creative environment. *A Performance Cosmology* combines perspectives that invoke aspects of the cosmological, the formal and the material; it explores senses of place, of experience, and it documents art as activism in interdisciplinary forms of writing and artistic reflections that we connected to how we were thinking about an ecology of dramaturgical practice. In theorizing performance as a constellation of past, present and future, this book is a helpful model for thinking about expanded and deterritorialized forms of thinking about dramaturgical processes. The book folds performance making into a multidimensional awareness of history that in many ways mirrors the associative sensibilities and interweaving flows of time, place and embodied presence, that are part of a dramaturgical awareness of how ideas find expression in the theatre. It gathers ideas, more imaginative than historical fact, but with a sense of creative negotiation and ecological interaction that we aimed to explore in our workshop.

We also worked with the idea of a 'decentred dramaturgy' as developed by the dramaturg Guy Cools in his work on performance, dance and visual arts. Cools argues that dramaturgy as a process of collaboration is both generative and invisible in the development of work. He argues that it is not the role of the dramaturg to give some kind of structural reading of a creative process, nor to assist in the organization of these elements into a unity. Rather, the dramaturg is *facilitating a process*. Cools is provocative because he refuses to make simple interventions that might give a new work more coherence, maintaining instead that the diversity of the process must be shown. To the extent that Cools's decentred approach governs the compositional plane of performance and is intrinsically dramaturgical, this is also a model of collaboration. Moreover, to struggle with the idea of decentring dramaturgy suggests a need to be responsive to interactive flows of ideas and how they create systems and patterns of production – hence operating with a model akin to our thinking about ecological practices and dramaturgy.

While this is an elegant theory, when working in small groups to try and identify a decentred dramaturgy in practical terms, we reached a series of quite divergent conclusions. The workshop produced associative and stylistically hybrid, intertextual works, that for all their decentring, found a certain coherence around the ecological sense of patterns and forms of life being emergent: sometimes these were more or less obvious, but they all had a poetic relationship to an awareness of performance as language and structure. Certainly the idea of decentred dramaturgy engages with questions of collaboration and ecology – arguably it makes the production of theatre centrally about this, and demonstrates the kind of process-based dramaturgy that is discussed above. At the same time, this idea was also taken as a kind of given. No one argued that the diversity of stimuli created a more satisfactory theatre experience. But the decentred approach was also considered to be unhelpful in some instances. What if work remained unfinished and therefore unable to communicate with an audience? Why propose a jumble of chaotic interactions as the only means of making theatre? There were also questions about form. Some forms of performance, certain kinds of dance, for example, might work better in decentred staging while others potentially become oversimplified. What happens in a more mediatised, complex performance setting where dramaturgy has such an important function in ordering and structuring theatrical representations? In the final analysis the notion of a decentred dramaturgy was both helpful and annoying to participants. It was a worthy provocation but only meaningful to some members of the group.

While these questions remain, Bruce Gladwin's presentation offered an example of work that broached both the fluid-ecological and decentred dramaturgies of collaboration discussed here. *The Democratic Set* is a film project by Back to Back, the Geelong-based contemporary performance group that Gladwin leads. The work is a template for participatory performance and is remade in different contexts and places. A camera focuses on one small plain room, open at the front and with a door on either side. People enter and exit the room and perform a simple action, singularly or in groups. Each action/performance is less than sixty seconds, and the film is edited to give the impression of a continuous peeling off of bodies and uncanny transformations of space. Perhaps this example demonstrates something about the compositional nature of decentred dramaturgical work. The template enables an endless variety of participation. The outcome is a series of hybrid performance films produced in diverse contexts. Although theatrical stimuli are provided and editorial decisions shape the outcomes, *The Democratic Set* can only utilize the performances that are provided by people. Collaboration is seen in the work via the participation of performers, via the design and sound elements used in the production of each small performance, and by the seamless creation of a longer work made from a series of single elements.

In the final session our intention was to have a concluding discussion to summarize our findings. Actually what took place was an activist staging of the various possible ideas and problems with the notion of collaboration. The group as a whole created a large-scale installation by taking down texts from walls and laying them as lines of paper across the floor. Other pages and objects were squashed and rolled into bundles or destroyed. A sense of frustration with the process was evident, but it was also evident that a construction with a dramaturgical order was evolving. The effect was to make an installation of the workshop, so that when the people from other groups visited our room they would experience a decentred dramaturgical process. The idea was spontaneous, and the event could be compared to an art happening. The final result was intriguing for its clarity as a record of the event and a demonstration of a collaborative dramaturgy, albeit in unruly form.

Dramaturgy and diversity

This working group aimed to explore how an awareness of dramaturgy as ecology could promote cultural diversity in contemporary Australian theatre practice, and vice versa. Our goal was to identify whether misconceptions about 'difference' exist, to create awareness about issues of exclusion, and to develop strategies to combat identified prejudices. We aimed to think dramaturgically about such questions as: How do we work from and celebrate difference? How do we negotiate difference within the context of an expanding cultural marketplace? Are we able to work within the existing structures and companies or do we need to transform these structures? In what ways can an understanding of a decentred and ecological model of dramaturgy assist in extending the parameters of theatre production in contemporary Australia? The fact of cultural diversity needs to be recognized in processes as well as outcomes.

At the beginning of the workshop participants *took time* to introduce themselves to each other. Bringing to the room their names, their family backgrounds, their histories and their artistic interests was a model of dramaturgy we wanted to promote, a compositional frame and politics in an expressive form of communication. Each participant shared crucial knowledge with each other in ways that were both dynamic and intimate. The tone of these introductions expanded on a keynote address to all participants by director Kully Thiarai, who wove her own cultural background and personal experiences into an understanding of her pathways and working life as an artist:

It would be nice to think that these issues were as simple or as 'Black and White' as sometimes commentators might have us believe. In the end though, I feel the world, and our place within it, is much more complex. Now more than ever, as our world fragments and yet at the same time becomes more globally connected, our ability to communally connect and engage is of paramount importance. Now more than ever the uniqueness of the collective experience, the power of live performance and the potency of the spoken word are necessary to help us shape a better future. Theatre has the power to help shape and facilitate change – its roots extend across the globe and serves our very fundamental needs to come together and act as witness to our desire to understand and share our common humanity. History shows that theatre and plays have not always sat in the comfortable settings of formal theatre spaces or arts centres – they have always had a historical connection with social and political struggles.[14]

The session discussed possibilities of how to encourage and support cultural diversity in Australian Theatre – whether that be at the edge of contemporary practice or at the centre. We also considered the existing pathways for making funded work, and whether they are productive and provide sufficient choice for a diverse range of practitioners. We discussed how contemporary non-narrative or non-naturalistic theatre practice allows for a multiplicity of voices and points of view, and how it has the potential to challenge and influence mainstream paradigms.

Rachael Maza Long, performer and artistic director of Ilbijerri (indigenous) theatre, spoke of her passion and commitment for 'telling her own stories'. She talked about Australia as a country that sees itself as white, and that anything outside of that is like a blind spot. She compared the theatre industry to a garden, and noted that for it to flourish it needed not only water but also good soil. She named culturally diverse artists as the soil that would enrich the industry, create a biodiversity of activity and bring points of view that would lead to more lush outcomes. Raimondo Cortese, playwright, spoke about how his own cultural background makes him stronger as an artist, and how he believes that the purpose of writing is to express one's personal vision of the world that is inextricably linked to one's experience. He talked about how in hindsight he relishes feeling alienated, as it has enabled him to be who he is. He talked about how theatre does and always has attracted the voiceless and the marginalized, and encouraged artists to embrace their 'difference' as an opportunity to be remarkable rather than see it as any form of 'disability'. Wesley Enoch, artistic director of the Queensland Theatre Company, spoke about how indigenous artists have 'claimed a stake' in the arts in recent decades, and encouraged members of the working group to assert their place in the industry on their own terms. He spoke of the way diversity makes economic and political sense.

The diversity theme gave voice to many perspectives on participation in theatre, some more developed than others. However, questions of how the broader politics of participation connects with dramaturgical practice remained less resolved. The final session was a good example of this, aiming to move from discussion to practice, but realizing in the process the continuing need among participants for further discussion. Of course discussion is a kind of practice too, and this led to a robust critical analysis of recent theatre histories and comments on questions of appropriation and cultural negotiation. These questions have been around theatre for a long time but in the Australian situation they are yet to be addressed thoroughly. A question then about the application of dramaturgy to diversity remains: what does a diverse dramaturgy look like and how does it function in the theatres of today? The working group confirmed the importance of identity and expressing ideas from diverse communities. The importance of enabling access and richly embodied participation was also stressed; to be witness to peoples' migratory, cosmopolitan and/or indigenous struggles and to equalities of gender, mobility, class and sexuality. In exploring these ideas, the workshop remained productively engaged in conversation and debate; thus, the suggestion is to recognize that a dramaturgy of diversity would continue to give awareness to conversation as a mode of creative production. The workshop showed that the question as to how these ideas can further develop as dramaturgical processes now requires our attention.

Pedagogy and the dramaturgical intelligence

The pedagogy working group focused on identifying the theatrical and cultural elements that are active in the ecology of dramaturgical practices we have been discussing, and how different aspects in this ecology can be learnt, taught and enriched.

We made a distinction in our discussions between focused learning *in dramaturgy* (that which always and necessarily exists whenever there is theatre/performance), and learning that prepares one to work *as a dramaturg* (a role allocated to a specific person within the creative process). But we also concluded that working as a dramaturg in this ecology of practice increasingly requires a fuller grasp of the broad and shifting field of dramaturgy. Working with 'new dramaturgies' seems to require an enhanced ability to work with complexity and uncertainty, with in-betweenness, cultural diversity and invisible underscore. It requires a heightened alertness to 'lines of force' or what Turner and Behrndt call 'red threads'[15] in the weave of actions that provide us with insight into both the compositional logic of the work and its ideological ideas, assumptions and assertions. The group asked what kind of pedagogy is needed to reflect, feed into and even instigate change in this ecology.

And while we recognized the rich dramaturgical learning that takes place in ongoing professional practice, there are also industrial factors at work in the profession that do make deep reflection difficult to find time for. We wanted, therefore, to turn our attention to situations of 'focused learning', by which we mean learning that arises from processes and explorations specifically dedicated to developing dramaturgical skills and understanding. We identified three settings in which focused learning takes place: Education (Performance/Theatre/Drama Studies departments focused on the study of theatre and performance), Training (immersive, studio-based training dedicated to making and doing) and Professional Development (the focused development of skills and understandings in professional contexts). Although sometimes seen to be mutually exclusive and antagonistic, one of our aims was to foster a more productive connectivity between these environments.

We focused our thinking on what we called 'the dramaturgical intelligence', a concept that encompasses the full range of factors involved in a diverse range of dramaturgical practices, and to identify how this intelligence can be cultivated. We identified five areas of engagement, each of which can be conceived of and developed separately. But importantly, the dramaturgical intelligence consists in a weaving together of these different threads, an ability to apply them productively to process and performance, and the ability to see both the micro and the macro levels of this complex ecology and the interconnections between them.

Given the increasing 'non-hierarchy of images, movements and word' in contemporary theatre,[16] the first objective of pedagogy in our analysis is a multidisciplinary understanding of theatre and performance. Because performance is collaboratively created and consists of multiple and shifting layers or inputs, an understanding of the way that the skills and material practices of different artists interweave, connect and potentially disrupt each other promotes the kind of agile creative negotiation increasingly required of an effective dramaturgical intelligence. There is a key role to be played here by training institutions, where embodied, multi-stranded and interdisciplinary learning, especially in postgraduate courses, has the potential to substantially mature the dramaturgical textures of our theatre culture. The key concept here is a multiplicity of practices and understandings.

Dramaturgical pedagogy also needs to better promote an understanding of, and skill in, composition, devising and collaboration. Not only is there an increasing focus in contemporary theatre on the kind of collaboratively devised work discussed earlier in this chapter, even where there is also a dedicated writer,[17] but as Turner and Behrndt note, it is in devising work that issues of dramaturgy are forcefully brought to the foreground.[18] Furthermore, in *collaboratively* generated and decentred dramaturgies, which tend to draw from a variety of disciplinary and interdisciplinary models, and in work that is enriched by culturally diverse perspectives and practices, these issues force themselves forward with even greater insistence, and in ways that disrupt habitual assumptions. While education and professional development settings are perhaps constrained in their ability to explore devised performance practice, training settings, with their greater supply of time and space, are ideally suited to the development of this aspect of the dramaturgical intelligence.

A third requirement of pedagogy is to better understand the interrelationship of aesthetic and critical dramaturgical practices. This involves the interrogation and disruption of circular and self-proving orthodoxies, a skill set that involves critical theory, philosophical thinking, historical analysis, and an awareness of the existence and need for cultural diversity in theatrical practice. As Kully Thiarai and the Diversity working group reminded us to ask: Who is not at the table or silent? What have we ignored or refused to recognize? All these considerations broaden our understanding of dramaturgy and its expansive possibilities and limitations, promote the recognition of internal structures and assumptions, and the ability where necessary to disrupt, bend and reorganize them for new insights and greater awareness. Education settings seem best placed to promote this aspect of the dramaturgical intelligence, but both training and professional development settings cannot productively advance practice without at least some significant exposure to it.

The fourth aspect for pedagogy to consider is audience reception as an aspect of dramaturgy. As creators and audiences, we are informed and shaped by the culture and world we live in, and theatrical meaning is negotiated between performance, audience and the world.[19] Understanding the role of the spectator in creating meaning, especially where deterritorializing dramaturgies and what Lehmann calls the 'aesthetics of undecidability' in postdramatic theatre are at play,[20] involves a keen sensitivity to the deep and surface structures in a work, its images and compositions, and takes all of these into consideration alongside the conditions of spectatorship, including the crucial spatial and psychic relationship between performance and audience.[21] The learner needs to develop an ability to interrogate the work in respect of its spectators, asking 'why this work, at this time, in this way', and in what ways does the work resonate within the matrix of sensibilities and receptions within which its life is manifested. Again, although all three settings need to engage with this aspect of the dramaturgical intelligence, perhaps education settings are best equipped to lead it.

Finally – and this draws on the skills and understandings of all the areas of engagement above – there is a need to consider the process of 'reading' a performance. This involves being able to identify what decisions have been made and why, and their affective and significative impact. Reading a performance involves both a synchronic perspective (all that is presented to the audience at that moment) and a diachronic perspective (viewing the performance in the context of the history of performance, culture and ideologies). As a textual metaphor, 'reading' is only a partially valid term here; we might rather say 'experiencing the performance as idea', or 'thinking through the body in response to performance', and so on, which asks us to make all of our senses available to the experience. The learner needs to be keenly attuned in this more inclusive way to what materials are active in the composition, and how their arrangement and treatment creates frameworks for experience and interpretation. In addition, the learner needs to be able to identify, understand and respond to underlying scores or blueprints (such as a question, idea, line of force, image, play text – hence the importance of skill in textual analysis, choreographic proposition and so on), and how these blueprints have been articulated in time and space. Being central to the dramaturgical intelligence, we suggest this aspect of the dramaturgical intelligence needs cultivating in all three focused learning settings.

What emerges from our analysis is that, of the three settings, professional development is the least utilized. While the five areas of the dramaturgical intelligence need to be taught and learnt across institutions and in professional development frameworks, the bureaucratic structures of tertiary institutions tend to prevent this cooperation from occurring. The potential for a structured, layered and mutually complementary 'curriculum' across more fluid institutional boundaries needs to be thoroughly investigated. Furthermore, effective dramaturgical learning is sometimes hamstrung by the need to assess outcomes, especially as some aspects of the dramaturgical intelligence might best be developed not through 'teaching' or 'training' specific skills and knowledge, but by setting up 'situations of difficulty' which the learner is required to pass through, thereby acquiring valuable shards of dramaturgical intelligence along the way. This strategy more closely approximates the learning promoted 'on the job' within the profession, but avoids the profession's industrial constraints. A strategy worth examining is the transferral of some aspects of dramaturgical pedagogy out of tertiary institutions and into professional development scenarios, where pedagogy is potentially more nimble, and the need to assess outcomes lower.

Closing

We have sought in this chapter to show how dramaturgy as a concept and a diverse set of practices is being progressed in Australian theatre, and proposed an ecological model to encompass the diverse ways in which these practices connect, complement and potentially deterritorialize each other. Issues of collaboration, diversity and pedagogy, the focus of the most recent event of *The Dramaturgies Project*, are currently central to theatre practice in Australia, and we aimed here to report on how we could think about these issues dramaturgically, as dynamic agents within a dramaturgical ecology. Collaboratively generated and decentred dramaturgies embody the notion of ecology as material practice; they ask us to be responsive to interactive flows of ideas and how they create systems and patterns of production. The emergence and recognition of cultural diversity in Australian theatre is a crucial factor in this ecological model, both because that diversity underpins the fabric of Australian culture, and because it is synonymous with a sustainable theatrical biodiversity. The pedagogical principles and practices we have outlined here seek to nurture a dramaturgical intelligence that flows through and enhances this dramaturgical ecology as its vital sap. If 'new dramaturgy' is 'above all else a constant movement' as Van Kerkhoven suggests,[22] then decentred and yet simultaneously integrating dramaturgies require a new attentiveness to complexity, to artistic ideas of ecology, to artistic practice as ecology. *The Dramaturgies Project* aims to continue developing projects both in Australia and internationally that further enhance this ecology of dramaturgical practice.

(The Dramaturgies Project gratefully acknowledges support from the Australia Council for the Arts and University of Melbourne.)

References

Boenisch, Peter M. 'Towards a Theatre of Encounter and Experience: Reflexive Dramaturgies and Classic Texts'. *Contemporary Theatre Review* 20.2 (2010), pp. 162–72.

Chaudhuri, Una. 'There Must Be a Lot of Fish in That Lake'. *Theatre* 25.1 (1994), pp. 23–31.

Christie, Judie, Gough, Richard and Watt, Daniel, eds. *A Performance Cosmology: Testimony from the Future, Evidence of the Past*. London and New York: Routledge, published for the Centre for Performance Research, 2006.

Eckersall, Peter. 'Towards an Expanded Dramaturgical Practice: A Report on The Dramaturgy and Cultural Intervention Project'. *Theatre Research International* 31.3 (2006), pp. 283–97.

Eckersall, Peter, Beddie, Melanie and Monaghan, Paul. 'The Dramaturgies Project'. *Realtime* 70 (December 2005–January 2006), special dramaturgy supplement (www.realtimearts.net, 'Dramaturgy Now' link).

—, eds. *Dramaturgies: New Theatres for the Twenty-first Century*. Melbourne: The Dramaturgies Project, 2011.

Freeman, John. *New Performance/New Writing*. Basingstoke: Palgrave Macmillan, 2007.

Geertz, Clifford. 'Art as a Cultural System'. *MLN* 91.6 (1976), pp. 1473–99.

Hardt, Michael and Negri, Antonio. *Empire*. Cambridge, MA: Harvard University Press, 2000.

Hewett, Dorothy. 'The Labyrinth', *Greenhouse*, Big Smoke Books, 1979.

Kershaw, Baz. *Theatre Ecology: Environments and Performance Events*. London and New York: Cambridge University Press, 2008.

Lehmann, Hans-Thies. *The Postdramatic Theatre*. Trans. Karen Jürs-Munby. London and New York: Routledge, 2006.

Thiarai, Kully. 'Cultural Diversity and the Ecology of Dramaturgy in Making Vibrant Theatre Practice'. *Dramaturgies: New Theatres for the Twenty-first Century*. Ed. Peter Eckersall, Melanie Beddie and Paul Monaghan. Melbourne: The Dramaturgies Project, 2011, pp. 11–19.

Turner, Cathy. 'Mis-Guidance and Spatial Planning: Dramaturgies of Public Space'. *Contemporary Theatre Review, New Dramaturgies* 20.2 (2010), pp. 149–61.

Turner, Cathy and Behrndt, Synne K., *Dramaturgy and Performance*. Basingstoke: Palgrave Macmillan, 2008.

Van Kerkhoven, Marianne. 'European Dramaturgy in the Twenty-first Century'. *Performance Research, On Dramaturgy* 14.3 (2009), pp. 7–11.

Wiles, David. *A Short History of Western Performance Space*. New York: Cambridge University Press, 2003.

Respect and Perspective

Art, Structure and Ownership

Alan Lawrence

The January 1994 edition of the journal *Theaterschrift* presented a double issue on dramaturgy. In her introduction Marianne Van Kerkhoven wrote that:

> It proved to be no simple task to answer the question 'what is dramaturgy, anyway?' It appeared … that dramaturgy involves everything, is to be found in everything, and is hard to pin down. Is it only possible to think of dramaturgy in terms of spoken theatre, or is there a dramaturgy for movement, sound, light and so on, as well? Is dramaturgy the thing that connects all the various elements of a play together? Or is it, rather, the ceaseless dialogue between people who are working on a play together? Or is it about the soul, the internal structure, of a production? Or does dramaturgy determine the way space and time are handled in a performance, and so the context and the audience too? We can probably answer all these questions with 'Yes, but…'[1]

Van Kerkhoven's list of questions and the implied diversity of functions suggested therein supplies a broad, if not entirely comprehensive, anatomy of theatre practice as a whole. Her answer, however, contributes to the very confusion to which her questions allude. A better response would be 'No, but …'

Before going any further I should clarify one important point. When I say 'theatre', I do not refer by any means exclusively to that which goes on in 'a theatre'. Rather, I refer to any form of performance that 'represents' and 'enacts', wheresoever and howsoever it is created or presented, but with the proviso that I understand it as art. Everything to which Van Kerkhoven refers (above) belongs to the 'art of theatre' and I see no separation between dramaturgy and theatre. For me they are one and the same thing and this, to a large extent, informs my thinking on the subject of dramaturgy 'old' or 'new'. Art is central to the discussion, which raises the next question – what do I mean by art? (I refer to art of all kinds; good, bad or indifferent; intellectually challenging, entertaining or just plain boring – it comes in all flavours.) This is a question that in my understanding can only be answered where art is apprehended through 'structure', and since the pairing of these interdependent phenomena is crucial to my perceptions of theatre (as well as music and all other disciplines), it deserves some detailed attention.

Everything in the natural world has structure, the aggregate of its parts, the record of its coming into being. Man-made artefacts too, material or conceptual, have structure which, when understood, reveals the processes by which objects are made. It follows that art of every kind has structure. But if everything, including art, has structure then how is art to be differentiated from everything else on a structural basis? The difference lies in the fact that art deals in the aesthetics of structure – in the weights and balances of abstract quanta. The manner in which the thing is put together is the justification for its being, not some subsequent *use* to which it may be put. This is as true for theatre as for any artistic discipline. When alluding to the structural elements of a playtext Lee Devin admitted, 'There's no denying that it's often difficult to use these imaginary parts creatively. It can be awkward and frustrating to treat a play as if it had no discursive meaning. This is a tricky part of dramaturgy.'[2] His comment holds as true for the production as a whole as for the playtext to which he refers.

But in the generality, I perceive art as a *model* of thought process – not as a representation of specific thoughts or ideas but simply as an abstract rendition of the structure of thought. The January 1994 *Theaterschrift* included a range of outcomes from a symposium held in Amsterdam during August 1993, concerning the 'context' of (then) current theatre. One of the purposes of the symposium was 'to close up the gap between theory and practice that still exists in theatre'. Van Kerkhoven suggested that, 'dramaturgy and dramaturgs ... are, after all, halfway between theory and practice, between thinking and doing'.[3] Clearly, I find this proposition difficult to accommodate. Art *is* thinking – the reification of thought; thought as organized elements of sound, as the disposition of shape and colour, as enactments that furnish or represent the spaces, balances, congruities and incongruities of ideality. To suggest the possibility of a gap between 'thinking' and 'doing' in art is to place oneself on the wrong side of a cognitive divide. All art, or so it seems to me, presents an analogue of the inegalities and balances, reconciled or irreconcilable, that contribute to the act of reasoning. All thought processes consist of idealities and their juxtapositions, sometimes deeply and confusingly nested, but nevertheless, providing the structure of how one thinks. And it is this structure made manifest, this *model* of thought process, which supplies the commonality across art of all disciplines.

The ability to recognize and concur with or refute the reasoning of others strongly suggests that people share similar rational processes. How else could debate and negotiation take place? Such activities are based on the ability to anticipate the thought processes of another. Because art, when considered as the *model* to which I refer, relates only to process, rather than to ideas, it will resonate with the thoughts of responsive recipients no matter what those thoughts may be about. The contours of this abstract *model*, reflecting as they do the comparisons and evaluations of an internal discourse, will resonate with the various sensibilities of the many. It is at this abstract level that the individual empathizes with the artwork, almost, or in fact, subliminally. The very lack of specificity allows each individual to experience a sense of personal engagement with the art.

This is the base level at which all art must operate. Could one otherwise explain the multiplicity of responses to art? Individuals may like or dislike a given work but when questioned, their reasons will vary considerably. Obviously, the greater the familiarity with the particular discipline or idiom, the stronger the power of association, but the effect depends on the quality of the *abstract thought model*, or, as I shall refer to it, the *abstractum*. One may feel disconcerted by the discovery that one shares an affinity for a particular work with someone whose opinions differ widely from one's own or whose actions one abhors. The particular preoccupations, preferences and prejudices in the mind of the recipient are irrelevant to the associative power of the *abstractum*, resembling, as it does, not the matter but the structure of thought process.

Although most artistic disciplines afford a narrative potential (indeed, many have clearly evolved from reportage, enactment and/or depiction), it seems clear that what we recognize as art is something other than or beyond mere representation. Indeed, there are disciplines – significantly music and abstract visual art – that, while they have no means of depiction, are nonetheless recognized as art. How then could such disparate manifestations as dance, sculpture, photography, music, painting, installations (aural, visual and even tactile) and drama in all its forms – how else could all of these share the name of art, were there not some common characteristic underlying their multiplicity of differences? I suggest that where one speaks of art, one recognizes that structure has primacy over signification. It is the *abstractum* that makes it art. Abstraction in the visual medium relies entirely on structure, and music, the most abstract of arts, signifies nothing but its own transient existence, nothing but structure conveyed on air. But what does it all mean? Claude Levi-Strauss has said that music is a language at the same time intelligible and untranslatable.[4] The captivating nature of a particular melodic line, the almost visceral experience of a certain harmonic progression, the arresting sonorities of unexpected timbral juxtapositions, these are all structural elements of music and are experienced only in sensation, not in meaning.

In linguist art, not least in theatre, things are a little more complicated. Where we have words, we have signification. And this is the difficulty referred to by Devin when he says, 'It can be awkward and frustrating to treat a play as if it had no discursive meaning.'⁵ For now, signification is one of the elements of structure. Significations, viewed as differentiable values, serve as materials in the building of the *abstractum*. Yes, these signifying elements have meanings but it is the intensities and, dare I say, colours of these meanings that serve the aesthetic character of the drama, not the specifics of signification. And this is of the utmost importance, as by no means all elements of theatrical production share an equality of signification with words, but *all* are threads in the dramatic weave.

Having outlined my understanding of theatre – the art of theatre, its congruity with dramaturgy and its indivisibility from structure – I return to the concepts of dramaturgy and new dramaturgy per se. Geoffrey Proehl has written that 'Dramaturgy, ... – this deep, often personal, even idiosyncratic understanding of the forms and rhythms crucial to a play as written or conceived and performed – is inseparable from theatre making, whether or not the word itself is ever used.'⁶ Proehl, like Devin above, is referring to the 'play as written or conceived', but his observations apply as much to all elements of theatre, to the entire structural edifice, as to the elements of playtext and production. Furthermore, I view this contiguity of elements as fundamental to my understanding of theatre. So no, there should not be a discrete dramaturgy for each and every aspect of theatre. Every part of theatrical endeavour is serving the same function and everybody involved in theatrical production is doing the same job; that is, to make theatre. To suggest a dramaturgy of speech, of movement, of sound, light, or space, may seem to confer some axiological equality, but in fact tends towards division rather than unification of creative and aesthetic thinking. I'm not suggesting that this was Van Kerkhoven's purpose, and to be fair, she did say 'Yes, *but* ...'. However, in a field bedevilled by definitions one should beware the introduction of terminology likely to imply compartmentalization of any kind. All of the 'dramaturgies' suggested by such thinking attach to activities in themselves artistic, and the unifying quality of the combined *artistic* objective completely outweighs any perceived disciplinary variations or any benefits that may accrue from democratization. Of course, there may still be a voice coach, a designer, a sound department and so on, but a dramaturgy of voice, a dramaturgy of design, a dramaturgy of sound …? Were one to replace the word 'dramaturgy' with the word 'theatre', one may start to recognize the misgivings to which I refer.

Cathy Turner and Synne K. Behrndt have written that:

> We should … be wary that our desire to expand the term 'dramaturgy' does not lead to an overly diffuse, vague and therefore unhelpful presentation of the term and its practice. Perhaps it might; we take this risk, since it appears preferable to a reductive approach, and we look forward to debating this further with interested parties.[7]

I applaud their cautionary note but differ from their conclusion and welcome their invitation to debate. I don't intend to spend too many words on terminological nit-picking but I believe that much misunderstanding is caused by the profusion of nomenclature attaching to dramaturgy, some of which I feel bound to address, albeit with reference to writers for whom I have the greatest respect and who I view as victims rather than as authors of the lexicographical morass through which they find themselves obliged to wade. But even so, Devin has said that, 'in order to make good theater, we need a vocabulary that will allow precise and helpful discussion among the members of a production team'.[8] This sounds like a reasonable observation but I sense the onset of new nomenclature. I'm a musician who has worked a good deal in theatre as both composer and performer and I've spent time enough in both the production meeting and the rehearsal room to have developed a feel for how these things work. The creative people involved, be they actors, designers, lighting or sound specialists, directors and all, are not only able, but usually enthusiastic to develop their own vocabulary, often unique to the particular production at hand. Furthermore, the theatrical world, be that the world of a given production or of theatre at large, is a metamorphosic environment in which ideas, practices and descriptions emerge through process, on a continuous basis. Such people, inhabiting such a world, have no need of a devised vocabulary to assist the development of their thinking or the communication of their ideas. In fact, the attempt to 'define', in this instance, is more likely to memorialize or even to ossify a concept than to liberate it.

And so, far from expanding the already overcrowded dramaturgical lexicon, I would prefer a drastic pruning of the nomenclature. And now new dramaturgy threatens to start, or has perhaps started, the whole confusing process over again. The problem with 'new' is that one never knows quite *when* it was new. For example, 'new criticism' is now very 'old hat'. As if things were not already sufficiently complicated, there can sometimes be considerable slippage between developments that are referred to as 'new' only after their somewhat belated doctrinal recognition. One can only wonder at residual references to the persistent constraints of Aristotle's poetics,[9] many decades after the arrivals of Pirandello, Beckett, Ionesco and Pinter, to name but a few, and concurrently with Martin Crimp, Heiner Müller, Tracy Letts, Patrick Marber, Mark Ravenhill, Complicite, Robert Wilson ... .

So far I've aired my misgivings regarding the proliferation of nomenclature in an 'expanding' or 'new' dramaturgy, and I've defined what I mean by theatre, that is, any performance that 'represents' and 'enacts', wheresoever and howsoever it is created or presented. I added that I understand theatre as art, good, bad or indifferent. This will not be everybody's definition of theatre but it is mine. And my perception of theatre as art, given my understanding of art as the aforementioned *abstractum*, raises certain difficulties vis-à-vis a particular strand of thinking on new dramaturgy. For if art is the model of thought process, one must ask, 'of whose thought process?' The answer must surely be that it belongs to the person or persons responsible for its creation. Now if a person is part of a creative team then their contributions will scarcely be thought of as interventions – intervention comes from without.

In his essay, 'Towards an Expanded Dramaturgical Practice: A Report on "The Dramaturgy and Cultural Intervention Project"', Peter Eckersall speaks of how expanded forms of dramaturgy might 'intervene in and transform aspects of contemporary theatre practice ... challenging contemporary theatre culture while also finding ways that the work of dramaturgs can become integral to systems of theatre production in a period of neo-liberal capitalist domination'.[10] He refers to the intention 'to grow the capacity ... for discussion and intervention' and to 'expand political and aesthetic dimensions of theatre'. He sees dramaturgy 'as a tool to challenge cultural norms and established systems of production'. If Eckersall is proposing to create 'new' works with the purpose of reorienting the contemporary theatrical canon then I applaud his progressive thinking. If however, he is suggesting that playwrights or theatre-makers of any kind should be urged towards, for example, a more 'political' stance 'in a period of neo-liberal capitalist domination' then I question his position and to whatever extent it represents an expanded dramaturgy, I question that too. My political thinking is decidedly left wing but political thinking has nothing to do with art or therefore with theatre. Without doubt, theatre can use politics as its raw material but to urge or cajole in this direction or that is to undermine the authenticity of the creative act. In any case, if we allow ourselves that privilege we open the door to those just as likely to push in the opposite direction.

I said 'No, *but* ...' – for indeed there are theatrical techniques appearing now under the rubric of new dramaturgy with which I have some sympathy, and which resonate with practices of my own. I turn first to site specificity. In 1991 I had the pleasure of designing and installing a soundscape to accompany an exhibition of paintings by French artist Jacques Pasquier that was mounted first in Holland and then in France. I collaborated with fellow composer, John Lambert, who, by way of an aside, had been my composition professor at the Royal College of Music in London, some twenty years earlier. The audio material consisted of music by Lambert and myself, and environmental sound collected by Lambert from around Pasquier's home and studio. The sites in both instances were deconsecrated medieval chapels, the first in the Dutch town of Warmenhuizen, and the second in the grounds of the Château at Caen, Normandy, William the Conqueror's fortress in that city. I was not unfamiliar with the concept of site specificity, having composed music for, among others, John Tasker's extraordinary production of *As You Like It*, in Albert Park Brisbane, in 1981. Here, for example, a distant horseman could be seen riding across the park, arriving and dismounting on the scene to deliver his perfectly timed first line. My sound was distributed to the four corners of the park, contributing to a large-scale environmental experience for the audience. But the exhibition posed different problems and opportunities. There's no room here for detail but suffice to say that experiments there with the dramatization and characterization of space have informed my thinking ever since. The ability to 'change' the dimensions of the building through the manipulation of sound and to relocate or redefine areas within the greater space – these site-specific techniques have informed my thinking regarding sound in theatre to the extent that I now view every production as site-specific, no matter where it is mounted.

Another attribute ascribed to new dramaturgy, and of interest to me, is that of the hierarchical/non-hierarchical nature of theatrical conception and production. I have to say that in my experience, the hierarchical nature of the 'established' theatre has been somewhat overstated. Of course, the autocratic hierarchical thinking that new dramaturgy seeks to remedy has always been there. I remember the director – it was at The Old Vic – who before the first read-through on day one announced that anyone with suggestions should feel free to make them at any time. All such contributions, he added, would be ignored but that this should not inhibit anyone so moved. And he wasn't entirely joking. A few years later, composing now for an Australian state theatre company, I approached the lighting designer. I asked if he could spare a moment some time so that we could compare notes and coordinate our thinking. I was somewhat dismayed when he told me in quite unambiguous terms that he could see no connection between his job and mine and that I had best not waste his time. And he taught in a university drama department (before becoming a taxi driver, that is). But the reason why these examples stick in my mind is that they were the exceptions. In general I have found cooperation and collaboration to be the preferred approaches.

But at the compositional level I have encountered, and attempted in at least some small way to remedy, perhaps the greatest hierarchical inequality in the gamut of performing arts – that between composer and librettist. Here we encounter a 180° inversion of the conventional dominance of text in theatre. When one thinks of *Don Giovanni* it's Mozart's name that springs to mind; very few think first of Lorenzo Da Ponte (unless, maybe, they happen to be librettists). *The Marriage of Figaro* offers an even more extreme disassociation of wordsmith and work. Once again Da Ponte provided the libretto, but this time based on the play by Pierre Beaumarchais, scarcely an obscure figure then or now. But even so, both Da Ponte and Beaumarchais are eclipsed in cultural recognition by the composer. It's true that for various technical reasons the libretto is usually a slim example of the wordsmith's art while the opera score is often substantial, but sheer magnitude has never been a useful gauge of artistic merit. However, there has been a hierarchical evolution in the history of opera from 'plays with songs' to 'music as stage drama' – from theatre music to music-theatre. What was originally the sung enclave has progressively devoured and metamorphosed the entire spectacle. For the greater part of the past two hundred years the opera has been seen as a musical work and its creative identity (particularly in the public perception) has rested with the composer.

Where the librettist has produced a text of poetic and/or dramatic merit, its qualities will often be lost on the audience for while it may have served well to inspire the composer the resulting music will regularly distort or simply drown the language to the point of extinction. This is borne out by the fact that whether or not an opera is presented in the local language producers these days deem it necessary to provide surtitles for the benefit of those incautious enough to have entered the theatre without first reading at least a synopsis and preferably the entire libretto. There is clearly no expectation that the words (or at least enough of the words) will be heard. One could suspect that a libretto of poetic merit may less well suit the purpose than something more mundane, as the former poses a serious axiological dichotomy. As often as I may take issue with the writer and critic Neville Cardus,[11] he summed the matter up precisely when he wrote that, 'If the words in a libretto are excellent enough in themselves as dialogue and drama, they don't need music, and in fact, are wasted on music.'[12]

I first read David Harsent's libretto for the one act opera, *The Hoop of the World*, some years after it had been first drafted. It was the orphan of an abandoned project with another composer. I was, perhaps naively, attracted by the excellence of the poetry, and by those very qualities described by Cardus as 'excellent enough in themselves.'[13] Having taken on the project I soon discovered (or at least so it seemed) that such words really 'don't need music and in fact, [may indeed be] wasted on music'. In any case, my respect for the text was such that I felt constrained to save it from the worst indignities of word setting. But, by the same token, I was intent on making a musical work that reflected my own creative impulses, as far as possible uninflected by excessive deference to verbal intelligibility. In fact, I confronted the very dichotomy outlined above.

The conclusion that suggested itself was that music may be either the medium for delivery of the drama or it may provide the whole world in which the drama exists. It may combine the roles of word setting, accompaniment and incidental music, or it may function as the indicative or typological agency for the whole work: a kind of meta-stage; not 'theatre music' nor quite 'music-theatre', rather *music as the theatre*. If the composer opts for the first approach (i.e. 'the medium for delivery') then the process may be characterized as somewhat similar to that of song. The music will attempt to mimic or illustrate signification and the necessary recourse to stereotypes will, one hopes, be invigorated by imaginative transgression and reinvention of those apriorisms, as with the best examples of song. The dramatic structure of the work will be underpinned by musical gestures that evoke the emotional, and thereby, perhaps even the argumentative progress of the narrative. This approach will however, to at least some extent, call for an illustrative and therefore preordained conceptualization of the musical endeavour. Where the second alternative is adopted (i.e. 'the whole world' or environmental approach) a greater degree of artistic integrity may be preserved for both words and music. Now the music may be imagined as the composer's *experience* of the libretto, not as illustration, amplification or explication but simply of how it is comprehended. It is as if the composer is saying to the librettist, 'I read your libretto, your drama, and this is the musical space on which it plays out in my mind.' Just as the composer's work in general will inevitably reflect the manner in which he or she comprehends and assesses experience of the world at large, so the opera music will relate to the world of the libretto. Equally, the libretto will be liberated from its subjugation to direct compositorial interpretation.

Having chosen the second, that is, 'the whole world' or environmental approach to the opera, I found myself better able to cope with the poetic language of the libretto since it would not now be hostage to my musical rendition, or I to its metrical and overall stanzaic structure. Harsent's libretto, written, as it is, entirely in verse, predisposes itself to a stylized, at times ritualistic dramatization. This was the quality above all that I chose to exploit for its aptitude to staged music. The ambiguity of the central character in the work allowed me to write entirely into an environmental rather than an illustrative mode of musical expression. I was able to view text (and especially the intelligibility of words) in exactly the same way that I would view the technical limitations on the performance of any instrument. In other words, I was able to focus on verbal clarity as a technical prerequisite rather than as an imperative for signification, interpretation or apprehension. This was the level of objectivity for which I aimed in the hope of creating an authentic musical landscape on which the drama could play out unmolested.

Based on my experience with *The Hoop of the World*, I would suggest that many hierarchical inegalities in theatre could be addressed, not by imagining *new* branches of dramaturgy attuned to particular sub-disciplinary needs, but by re-envisioning the structural relationships between the dramatic elements. Structure is ultimately as much to do with boundaries as it is to do with components. If we draw the boundary around everything that constitutes dramaturgy I contend that we will see the same boundary that encloses everything that we call theatre. If we view the structure of theatre and its elements in the same way that we view the structure of the production and its elements, just as we might view the structure of a playtext and its elements, I think we may see that there is one dramaturgy, one theatre. When I answered Van Kerkhoven's list of questions with 'No, but ...' I took issue with certain of her implied propositions but there is one with which I have little disagreement. When she asks, 'Is dramaturgy the thing that connects all the various elements of a play together?',[14] the answer is an emphatic yes – and all the elements of production and presentation besides. And that's theatre – no 'buts' about it.

In 1993, a symposium was organized in Amsterdam to discuss the contemporary 'context' of theatre and to, among other things, 'establish a new vocabulary ... to name and define the radical changes that have taken place in theatre'.[15] In Brisbane, during 1986, an ad hoc working group assembled, bringing together in one room a representative collection of performance-oriented individuals. The purpose was to consider the possibilities of a theatrical fusion of ideas where each could contribute a particular skill but where each would participate equally in the development of a performance piece, from text (in the broadest sense) to production. We were, Jean-Michel Raynaud (poet and semiotician, then at the University of Queensland), Carol Burns (actress), Alan Edwards (then artistic director of the Queensland Theatre Company), Mark Ross (performance maker, now international design consultant), David Walters (lighting designer) and myself (composer). We were three nationalities in all. We met on a number of occasions and centred our discussions loosely around the idea of a wall, the notional boundary between our different disciplines. No production materialized from these meetings and I'm not sure that anyone expected that it would. The object was, as I remember it, more an exploratory exercise; an investigation of this approach to performance. No one felt confined to their own field and all were open to suggestions and queries. Raynaud's semiotics illuminated cross-disciplinary parallelisms and resonances. Ross introduced us to some extraordinary possibilities of both technical and aesthetic site specificity. Each person present brought his or her own perspectives to the table, but each was there to share in a combined catalytic process of creativity. It seemed to me that this was not how theatre could be, but how it already was (albeit informally) and still is. No new vocabulary was developed and none was needed. As usual, the common creative agenda generated its own world, its own terminology, sufficient to itself and, like all practical manifestations of theatre, ready to stand down in favour of the next project. The significant attribute of the group in Brisbane was its composition not its topic. One has to ask, why were those particular individuals drawn to that particular discussion? And the answer is that it was they who already understood and pursued the making of performance in that way – it was more an act of affirmation than of discovery.

References

Cardus, Neville. *Talking of Music*. London: Collins, 1957.

Devin, Lee. 'Conceiving the Forms: Play Analysis for Production Dramaturgy'. *Dramaturgy in American Theatre: A Source Book*. Ed. Susan Jonas, Geoff Proehl and Michael Lupu. Orlando: Harcourt Brace, 1997, pp. 209–19.

Eckersall, Peter. 'Towards an Expanded Dramaturgical Practice: A Report on "The Dramaturgy and Cultural Intervention Project"'. *Theatre Research International* 31.3 (2006), pp. 283–97.

Katz, Leon. *Cleaning Augean Stables: Examining Drama's Strategies*. Encino, CA: CreateSpace Independent Publishing Platform, 2012.

Levi-Strauss, Claude. *Le cru et le cuit*. Paris: Plon, 1964.

Pasquier, Jacques. Peintures récentes, Oude Ursulakerk, Warmenhuizen: Holland and Peintures récentes, Chapelle, Saint Georges, Caen: France, 1991.

Proehl, Geoffrey S. *Toward a Dramaturgical Sensibility: Landscape and Journey*. Cranbury, NJ: Associated University Press, 2008.

Shepherd-Barr, Kirsten. *Science on Stage: From Doctor Faustus to Copenhagen*. Princeton: Princeton University Press, 2006.

Turner, Cathy and Behrndt, Synne K. 'Introduction', *Contemporary Theatre Review, New Dramaturgies* 20.2 (2010), pp. 145–8.

Van Kerkhoven, Marianne. 'Introduction'. *Theaterschrift, On dramaturgy* 5–6 (1994), pp. 8–34.

Part Two

Text

Telling Stories Across Forms

Interview with Brian Quirt
(artistic director, Nightswimming, Toronto)

Yolanda Ferrato

Established in 1995, Nightswimming is devoted to theatrical research, creation and performance. The company commissions, develops and workshops new Canadian performance. Rather than producing these new works itself, Nightswimming seeks out other established performing arts companies as partners in an extended development process leading to premiere productions by their partner companies. Through the creation of these new works, Nightswimming is devoted to advancing the field of dramaturgy – the exploration of theatrical stories and how they are told – and play development in Canada.

Nightswimming's work has premiered at some of Canada's leading theatre companies (including Tarragon, Factory, Theatre Passe Muraille, National Arts Centre and Arts Club Theatre), toured the country and appeared at the Magnetic North Theatre Festival, On the Verge, Canada Dance Festival, ATP's playRites Festival, Summerworks Festival, Rhubarb Festival, Harbourfront's World Stage and World Moves Dance Series.

Along with being Nightswimming's founding artistic director, Brian Quirt was president of the Literary Managers and Dramaturgs of the Americas from 2006 to 2008, and twice received the LMDA's Elliott Hayes Award for Dramaturgy. In 2012 he was appointed director of the Banff Playwrights Colony at the Banff Centre.

Yolanda Ferrato:
Tell me about Nightswimming and what you do?

Brian Quirt:

We define ourselves as a dramaturgical and commissioning company, devoted to new work in theatre, dance and music. This came from my desire, as a co-founder, to do work I couldn't do anywhere else. I wanted an environment where, by commissioning new work, I could look at how stories are told on stage, across different forms and disciplines, and have the opportunity to address questions that intrigued or concerned me.

Partnership is equally central to the company. Being a non-producing company frees us from the financial requirements of producing the works we commission, and that compels us to partner with other companies during the development process who will ultimately premier the work.

The company has adhered to these premises for many years. This has ensured a huge amount of flexibility in the work we do, and adaptability in how we work. It enables us to explore the central question of the company: How do you create an environment where you can customize the process for each show?

Our commissioning enables artists to create work they couldn't have created anywhere else. That feels like a good reason for a company to exist.

YF:

Your work comes from many different starting points. In the case of Lake Nora Arms, *the source was a book of poetry by Michael Redhill. Adapting written verse for performance is a great example of exploring how a story is told onstage. Tell me about your process for adapting* Lake Nora Arms.

BQ:

I was attracted to its beautiful, evocative language that I felt would work onstage as spoken text. It also had an accessible environment about people's experience of Canadian landscape and cottage country. The combination of accessibility and heightened language interested me. I thought: What's an equivalent way to put that on stage? Song was a way to explore that in parallel. Song continues to make it accessible.

The form the show took, an a cappella musical, is heightened. But how do you find a narrative pathway through a book of poems that wasn't written with that in mind? How do you find a pathway musically through a piece?

To begin the project, I commissioned songwriter Jane Miller to select poems to compose songs for. It was more interesting to ask her to choose the songs, to see what her choices revealed and draw on her instincts as an artist and collaborator. Giving other artists authority to make choices that will shape the piece down the line is one of several threads running through Nightswimming's work.

We constructed a half-hour piece from the original songs Jane composed and presented it in Toronto to test certain questions I had about the piece. Was there enough material in this book of poems to be the core of the piece? Could I construct a narrative onto this non-narrative set of poems and find individuals who could voice it, even though the book has no individuals in it? What rewards are there for an audience in watching the actors/singers take that pathway through the piece?

We came away with a set of songs we loved and the audience really enjoyed. We also had a basic premise for character archetypes that fit some of the threads in the book.

I asked Jane to look for other poems she thought could be songs, and we built a repertoire of twelve or thirteen songs. The songs are the touchstone moving through this piece. Now the question is: What are the textual elements that carry us from song to song? We drew from the book, with the restriction that we couldn't change the text of any poem, but we could change their structure.

We did a series of workshops and public concerts of the piece. Those were designed to test the storytelling and musical journey through the piece, and to determine how audiences were interpreting what we were presenting to them.

YF:
Is the audience an important tool in your dramaturgical process?

BQ:

Yes. With almost all of our pieces, we do workshops from the first draft. I believe plays are meant to be spoken, and I like hearing them earlier rather than later.

I don't solicit feedback from audiences directly. I don't find talk-backs or written responses useful. As a playwright said, what's useful is just being in the audience, experiencing the story with them as it is today. You can glean a lot of information from listening or watching a story through the eyes of other people. That's a very valuable tool in continuing the work on a theatrical story.

YF:

How long was the process for Lake Nora Arms *from conception to production?*

BQ:

Lake Nora Arms took eight or nine years ultimately. That's partly a reflection of how long it takes to compose and score a piece, to find an ultimate producer and to determine which elements of the book of poetry to use and how to structure it.

YF:

Is it a luxury to spend years developing a piece?

BQ:

At Nightswimming extended workshops aren't a luxury, they're a product of a set of choices we made to focus entirely on dramaturgical work and the development of the pieces. Sometimes, they're choices forced by a set of circumstances. If we don't have a producer for a piece, we take advantage of the time that offers us to continue working. Sometimes the resources aren't available when you most want or need them, so you defer the work, then return to it a year or two later. While that's not intentional, often that turns out to be valuable.

A show that happens more quickly is not necessarily better. That's part of the equation of knowingly commissioning shows outside of common conventions. If you're pursuing work whose form is a little unusual, you have to accept it may take longer for that work to find a home.

YF:

The Whirlpool *is another piece where you combined forms, in this case dance and theatre, to adapt a tale of entangled lives set in Niagara Falls. What was your starting point for translating Jane Urquhart's novel to the stage with choreographer Julia Sasso?*

BQ:

My instinct was that because there was relatively little dialogue in the book, a different form was needed to express the story, and choreography might be it. In the first step of the process we focused on one of the book's threads with a group of three actors. We read each chapter aloud, focusing on those three characters. As we worked through the chapters I would ask Julia to choreograph or physically explore elements of those chapters. The process generated a physical vocabulary for how characters interact with each other, and a metaphoric vocabulary about the thematic world of water and whirlpools the book was exploring and also the literal setting of the whirlpool by Niagara Falls.

Those sessions convinced me there was a way to draw out the unspoken story. Choreography was our way to convey some of the images, ideas, interactions and dynamics that a novel reveals through prose.

Having concluded that was a profitable way forward, Nightswimming set up a larger workshop where we did the whole version of the first thread, knowing there was a parallel story which intersects with it at the end. In subsequent workshops we focused on that second thread, which led to further workshops about integrating the two threads of the book. Each stage moves you closer to something. In this case, the discreet elements of the book allowed us to do it in phases.

YF:

In scripting The Whirlpool, *how did you translate dance and movement to the page?*

BQ:

During the workshop process we extracted and adapted the dialogue, along with very basic stage directions to suggest the main actions. After the production there was interest in publishing the adaptation. I spent a long time determining the criteria for describing the choreographic sections of the production. Ultimately, I didn't describe any of Julia's choreography. Instead, I used her choreography to articulate the principal actions that happened between characters physically and what the choreographic sections had to achieve. If someone else were to produce *The Whirlpool*, they could invent whatever choreography they wished. My work was to make clear that certain sets of actions and parts of the narrative voice were choreography, not spoken.

The only addition Julia made, ultimately, to the published version was at the beginning of the text. It seemed important for the audience to enter the story physically, not through words. The piece opens with a scene between a mother and child that is completely physical, so the book now opens with the words, 'The play begins with a dance,' which captures the status of physical, choreographed action in the production, as conceived, without saying what it was.

YF:

Blue Note *must also have been an interesting piece to script. On this project you collaborated with actors, musicians and architects to create an installation performance about a choir in rehearsal, where the audience could watch the performance evolve over the course of the exhibit. In its publication you referred to the text as a* score for performance *rather than a script. Can you explain that idea?*

BQ:

Blue Note came from an idea about what happens to a small ensemble of singers when one of them leaves, and in this case has died. You're dealing with loss on two levels: the physical, tangible loss of voice in the ensemble, and the emotional loss of the individual, period.

I collaborated with actor, playwright and musician Martin Julien. We decided early on that we did not necessarily want it to become a play. We feared if we continued talking about it as a play, we would become beholden to psychological narrative or character-driven psychology, and would feel drawn to conventionalizing the narrative of this piece. Who are these people? Do we know enough about each of these seven or eight individuals? What are their back stories? What are their motivations? None of which was interesting to us. It took a lot of work to say to ourselves that this wasn't a play, and therefore we could give ourselves freedom not to worry about these things. If you're not worried about any of those things what then are you offering an audience? What are the rewards of watching? What are you actually exploring? That's why, when it was published, we didn't call it a play. We decided to create this piece in a different way, and we felt that the written version should also find its own form.

YF:
How did you find the written form of the piece?

BQ:
In thinking of how to score *Blue Note* we thought of Terry Riley's musical score *In C*. It has a musical notation but it also has a set of tasks or conditions under which the piece has to be performed. When we encountered *In C* and incorporated it into a workshop, it offered us a lot of interesting musical opportunities for the play because it's about a group that is together but fragmented. It expressed part of the emotional world of this choir who are together but separate, in that each member had different emotional responses to the death of their colleague, as we all do. We all try to be uniform in our public presentation of grief, but of course we never share it all completely.

Parts of *Blue Note* had conditions, or rather tasks: sometimes performers were to play different parts each night; scenes were conducted live by different performers each night. That had to become part of the score. *Score* became something more interesting to us because a score is shaped and conducted live each time it's presented. We wanted to capture that fluidity on paper and *score* seemed the better word than *play*, which somehow feels like it is set.

YF:

The score contains footnotes describing the tasks and how they varied from performance to performance, one even mentioned the effect a child's laughing had on a performance. Has the audience become part of this finished product?

BQ:

Those are offered as examples of how the performance can be a partnership with an audience. We wanted to capture things that were important to us: proximity, intimacy, direct address at certain points, and that an audience has their own series of choices to make.

YF:

Often, you direct a piece you dramaturged. Are you always the dramaturg during the process or is there a moment when that hat comes off?

BQ:

I don't think the hat can ever come off, but other people take on more of the role. Dramaturgy happens whether there is someone with the title of dramaturg or not. Sometimes Nightswimming's long-time producer Naomi Campbell played that role. Many producers are very smart dramaturgs but don't think of themselves that way. They have a very precise and clear-eyed vision of storytelling and an ability to feedback usefully on how that is being told on stage. You never do it solo. Ever.

YF:

When Nightswimming commissions a playwright, how do you support their project?

BQ:

The relationship between the playwright and the dramaturg is about three things: ideas, communication and process. What are the core ideas that person is trying to investigate and ultimately express? 'Heart ideas' is the word I use sometimes. Part of my work as a dramaturg is to discern, illuminate, discover and begin to develop a set of opinions about those ideas. You can't be objective about them; you become more subjective as you learn about them, and your opinions will help shape what the thing becomes.

In Nightswimming's world that part often begins before the commission, because you're not responding to a script, you're responding to an artist. Just as I'm interested in things I don't know how to do, I'm interested in things artists want to do but don't know how to do, or are afraid of doing, or feel they will never get to do otherwise. If I can help them do that, we have a reason for a partnership.

YF:

How did this partnership work, for example, when Nightswimming commissioned playwright Judith Thompson for Such Creatures?

BQ:

Judith wanted to revisit the set of masks she had created for her when she was a student at the National Theatre School, which she now uses when teaching. She didn't know where it might go, and asked if Nightswimming could support her in sessions to work with those masks. I said yes, that's exactly the sort of thing Nightswimming can do, because it's something she needed to do, that she couldn't do somewhere else, and that fit with the flexibility that Nightswimming can offer. It was a way for us to get to know an artist better, it wasn't about a show yet.

We set up the studio for her to improvise with her masks alone over the course of three weeks. I would check in occasionally. At the end she wanted to do it again. This time, she wanted me to be more involved in the second part of each session. I would interview the characters she created each morning, improvisationally. None of it was about making a play.

Ultimately, one of the characters asserted themselves, the character who became Blandy. She's a teenager from Toronto coping with an extremely damaged family. We commissioned her to write a play with Blandy at the centre. We didn't know if it would be a solo play or other, but we said there was enough there to go on.

At a certain point, Judith decided it wasn't a solo play anymore. She wanted to combine it with another ongoing obsession; this character who became Sorel: a woman who as a teenager was part of a rebellion in Auschwitz.

YF:
Did the character of Sorel also come from the mask work?

BQ:
Completely separate. Much more research-driven. I said to Judith, don't think about how they fit together, just write it and see what happens. She started writing the Sorel monologue. Equally powerful, very different. Originally it was thought one half of the evening would be Blandy, one half Sorel. We did a reading of them separately, and Judith had an instinct we should weave them together, so we started doing that. What were they saying about each other? What was the conversation between those two characters across time and speeches and theatre? The last year of the process was about how the images, the ideas and the friction between them work, and then how they get realized onstage together.

YF:
How do parallel stories work in conversation with each other?

BQ:
Even if stories alternate, we watch them simultaneously. On some level, any audience member is comparing and contrasting them and, whether we like it or not, looking for clues in each about why they are together. You hear something in one story, the next time someone speaks, you either know something different or deduce something additional, or wish you did. Our job is to not leave it in the realm of wish, which creates dissatisfaction. You can't stop an audience from asking how the stories are feeding each other, so you have to pursue that instinct, but also monitor it, and reward it on some level.

How do images refract or link up or not link up? How do thematic ideas relate the stories? And word choices. All of those things have to be parsed and considered. We also have to look at potentials for misinterpretation. You are putting stories together for some reason, you want a conversation between them, but you also have to acknowledge that the audience will be looking for one; those may or may not be the same conversations.

YF:

Many pieces you've worked on recently involve parallel stories. Is there something about them that inherently interests you?

BQ:

Apparently. I don't pursue them, but I think there's something inherently dramaturgical about the challenge of pieces with multiple threads. The dramaturgy of how they work together exposes issues about how stories are told and how stories work together. Plays that are puzzles intrigue me. How does an audience assemble them? The reading of two stories together adds something. It's a multiplier effect. It asks us to be engaged in both, and the collision of stories gives opportunity for the audience to assert a place for themselves in the experience. Lots of stories are passive, and that's great, they might even be better. They allow a degree and quality of focus that is different. Stories that have multiple threads where the friction is a third component, that really intrigues me.

Trying to manage that third component, how an audience interprets the relationship between those components, is exciting. It puts dramaturgy at the centre in a stronger way. It forces you to make interesting choices about how that functions, and how that articulates something about the world that you're exploring. And the theatrical challenges of telling multiple stories on stage are very real about how you keep them alive, how you weave them and how you tell them. It's a harder way, but it's fun.

YF:

Do you ever think you can't stage a certain play?

BQ:

Yes. In the case of *City of Wine*, Ned Dickens's cycle of Greek plays. There are plays, the challenges of which are better served by other people. As the cycle grew from three to seven stories, I became aware that I couldn't direct any one and still dramaturg the whole. That, however, didn't stop us from pursuing these shows that are enormous.

YF:
Could you define this project a little?

BQ:
It started with Ned doing his version of *Oedipus* almost twenty years ago; I was the dramaturg. Ned and I spent a lot of time talking about what happens before and after the story of Oedipus. I was interested in the pre-story of Jocasta. Our conversations ultimately led to Nightswimming commissioning him to write *Jocasta* which tells the story of her marriage to Liaus, the conception and birth of Oedipus, his return as an adult and the moment they meet and fall in love. It ends with their wedding, it's happy, it's a comedy. Then he wrote the sequel to *Oedipus*, which is *Creon*, a version of *Antigone* from Creon's point of view. Ned wanted to investigate the moral and civic choice Creon faces, less so the emotional one. Antigone doesn't have a choice; she says what she's going to do from the very beginning.

We started to conceive of a seven-play cycle that would tell the story of the City of Thebes from its conception, which is the story of Cadmus and Harmonia on Mount Olympus, through its demise, to the end of its people documented at the siege of Troy.

YF:
What can these stories offer modern audiences, what questions are you putting to them?

BQ:
City of Wine is about a city, a civic community. It's actually about its evolution from its founding to its demise, so it's about how a culture evolves and changes over time. Most importantly, it's about leadership, but not about leadership during war. That's what the Trojan plays are about. Not surprisingly, they were popular in the twentieth century. The Theban plays are about civic issues. How are we led? Who leads

Figure 2 Kristian Messere in *Harmonia* by Ned Dickens from the *City of Wine* cycle. (2009, dir: DD Kugler). Photography: John Lauener.

us? How is leadership shifted from generation to generation? What are the responsibilities of the leadership to the leadership class and to the people they lead? What are the responsibilities of the citizens to their own community, to the leadership of it?

The Theban story has two civil wars, they're certainly war, but the issue is different because it's a struggle about the future of yourself and your place, and whose agenda will triumph. Who's responsible for shaping the future of a community? That seemed to us thrilling and important and exciting, and something that wasn't getting written about explicitly here over the last fifteen years. They're so explicitly about leadership, but they're also in the best sense fantastic, rollicking stories.

YF:

How important is entertainment in developing work?

BQ:

Pretty important, but not every story is a rollicking good story. I tend to think of it in terms of rewards. In *City of Wine* the rewards are partly about following people over time through sequential events, and seeing what will happen to them. That's a reward most humans like in lots of forms of storytelling.

YF:
What other kinds of rewards do you offer audiences?

BQ:
Beautiful music well sung is a reward. Laughter is a reward. Surprise or reversal is a reward; expectations are challenged and audiences are rewarded by that. Beauty is a reward: visual, physical, thematic beauty. Suspense is a reward. Intimacy, as in *Blue Note*, can be a reward. Not for everyone, frankly, but for some it absolutely is.

One benefit of a reward is the audience retains engagement or becomes more engaged. I think of that a lot. What are the rewards I'm offering in return for the work I'm asking from the audience?

YF:
What do you see as the way forward for storytelling and play development?

BQ:
There are times when the playwright-driven play form feels insufficient for telling particular stories. Right now, some of the most exciting energy is from hybrid forms. I think it's also true that audiences are interested in events in a different way now; the growth of festivals in the last thirty years has accentuated that. A lot of our theatres and perhaps our plays haven't figured out how to use or compete with that.

Playwrights that find the right pathway through a powerful story with characters confronting the things we don't say often enough in the real world will always be important and will always rise to the surface. I just wonder whether we accept too many of the ones that aren't quite at the top, and whether there are other options we should be pursuing, but we're a little scared of our audiences. Nightswimming creates in both the playwright-driven and devised theatre worlds, and the balance between them in our company is always shifting.

You can say the same thing in a playwright-driven play, or a devised play, or in this interesting hybrid form. How do you tell stories in these different ways? How are the stories different and how are the forms different? How do they contribute to each other as well? That's where Nightswimming has always wanted, liked and continues to live.

(The interview was made in Ottawa, on 29 March 2012.
Many thanks to Brian Quirt for his participation and generous insights.)

Towards Performed Dramaturgy

Duška Radosavljević

What is the relationship between the discipline(s) of dramaturgy as we have come to know it in Europe and the practice of performance as it emerged in the latter half of the twentieth century in the English-speaking world? One, potentially oversimplified, way of viewing the distinction between the two is that dramaturgy is traditionally associated with text-based theatre, from which performance, in turn, has struggled to emancipate itself. In her study of the genealogy of Performance Studies in the United States, Shannon Jackson noted elements of rebellion, opposition and adversarial rhetoric deployed by some proponents of Performance Studies such as Richard Schechner in relation to theatre and Theatre Studies in particular.[1] From a European perspective, this adversariality can appear entirely baffling.[2] Nevertheless, in his investigation of the tension between Performance Studies and its 'abandoned child/parent' – dramaturgy – the Croatian dramaturg Marin Blažević has raised several pertinent questions:

> What is it that, despite evident parallels, keeps performance studies at a secure distance from its abandoned child, or perhaps more accurately – its abandoned parent? Is it possible that the reason for circumnavigation of dramaturgy is not solely contained in the fact that performance studies – as a paradigm dominated until recently by Anglo-American academics and artists – simply mistook dramaturgy for literary management (due to the expectation levelled at it within the Anglo-American system of theatre production)? Or could the reason be that dramaturgy has the potential to interfere with the perception

that performance studies have cleared up their territorial issues with theatre studies and dramatic literature studies? Above all, could it also be that performance studies are avoiding dramaturgy because it constantly reminds them of the shared departure point, which is the subject of all three disciplines contained in the terminological potential of the word 'action'?[3]

Eventually, Blažević borrows the notion of 'in-betweenness' from Richard Schechner via McKenzie[4] – originally ascribed to the field of Performance Studies – and deploys it to characterize both fields thus facilitating a speculation on the possibility of their reconciliation.

I was oblivious to the potential cross-cultural complexities contained within the encounter between the practices of dramaturgy and performance-making when I volunteered to work as the dramaturg on *Imagining O*, a 2011 performance that Richard Schechner created with staff and students at the School of Arts' Jarman building at the University of Kent. Inspired by Shakespeare's character of Ophelia and the 1954 erotic novel *The Story of O* by Pauline Reage, this piece would ultimately constitute an inter-textual dialogue between the characters of Ophelia and O.

Instead of acting as a production dramaturg in a conventional sense, in this project, I was tasked with creating a seminar that would unfold during the live performance in one of the building's seminar rooms. My job therefore acquired the function of what I have defined elsewhere as 'Reception Dramaturgy'[5] – a process whereby the inner dramaturgy of the piece is made more explicit and accessible to the spectator. To ensure the presence of an audience, capitalizing on the erotic content of the piece, I had the dramaturgical seminar streamed live through Chatroulette, a social networking site often associated with erotic web-based interaction. In analysing this particular case study with regard to the fact that, contrary to some of the pre-existing notions of dramaturgical practice, my process unfolded simultaneously to the live performance of the piece, I will argue that this project created space for a category of 'performed dramaturgy' to emerge.

Departures

As a director, Richard Schechner appeared open to the possibility of working with a dramaturg. We had our initial meeting on Skype about six months before he came to the University of Kent to take up his Visiting Professorship and to work with a group of students and staff on creating a new piece based on *Hamlet*. I volunteered my time because I was just embarking on a research project in which I was going to consider the relationship between text and performance in contemporary theatre. I was hoping that the founding father of Performance Studies – and of the Performance Group – would be a good source of wisdom. Plus, I had hoped that I could bring into the process useful experience of my own as a dramaturg, a member of the theatre profession in the United Kingdom, and a long-standing fan of that particular Shakespeare's play.

As someone who had fallen into the profession of dramaturgy having done a Theatre Studies degree in a British university, I was always in two minds about whether the dramaturg's place in the UK theatre system was worth fighting for. I care about the process of making, more so than the process of finishing a show and putting it in front of an audience – this is why I have opted for the job of a dramaturg rather than director. I also enjoy offering a personal response more so than initiating an idea. In this way, I have always thought that the jobs of an actor and dramaturg were closer in their nature than the jobs of the director and dramaturg. I have encountered refined dramaturgical sensibility in some actors I have worked with, and in addition – even though the dramaturgs are often perceived as being linked to the written word – I have come across several dramaturgs who had originally trained or worked as actors (Hanna Slättne, Peter Eckersall) as well as some who continue to juggle their acting and dramaturgy roles (Joeri Smet, Adriano Shaplin). However, I have never enjoyed having to defend the existence of a dramaturg, engage in advocacy for the usefulness of this post or negotiate space for it in the rehearsal room. I had hoped that I wouldn't necessarily have to do this with someone as experienced and self-assured as Richard Schechner.

Our Skype conversations, which also included Kent PhD graduate Pablo Pakula in the capacity of Schechner's personal assistant, unfolded on a weekly basis from January to May 2011, when the director came to Canterbury to meet the rest of the cast and creative team. Having previously worked on *Hamlet* on several occasions, Schechner was keen to focus on the character of Ophelia, and therefore he gave the project a working title of *Imagining O*. One starting idea was to make a piece in which only the women spoke and men were silent. At first he wanted to borrow from all the other Shakespeare's women to help Ophelia articulate herself, but then because someone misread the title as implying association with the French erotic novel of the 1960s *The Story of O* by Pauline Reage, he decided to bring this female voice into the mix too. Later the visual world of Balthus (Balthasar Klossovsky) and his paintings would enter the rehearsal room. The project also involved Schechner's associate director Benjamin Mosse and Kent PhD student, choreographer Roanna Mitchell. Following the principles of 'environmental theatre'[6] the piece was envisaged as taking place throughout the Jarman building which was erected less than two years previously, in 2009, and for this occasion the billing of a 'dispersed performance' was coined.

In his first reconnaissance tour of the Jarman, Schechner motioned at a seminar room, instantaneously deciding that this would become the 'dramaturgy room', in which – unlike anything that had ever been done before – a dramaturgical seminar would be taking place during the performance itself! This was both exciting and unsettling. Up until this moment I had been tasked with routine text-related jobs – to compile all female lines in all Shakespeare's plays being one of the more substantial ones – but at this moment it became clear that Schechner's idea of a dramaturg was close to a variety of scholar. My view, on the other hand, has always been that – while the dramaturg's job may involve it – research is not a defining characteristic of the dramaturg's contribution. Schechner's gesture described above could be read in a number of ways: as indicative of the director's desire to segregate the dramaturg from the creative process, as a compromise, or as indicative of a certain generosity and desire to give his collaborators autonomy.

I opted for the latter reading. Indeed, in one of the rehearsals which followed a few weeks later, Schechner underlined the importance of autonomy, using the analogy of the piece as a globe where he is in control of the globe and his associate and movement directors are in control of individual continents. The performers too were invited to come to the first rehearsal with their own compilations of female Shakespearean lines – thus making their own contributions to the dramaturgical process. As the process evolved, I found my place to be something of a satellite – to pursue the above analogy: a moon to this globe, inextricably connected to it by the force of gravity, but an entirely separate cosmic entity. This was partly an organic development resulting from the fact that the piece had three directors. Instead of acting as a production dramaturg in what I would consider to be a conventional sense – that is, working closely with the director on shaping, evolving and executing his vision through the rehearsal process – as mentioned above, I began to see my job as being closer to 'Reception Dramaturgy', a process whereby the inner dramaturgy of the piece is made more explicit and accessible to the spectator through workshops, talks or accompanying materials.

The process

Early on in the process we came up with a general structure for the dispersed performance. The principle of interactivity between the audience and the actors emerged as an important theme and the structure was envisaged to facilitate the audience's participation. This resulted in a five-part structure:

1. The exposition occurs in the foyer, on and around the staircase of the building. Here, all of the conventions of the piece are introduced – site-specificity, a section from *Hamlet*, a section from *The Story of O*, a dance inspired by Balthus's nudes, the use of film.
2. The audience are ushered into a studio space where a filmed dialogue scene is played out between Ophelia and O.

3. Then the audience are divided into groups using a single-digit number they were given on arrival and they follow a particular journey around the building which consists of three short site-specific scenes. This section was called the 'First Dispersal'.
4. The middle section ('The Tipping Point') has the audience back in the studio space where a second interaction between Ophelia and O takes place at the end of which the audience are sent off on their own individual journeys – referred to as the 'Second Dispersal'.
5. Finally, the audience are gathered together again for the finale which gradually takes them outside the building.

It was the Second Dispersal, lasting around twenty minutes, that featured an active dramaturgical seminar in the Dramaturgy Room. The audience also had the option to visit the Dramaturgy Room as a kind of a live Programme Note before the show, and again afterwards for a post-show discussion with the director and cast members.

In conceptualizing the Dramaturgical Seminar, Schechner remained keen on the idea of a scholarly rendition of the process using various rehearsal materials and a live feed of the performance via TV screens – thus perhaps limiting the dramaturg's role to an archival rather than a creative one (and evoking the conflict encapsulated by Blaževič's quote). On my part, I was intent on using the intellectual and artistic autonomy which I understood I had been given. I wanted to interpret the notion of the 'seminar' – using its Latin root 'semen, seminis' – as a seed garden, or a nursery. Having been delegated a cosmic entity of my own, I assumed that I could utilize my otherwise unutilized dramaturgical skills and impulses thus far, within an autonomous conceptualization of the Dramaturgy Room. For example, I wanted to have sprigs of Ophelia's flowers in this room, and an O-shaped seating formation for the audience rather than seminar room desks. I also wanted to extend the notion of autonomy to the audience's process of meaning-making by 'seeding' certain ideas with them so as to facilitate individual appreciation of the piece, rather than serving them with digested information. There was something thematically justified about providing a space for 'semen' in a piece otherwise dominated by female expression only. I offered that, in the absence of male voices in this piece, the only place where men could speak would be in the seminar room. Technically, there was some concern about whether or not the audience would want to attend a seminar during the performance. My response to this – once again in keeping with the thematic world of the piece – was to also stream the seminar via Chatroulette, thus at least ensuring one audience member at a time (another thing that, to my knowledge, had never been before). As Chatroulette is often used for sexual exhibitionism of people (mostly men) who are seeking interaction with strangers via the internet, I thought it would be interesting to provide to potential website users the kind of interaction made available by a dramaturgical seminar (even though the nudity in our show was never actually streamed to any of the monitors in public spaces). Ultimately, in keeping with one of the formal characteristics of the piece, I wanted the seminar to be truly interactive rather than presentational in its format.

Benjamin Mosse and Roanna Mitchell were initially more supportive of this idea than Schechner, who maintained a surprisingly conservative view that the Dramaturgy Room had to hold all knowledge concerning the piece. But how could this be done to fit the twenty-minute slot made available by the Second Dispersal? Even in my teaching, a lecture format is in any case my least favourite form of interaction with people as I believe strongly in the value of kinaesthetic and experiential learning. In conceiving the format for the content of the Second Dispersal, Mosse and Mitchell provided a useful rule which was applied to all of the dispersed scenes taking place at the same time – each segment of material should last for three minutes only. The rationale behind this was to enable individual audience members to visit several dispersed scenes within the twenty-minute interval.

I therefore devised the following game, using some of the elements of the process and of the performance itself:

You pick a number from 0-9. Each number determines a particular topic concerning *Imagining O*, its development, its themes, and its connection with you. We talk about each topic for three minutes; the time is measured by this egg timer. We can only cover six topics before you leave this room.

Sometimes 'rules are there to be broken'.[7]

The Rules of the Game were made available under number 1. Laminated A4 sheets of paper with a single-digit number from zero to nine were arranged in a circle inside the circle made by the chairs on which the audience sat. On the other side of the sheet there was a script I would use for that segment. A laptop through which the seminar was streamed on Chatroulette was in the middle of the room and behind me were the monitors which streamed the performance live and which I could also use to screen some documentary material from rehearsals.

Other topics, represented by other numbers included:

2 – Travelling – the notion of spectating as a journey, the notion of 'Canterbury as a place of pilgrimage'.[8]

3 – Balthus – Roanna's Power Point of the images which inspired the choreography.

4 – Nakedness – Schechner's ideas on nakedness and nudity[9] drawn from rehearsals and from his writings are offered up for discussion.

5 – Text and Performance – explores the use of text as pretext for an element of the installation as a whole, offers some theoretical ideas[10] and some practical approaches to text used in rehearsal, specifically Schechner's interest in 'Concretisation rather than psychologisation of language'.[11]

6 – Imagining/fantasy – I ask the audience to close their eyes and take them on an imagined journey towards pleasure (using some key terms from the play such as the 'inner eye').

7 – Death – Both Ophelia and O commit suicide; we take the three minutes to reflect on some aspects of death and suicide, including the Early Modern usage of 'death' as a euphemism for orgasm.

8 – Film – I play a short section of documentary footage from rehearsal, focusing on Schechner's methodology of Rasa Boxes.[12]

9. Your questions, comments, 'remembrances' – the audience leads.
0. O – O'clock. Ophelianess. Orifices. Openness/Emptiness. Endless-ness/Completeness. Eau. We read together 'O, what a noble mind is here o'erthrown'.

Allowing for the possibility that the rules may get broken, I would allow an audience member to be in control of the egg timer, thus deciding whether to move on after three minutes or dedicate another three minutes to the same topic. The audience members on Chatroulette were free to stay or go as they pleased, but I am happy to say that the Dramaturgy Room had good traffic throughout the run of the piece.

Performed dramaturgy

The invisibility of the dramaturg's contribution to a process is an often-noted feature of his/her work.[13] While Turner and Behrndt relate this problem to the dramaturg's 'in-betweenness', Hartley notes that this invisibility is contained in the attention to 'detail' which may seem insignificant in relation to the 'sprawling monolith' of the show that is nevertheless composed of and held together by the detail itself.[14] He warns however that a dramaturg should avoid making the mistake of being 'self-effacing to the point of invisibility'.[15]

Marin Blažević applies the notion of 'in-betweenness' to the condition of dramaturgy due to its 'particular twofold competence' and a process of 'mediation' between theory and practice, critical reflexion and embodiment, academic research and the production of knowledge, and ultimately – artistic inspiration and technical execution:

> If we understand dramaturgy in this way, we can see that in the absence of the visible field of autonomy on both ends of the scale, dramaturgy can derive its own power precisely from its deficiencies, its inability or unwillingness to constitute itself as a discipline or to institute itself as an authorial (e.g. directing) or executive (e.g. acting) activity.[16]

The parallel drawn between the 'in-betweenness' of Performance Studies and dramaturgy thus leads Blažević to ask whether dramaturgy can work within Performance Studies, or whether its 'in-betweenness' could be deployed in 'harmonising the three disciplines (of Theatre Studies, dramatic literature and Performance Studies) while simultaneously continuing to create fruitful provocations in their further polemics'.[17]

As mentioned above, I resolved to embark on the project of *Imagining O* without any preconceptions of political relations between Performance Studies and Theatre Studies. (My own studies of theatre in the mid-1990s in the United Kingdom featured a healthy mix of Schechner's theory, Grotowskian physical theatre, British theatre history and contemporary drama without any apparent internal conflicts). I was keen to discover – in a way which would be as unbiased as possible – how the function of dramaturgy manifested itself in a performance-making process led by Richard Schechner. The best I could glean was that, due to the mechanism of increased autonomization which this process made possible, dramaturgy became both an authorial (in the case of the directors and actors) and executive activity (in the case of the actors, and exceptionally, the dramaturg). In such a situation, everyone assumed a dramaturgical sensibility and the dramaturg was not strictly speaking indispensible.[18] But ultimately, the process of dramaturgy was here explicitly performed rather than being simply intrinsic (and therefore invisible). Thanks to a set-up like this one, dramaturgy could move away from ontological questions concerning its own existence and towards more pragmatic issues of its operation: not whether and what it 'is', but how it 'does' what it does.

Harding and Rosenthal's introduction to their recent collection of essays offering a reevaluation of Schechner's body of work highlights that, prior to doing a PhD on Ionesco and eventually dedicating himself to the promotion of Performance Studies as a discipline, young Schechner himself had begun his theatre practice as a playwright and director of his own plays.[19] By maintaining its in-betweenness, Performance Studies forged its way ahead and abandoned (or at least appeared to want to abandon) traditional theatrical models of professionalization and division of labour into acting, writing and directing. Through the 'environmental theatre' conception of staging, Schechner's own directorial work also abandoned the distinction between the performance space and the auditorium. Ultimately, Performance Studies has allowed us to conceive of the possibility that we are all performers, and possibly in a process of making and watching a performance, we are all performers of dramaturgy.

What is left to say about the role of a dramaturg in a contemporary performance-making process? That – maybe thanks to the influence of Performance Studies – s/he has long ceased to be seen as a guardian of the written word, a researcher or a scholar. That through the works where the audience are increasingly given a co-authorship role – in pieces such as *You Me Bum Bum Train* in the United Kingdom or the work of Ontroerend Goed in Belgium, for example – the job of a dramaturg is equally increasingly linked to a facilitation of this changing communication process. And, finally, returning to the opening question of this essay: that, working in a globalized context, the contemporary dramaturg will often discover that the theatre-makers' (and audiences') methodological relationships to text and performance are often culture-specific rather than necessarily universal. Although 'dramaturgy' may be broadly understood in similar ways across the world, 'being a dramaturg' will vary in its use and understanding.

References

Blažević, Marin. 'Međutnost dramaturgije - od Batušićeva 'redatelja-teoretičara' do Gevelle-dramaturga', in Sibila Petlevski, Boris Senker and Marin Blažević, eds. *Trajnost čina – zbornik u čast Nikoli Batušiću*. Zagreb: Hrvatski centar ITI, 2011.

Harding, James and Rosenthal, Cindy, eds. *The Rise of Performance Studies: Rethinking Richard Schechner's Broad Spectrum*. Basingstoke, New York: Palgrave Macmillan, 2011.

Hartley, Andrew James. *The Shakespearean Dramaturg: A Theoretical and Practical Guide.* New York: Palgrave Macmillan, 2005.

Jackson, Shannon. *Professing Performance: Theatre in the Academy from Philology to Performativity.* Cambridge: Cambridge University Press, 2004.

Luckhurst, Mary. *Dramaturgy: A Revolution in Theatre.* Cambridge: Cambridge University Press, 2006.

McKenzie, Jon. *Perform or Else: From Discipline to Performance.* New York: Routledge, 2001.

Radosavljević, Duška. 'The Need to Keep Moving: Remarks on the Place of a Dramaturg in 21st Century England'. *Performance Research, On Dramaturgy* 14.3 (2009), pp. 45–51.

—*Theatre-Making: Interplay Between Text and Performance in the 21st Century.* Basingstoke: Palgrave Macmillan, 2013.

Schechner, Richard. *Environmental Theater.* New York: Applause Theatre and Cinema Books, 1973/94.

—'Rasaesthetics'. *TDR: The Drama Review* 45.3 (2001), pp. 27–50.

Turner, Cathy and Behrndt, Synne K. *Dramaturgy and Performance.* Basingstoke: Palgrave, 2008.

Worthen W. B. *Shakespeare and the Authority of Performance.* Cambridge: Cambridge University Press, 1997.

Disruption as Revealing the Essence of Truth

Gad Kaynar in conversation with Ruth Kanner

Ruth Kanner has been a creator of experimental theatre in Israel since the early 1980s. Currently she leads her own group, an experimental theatre team, searching for a local theatrical language, interweaving storytelling, physical theatre and visual imagery. The group's re-examination of Israeli hegemonic narratives is performed through literary and documentary texts, creating innovative storytelling theatre. Kanner works internationally (Tel Aviv, New York, and Tokyo). Among her productions are: Discovering Elijah – *a play about war (2001);* Bathers – *a project with actors, dancers and specially designed sound instruments, based on women's casual conversations in the dressing room of a swimming pool (2004);* Dionysus in Dizengoff Center – *a penetrating investigation of the historical layers of a shopping mall in Tel Aviv, performed as a storytelling theatre that engages various theatrical means to ask challenging questions about the roots of the Zionist existence in Israel (2004);* Mother Courage *by Bertolt Brecht (2005);* Signals – *an original interpretation of traditional and modern Hebrew texts, with vocal artist Victoria Hannah (2005);* At Sea – *an adaptation of two stories about love, life and death at the sea shore by S. Yizhar (2005);* Disgust – *a search into the anatomy of a basic human emotion, as expressed by ordinary people stopped and interviewed on a street (2006);* Eumenides *by Aeschylus (2007);* Cases of Murder *by Manfred Franke (2008);* Sakura No Sono Nippon – *a free adaptation of* The Cherry Orchard *by Yoko Tawada (2010);* The Flight of the Dove – *two parallel stories by Yuval Shimoni (2011).*

Ruth Kanner serves as an associate professor at the Department of Theatre Art, Tel Aviv University. She also presents, in Israel and abroad, workshops on storytelling theatre, movement, semiotic techniques and pragmatic speech act theories as sources for staging and directing techniques.

Gad Kaynar:
What would you in general regard as dramaturgical elements in your work?

Ruth Kanner:
If I could mention one key word – it would be 'distortion'. I do find out that the more you disrupt or disturb the work, any element of the work – you find the true essence of whatever you deal with: a specific text or idea or movement. Walter Benjamin is writing in such a wonderful way about the concept of interruption. He claims that that's what Brecht is doing – to disrupt the continuum. I guess I am attempting to follow these inspiring ideas in my work.

GK:
Could you give me an example from your work?

RK:
The one that comes to my mind is the story *At Sea* by the great Israeli writer, S. Yizhar. It is a love story about two youngsters. They go together to the Sea of Galilee, where they begin to discover each other. It's a very pure story, also in the way we deal with it on the stage – the whole stage is a huge, white paper, suggesting the purity of the primary moments.

But when we were rehearsing, I felt that the story needed a countermovement, it needed to go against something. This purity and these innocent first moments – what would interrupt it? I was trying to find it in a visual image. I tried to discuss it with the scenographer – Roni Toren – we live in a very vulgar world, and we see all these vulgar images around us, so maybe this is something we should struggle with, with how we are searching for our point of purity, which was actually lost. But we didn't find an answer in a visual image.

And then I did the most impudent thing I ever did: I asked one of the actresses to start the performance by sitting, holding a microphone, looking at the audience coming into the hall and counting the expected income from the box office. She is doing all kinds of calculations. She says: 'There are such and such seats in the hall and each ticket costs this and this, and students get reductions, so we lose such and such money.' So she does a very clear down-to-earth act. And it goes on! At the most fantastic moment, the very peak of the story the most sensitive and erotic moment – the dissonant voice of counting the money earned is invading the scene again. These noises of calculations are indeed something that exists in our world, although we strive to reduce them. But they are there. A part of my own conflict, too. So, this story with this provocative counterpoint is an example of what I would call an important dramaturgical 'disturbance'.

GK:
You choose to work with non-dramatic texts. What are actually the benefits of choosing a literary text and rejecting texts which were actually written for the theatre?

RK:
The painful truth is that the more I work with non-dramatic texts, I realize how good the dramatic texts are for the stage. They want the stage and the stage wants them, and it's so appropriate. And every time when I start again with literary or documentary texts – I suffer a lot, because it takes many, many weeks to find the dramaturgical line. Because it is as if the stories resist, they don't want to, they are not meant to.

GK:
So why all this stubborn insistence on taking them?

RK:
Because what I learnt again and again is that when you deal with these things that don't fit – it forces you to renew or expand your theatrical language. Somehow I think this very challenge is quite brutal: it's a force you invite for yourself, and then – you can't avoid it, you can't escape

from it, because the story doesn't work, so you have to ask challenging questions, especially questions about modes of representation.

For example – we worked on a story by Orly Kastel-Blum. She is a contemporary, postmodern Israeli writer. Her writing is very surreal, dream-like structures. Things are not stable, such as the story of this woman who is searching for food in an apocalyptic world. Everything is ruined – including human values. And this short story takes us from place to place. Places change repeatedly, also characters, like in a dream. Suddenly this woman meets a fish, then she goes into the bank of 'let-downs', then into a field of carrots, etc. You can't do that on stage, you can't build a bank and then a field of carrots. So it is wonderful, because it forced us to realize that the magic of the writing is the magic of a dream – the power of transformation. So we developed our ability to transform, and to transform within the rationale of a dream. We have to find these techniques of giving voice to unusual texts.

GK:
What are your criteria of choosing a specific text? Do you have any preferences for certain, specific texts over the others?

RK:
I feel that a choice of a text is always a political choice. Even more so, because we live in such a hectic place – every move turns to be a political move. Sometimes in a hidden way, not always in an explicit way. But I think my choice is always dealing with some dilemma, some wrong that is being done here. One of many, many wrongs that are being done here.

GK:
But this political approach is what defines only a part of what works you are doing, like Discovering Elijah *or* Dionysus in Dizengoff Center. *Other things are a little less obviously political.*

RK:
They are, but not always obviously so. My choices are also very instinctive. I choose something and somehow I tell myself: 'I have to do

it, I'm burning to do it.' But then I check myself, the dramaturgical side
of me is checking the more intuitive childish side of me.

I'll give you an example, something which was not at all political
to start with, but then. ... My work *Amos* is a story about a field
mouse that finds himself locked up in a trap, in a system of irrigation
pipes. And the whole story is his struggle to get out. I love animals
and the story is written in such a fantastic beautifully rich language,
yet, I was not really aware of my motivation of choosing it. Only
afterwards I heard people speaking about the essence of the story:
that you are trapped by a force which is much, much bigger than you,
which is blocking your freedom. So there were people talking about
Palestinians and Israel, but also people talking about the Holocaust,
and people who were trapped in tunnels, in the underground sewage
system there.

GK:
Or being trapped in and by memory.

RK:
Yes. On the face of it nothing seems political, it's rather a very personal
story in the fields of the Kibbutz, and all the colours and everything is
very Israeli. But maybe because it is located here, your mind starts to
search for something beyond and you take the mouse as a metaphor.

So one aspect of the choice is the political one, and its relevance for
our lives. The other aspect is the quality of the text. I would choose a
text only if it is written in a language that has truth; not pretending,
not imitating, but something that has its own inner truth. And also – a
text through which I can hear speech actions. Some texts just describe
things, and this for me becomes so boring. For me a good text for stage
– even the ones not written for the theatre – is rich with actions. And
this is crucial for me.

Only lately I realized that the very search for speech actions – is in
itself a sort of a political act. I read *The Human Condition* by Hannah
Arendt. There is a fantastic chapter entitled 'Action'. The way Arendt

describes action is a very broad definition of it. For her an action is always something you do to someone, it's not something which only stays within yourself. So it's always an opportunity to change something in the world.

So, a true action is something that you can never know where it is leading to. You start something. If you trust your fellows, the human beings, then it echoes. Something will happen to it, you can't control it – true actions can't be controlled. And this is such a fantastic lesson for theatre, for acting.

So it comes to the point, eventually, that I guess the dramaturgy of the theatre that I'm searching for, is hidden in texts that form practical and professional techniques and ways of doing. They do carry ideology, they do carry ideas, so actually – I began to speak about two different points that underlie my textual choices. One point is the political, the other is the existence of inner actions and action. But while talking, eventually realizing what Hannah Arendt is writing about, I begin to think that they are actually the same point.

GK:
Your dramaturgy seems to be first and foremost a dramaturgy of form and not of theme.

RK:
My father was an architect. I think I grew up with a very strong sense of form and structure. So my tendency would be working with colours, with movements, with patterns, with compositions. Sometimes the order of the working process would be playing with forms to start with, and only then beginning to structure the dramaturgical thought – listening to what the forms are talking about.

For example my work *Discovering Elijah*. This is a story about war. A specific war that happened in Israel in 1973, but also about any war. But, one of the first things I did was the decision that on stage there will be no weapons, no war machines – no tanks and war apparatus. And it's actually insane because the text is full of it – naturally it's dealing with bombs and noises etc. But it was obvious that I won't use it – because for me it's a ridiculous way of representation. When I see an actor holding a gun, I can't believe it, I can't trust it, I know it is fake. I can't trust this faking reality. So it was a very obvious decision not to use any weapons and so on.

But then – what? I played with several options in my mind, and it was hard to choose, but I kept telling myself: 'You have to be consistent and choose what is the one and only level of reality'. But something in me rebelled against this tyranny of a one and only logic, and I realized that I don't really want to go with one single principle during the whole play, so, eventually, for the ten different scenes, I created ten different ways of representing the weapons and apparatus of war. And while working, I understood more and more that the choice of representation is also a sort of a discussion about the issue itself. So in the course of the performance there are ten different signifiers, thus ten different discussions on different aspects of the use of weapons. It's like opening a discussion about morality through theatrical forms.

GK:
This is a very interesting aspect. What I remember from that production is using limbs, different limbs – like the arm as a gun. To objectify the body, alienate it. As if this is what war does to soldiers. And working with intermedial means, like using concrete music on stage, I felt as if there was an attempt to use the different medium as a kind of a commentary from a different point of view, not a human kind of view. It's like a dialogue between human elements on stage and the music, the sound elements.

RK:
Yes, I can mention two or three representations or signifiers. It started by the way that the first performer was just using the word 'fire'. This is actually what they do in the army, they take the real weapons, but without their ammunition. They run but they only shout 'fire, fire, fire!!' instead of actually shooting. It is called a 'dry exercise'. And then

Figure 3 Bombardment from *Discovering Elijah* (Ruth Kanner Theatre Group). The actor Yussuf Sueid with a big 'black hole' representing the holes left by a bombardment in which the fallen, in the next scene, will be swallowed up. Photography: Gadi Dagon.

I remembered a play by Eugene Ionesco, *The Lesson*, where the word 'knife' is killing. And then you begin to think – the word can kill. And the same is with the isolated limbs – when it's my own hand doing to the other arm this cyclic action of charging the rifle. So it's me, it's realizing something about the personal responsibility. This is one side of the use of weapons in the performance.

The other part is, when the actors take cover under fire. Of course I didn't want to imitate the bullets – but there is this kind of play balls that are made from a special rubber, that move randomly – you can't control their movements. So for me it wasn't the bullet, but the uncertainty principle, the horror of being there and not knowing if your eye will be lost, or your head, or your leg, or your whole life.

When I worked on this scene with the random balls jumping on the stage, I wanted the actors to discover the real horror of fear of death. I evaluated that the conventional techniques of finding the horror in yourself – would never be enough. So what I did was to ask all the actors to learn the same text – which is a wonderful monologue, and when one actor gets hit by the ball, he stops the monologue, and the other one will carry on. So it's actually the death of the actor. Since the movement of the balls is random – this principle created a real horror. It may sound nothing compared to really losing your life, but – the reactions were amazing. It was pure theatre. It was very powerful in rehearsals and then we did the same 'game' on stage. Sometimes we had soldiers in the audience, soldiers that have been to the battlefield, they told me: 'I could feel the war' – and this is so interesting that they felt a sense of reality although we didn't use any imitation of reality.

I'd like to say something about the music you mentioned before. Of course a war – and especially the war which is described in this novel of Yizhar – is a very noisy thing. But the last thing I wanted was to use recordings from reality. Because again, it doesn't work for me. So I approached the musician Ori Drummer and told him: 'We need noise. How can we produce a very big noise?' And he was so fantastic. He built a construction of pipes, and in it he worked with a torch of fire. The fire in the pipes created horrible sounds of scratching, of suffocating. So the sound is very physical, and it happens here and now. He also had two vacuum cleaners, and he blew their air into the pipes. So he had air and fire mixed in the work. This was for me a very powerful solution.

GK:
I also remember the rhythm. There is a scene where they run and shoot, that's what I remember the most. The sound of running; of not being able to stop the running. That's actually what recreated the memory of war in the strongest manner.

RK:

This is also my way of trying to use language not as something which describes but as the action itself. When the actors repeat the same text, 'running and shooting, running and shooting' again and again – the repetitive text plus the repetitive physical action creates the pulse of the event and this is something that has an autonomous significance which is beyond content.

GK:

The dramaturgical work of structuring the project, the thought about the techniques you described, thought about images and so on – are these pre-production deliberations? Do they emerge before you meet the actors, or is it something you devise while working with the actors? How much do you draw from their suggestions and intuitions?

RK:

There is still a gap between my true desire and the course I have taken so far. My dream is to come totally open to the rehearsals. And the dream of dreams is to come with nothing. But you need a lot of courage for this, so I'm growing and I'm collecting my courage. Up to now usually I would not start to work with actors before I had a very solid approach. First of all, the text – structuring the text – and at least the basic approach of what theatrical devices would be engaged. Because when I take a text from literature I don't transform it into dialogical words or a play, so actually the surrounding – the idea of how the theatrical world will surround the text – is highly important.

I usually come with a very solid idea, but then the actors never know what will happen. I don't talk with the actors beforehand. On the contrary, the actors usually don't even know what the text is going to be; I only come with little fragments and encourage them to explore freely. Within my vision I try to open as much as I can to their creative suggestions. But not through talking. It's always through work, through very physical work. I try to shake the actors' bodies, their minds, with words or with objects. And then, when I get more and more material from the actors, I try to see whether I can include it or whether it changes the original approach. So it's two parallel processes, I guess.

GK:
You work with a more and less permanent ensemble. So you have your own codes, a language of your own.

RK:
That's true. I am blessed to be able to work with amazing people whose expertise is to penetrate into the unknown. They are real artists that can come open to the process and remain open throughout. We conduct long processes, quite a lot of months for these projects, sometimes even a year or two of rehearsals. So the first weeks or months of the work are a period where we open things. Then, the actors move to the other aspect of the work – when I begin to structure very exact phrases. Eventually every breath, every action of the words, and every moment is crystallized and composed.

GK:
Would I be mistaken if I would say that the most predominant level in your work is movement, or choreography of movement? Can you tell us how that movement relates to the text?

RK:
The movement and the body are very important for me. It's the deep essence of humanity. I work a lot with actors around movement and the body – but it's not a goal in itself. Although my work is very physical, the physicality is a support of the text. Eventually, my main interest is the text, and the text receives its amplitude from the body and the movement. But it's true, each rehearsal starts with – I would even say – a violent way of working on movement and body. We're working in a way that shakes the body. The Israeli *Shabak*, the Intelligence Service, does this horrible thing: when they find a suspect and want to get the truth out of him, they shake him. It is a violent thing because when a person is shaking, he can't pretend. The truth will come out of him.

And that's what we do with actors in a way: take the body out of its natural balance. And in the moment of unbalance there the text starts to flourish.

GK:
Is it a kind of an inspiration of Jerzy Grotowski?

RK:
Of course. This is a very deep part of my education. I grew up in the 1960s, I was a theatre student in the 1970s, so Grotowski was a very powerful mentor.

The main feature of my method is the deep work of the actors. But most of the energy is invested in things that you would not see on stage. Because on stage it is very structured – you would never see us shaking. But if you go to the rehearsal you would think we are all a bunch of nuts, because we do such strange things. But it remains as a hidden level under all the other elements. It echoes. So I think that the real dramaturgy that I am doing is the hidden dramaturgy. Because I work on these streams of events, actions, flows in the body, in the text, that you don't directly see on stage.

GK:
Can you illustrate it?

RK:
There is this moment in the story 'Swimming in the Sea' that is the second part of *At Sea*. It's the story of a man that is drowning in the water. Of course on stage we don't have no water, no nothing. The performance starts with a flow of words. In a way the fear of the actress who had to learn so many words, so much text, is the thing that is threatening her. The stream of words is standing for the streams of water.

But then, my way to continue and create the dangerous surrounding, is working with a group of actors that oppose this actress. So that there are people, which puts the whole story on the level of people and not of waves. And then, there's a sentence about the sun: 'And even the sun was suddenly filling his eyes with the wickedness of a direct glare, too bright to handle.' This is the text. What I try to do on stage is to take the actress out of her balance through another actress, who is coming on and slapping her in the face. A real slap, not a theatrical slap – it hurts, it really hurts, and it throws the actress back into a very shaky moment. It is also an important moment, because of a person realizing that the world is indifferent to her suffering, to her misery. And then there are no words, no movements, she's not doing anything but the whole stage vibrates with all this inner hidden givens working for her – and we experience a very powerful moment from the depth of her soul.

GK:
Tell me something about how you combine music, non-human elements in the show. How do you combine all these subsidiary elements which I think are equal elements, egalitarian moments in your work, like choice of space, sound, lighting. In which stage of your work do these things come in? Are they integral to your process or do they come after you work with the actors?

RK:
I do work with these elements altogether and they do have equal value. Let me jump for a moment to the end. I strongly reject what I hear sometimes in the theatre: they call the last weeks 'the technical weeks'. I resist the term 'technical' in this context. Lighting is the moment where light meets a body of an actor on space, and thus it deeply influences the whole process. When I work with fellow partners, designers, musicians, I try to start to meet them as soon as possible, so we can dream together this mutual interweaving of the theatrical elements. Usually in my works there is not much on stage, but whatever is there, it's used to the maximum.

GK:
Can you describe one of your works in which these other elements, non-histrionic elements, influenced the work in a very special way?

RK:
I did *Mother Courage* in Tokyo. This is unusual for me, to work with a play and not with a story. My first instinct was: I don't want a wagon. It has become such a cliché. The stage should consist of a simple element

that could be multiplied, so everything could be made of everything – to reflect the idea that you are not functioning as an individual but within a specific social context.

I had a long conversation with Roni Toren, a wonderful Israeli designer whom I invited to work with me in Tokyo, and he came out with the idea of a suitcase. If I would do this play in Israel, I wouldn't use a suitcase because it's too overloaded as a symbol.

GK:
Too overloaded with the Holocaust connotations?

RK:
Yes. But I knew that we were going to do it in Tokyo, and that these connotations don't exist there. So a suitcase would be just a signifier for travelling, for changing locations, which is very relevant to the play. The whole stage became – we had around hundred suitcases – a wall of suitcases. And then one of the actors destroyed this wall. This was really a big gift from Roni, because the set became so active and valuable in the way it aroused the creativity.

GK:
Did you have to make changes in the text because of this idea?

RK:
No. Because to change means: 'I can't'. And I like these moments when it clashes, that, for example, the designer's idea clashes with the text. These are the moments that call for a creative jump.

GK:
In what ways do you consider the spectator?

RK:
I consider them more and more, but maybe in a different way than they are considered around me. In my group I never use the word 'audience', not because it is a bad word in itself, but because it has become a symbol, it signifies this master-slave relationship. So in my group I would say 'guests', and my tendency is to work more and more in small spaces, so

the guests are seen, they are left with a little bit of light and we see faces – it's more and more important to me to reach, to touch the minds of people. And most important – I think about it in terms of a dialogue.

The text is a dialogue; we don't carry out a monologue. Especially when you deal with storytelling theatre, the dialogue is not with another character but with the audience. So it's very important for us to talk to the people. And one part of my, or my actors' attitude, is to treat them as if they were another voice of ours.

GK:
You are working very much with Israeli texts, and they are overloaded with very indigenous local associations, emotional burdens and so on. And you are in a way dependent on this audience. When you go with the same play to, let's say, New York to perform, then New Yorkers don't have this local associative background.

RK:
Of course, there are some things that are lost in translation, but others are gained. For example, there is a work that we did – *Cases of Murder*, which is a text by a German writer, Manfred Franke. The text is about the Reichskristallnacht in 1938 in Germany. He collected testimonies from people who attended this horrible night. But when we performed it in Israel it was something like – I do it here and now, in my society, for my people. It was about what we experience here – in order to explore the mechanism of us as a society witnessing the wrongs that are done around us.

For example there was one scene in the original text with people laughing at an anti-Semitic joke about a Jew. I didn't change the text at all, in my work the actors told the same joke about a Jew – yet their costumes were contemporary Israeli costumes, and they were cracking sunflower seeds, which is one of the most conspicuous of social Israeli habits. It's something many, many Israelis would do when they sit and watch television or when they sit with their friends. So when we performed this piece in New York, I knew that this hint wouldn't be understood – but eventually the disposition of the text and the visuality is developed throughout the whole play – so there are all kinds of hints: visual hints, textual hints, etc. about these parallel societies.

It's not only the Hebrew language that I love, but I try in our works here to let the influence of the whole place seep into the work. For example, the actors would never wear black suits – that belongs to Europe. I try to bring to stage the colours of this country, the forms, the sounds. Thus I try to make the works very local. And in that sense the codes could be fully understood only for Israeli people.

On the other hand, only a few months ago we performed our work *At Sea* in Beijing. And at the general rehearsal there the technicians began to cry. Although they didn't understand the codes, other structures or human events could be understood, and it was so very significant for them!

GK:

One of your last enterprises was the Brecht's Lehrstück He Who Says Yes, He Who Says No, which started actually as a communist parable, which is also something more complex. What's your approach to this quite well-known piece?

RK:

I went back to the original source, a Noh play, entitled *Taniko – The Child of a Valley*, and I compared it with Brecht's play. It was very important for me to play it here in an Israeli context, where the question of consent is a very delicate question, because we're all the time in crisis or emergency. We have to obey all the time: have to be good children, go to the army and do what we need to do. And the play is challenging these thoughts. So my way of bringing it to the here and now was first of all to combine it with a folktale that we tell here in Israel. It is called *The Story of the Golden Heart Flower*, and it is about a child whose mother is sick and he has to bring her a remedy. The story ends with a happy ending: the child finds the flower, and the mother is healed. What I did was to confront on stage the happy ending with the very harsh and terrible ending of Brecht's play in which the child is thrown to the valley and dies.

This is one dramaturgical way: letting the play collide with our hidden demands – the child should bring remedy to his mother and risk his life for his mother/his country. The other strategy of the work was to play with the gestures of a teacher and schoolchildren, and through working with these gestures, encourage the actors to switch roles. So a teacher is someone who had, at a certain moment, the authority to be a teacher. But if he loses his authority for any reason then he loses the role, and somebody else becomes the teacher.

Into all of this mess I also asked the actors to bring their real school reports from elementary school with their notes from their teachers and it became part of the text. So eventually we incorporated the original texts, the Brecht texts, the folk story, and the actual documents from school, dealing with oppression in the family, in the class and in the society.

GK:

What are your main inspiration sources?

RK:

My inspiration is not so much from theatre. I rather open up more and more to other fields, for example, literary criticism and analysis. Maybe because I'm dealing with storytelling theatre and not with dramatic texts. I also gain enormous inspiration and nourishment from reading about science.

I started with reading about physics. It sounds strange and unrelated – but I talked to you about the uncertainty of the soldiers in the field, and that concept comes from the uncertainty principle of Heisenberg, which is a very intriguing principle in physics. When I first read it, I just enjoyed it, but then it came to the work somehow.

In the work of the theatre you have to be passionate for influences. I think you can never get prepared for a specific project, all your life is a preparation and you never know what will come out.

I'm very much interested in ethology, reading a lot about animals. There is an Israeli scholar, Amotz Zehavi, who wrote a wonderful book called *Peacocks and the Handicapped Principle*. He actually discovered a principle in nature that seems to go against the Darwinist principle. He discovered that sometimes animals would do things that are not good for their survival. And you ask yourself: 'why?' For example, the peacock has a huge tail, but it hinders him while running. So what is the signal that is being given by having this big tail? It says: 'I'm so powerful, that I can cope with such a big tail and not get caught by an enemy.' Or think about rich people, they usually have white carpets at home. And you ask yourself: 'why?' Because if you don't have enough money for a maid or energy to clean it every day, it would be dirty. So the carpet is a signal that you are either a hard worker or you are very rich. Or a young woman that walks on very high heels. It signals that she has a great balance.

Zehavi is writing about this phenomenon: that animals give signals that they are doing something which is actually very difficult, but they have a reason to choose to do it. It made me understand some of my choices. Usually I would choose the more difficult thing, like to get trapped.

In a way taking this hardship is to say: 'my dramaturgy is strong enough to cope with very bad conditions'. So the attempt is to deliberately look for uncomfortable situations on stage and yet – create a significant dramatic world. And with all that – have the people – audiences, visitors, guests – get caught in a dramatic human situation, because the theatre I try to do is not an abstract one. It deals with human beings, with their sufferings, their desires. So it's really like this handicapped principle: to do it, but with as little help from external or conventional measures as possible.

(The interview was made in Tel Aviv on 2 April 2013.)

Part Three

Devising

The Feeling of Devising

Emotion and Mind in the Devising Process

Jackie Smart

Introduction

In *Devising in Process*, Alex Mermikides and I proposed a tentative definition of devising 'centring on a certain playful openness: to a range of stimuli; to creative risk and experimentation; to the views and input of a variety of participants … '.[1] In this chapter, I probe this notion of 'playful openness' further, focusing in particular on the interpersonal, interactive aspects of devising as a collaborative creative process, and framing my exploration within current perspectives on the relationship between emotion and cognition drawn from neuroscience and psychology. I go into these perspectives in greater depth in the next section; for now Bruce McConachie offers a useful statement of the key insight of the field:

> Cognitive neuroscientists and psychologists now affirm that emotional drives undergird and sustain even the simplest of intellectual tasks, such as adding two numbers together; the old separations between reason and emotion no longer hold.[2]

Put simply, I am interested in the way people feel when they create collaboratively and how these feelings affect their contributions to the theatre-making process. I focus on two key issues of particular relevance to the dramaturgy of collaborative devising processes, which I characterize in terms of tension. The first tension is between divergence and coherence, which is to say between the interpretative openness that comes from a multiplicity of voices and visions and the need to shape these into a coherent theatrical experience. The second tension is between the need for trust, openness and free-flowing communication between participants in devising processes and the fact that the process itself can produce anxiety and insecurity.

It might seem obvious to say that I think dramaturgies of devising process should be emotionally intelligent and emotionally ethical – which practitioners would imagine their processes were not? Academic literature on devising tends to emphasize its positive aspects: the sense of liberation from conventional restrictions; the satisfaction of connecting with one's 'deeper' self; the excitement of working closely with others, sparking off their ideas and sharing your ideas with them. All of these are important elements that draw artists towards collaborative creative working methods. However, over more than twenty years participating in, observing and teaching devising, I have learnt that these undoubtedly appealing qualities of the devising process can also be sources of confusion and distress. I acknowledge that I come to this discussion from a personal standpoint, drawing on my own observations and experiences. In part this is precisely because devising practitioners are unwilling to talk (publicly at least) about the more emotionally difficult aspects of their experience. This is understandable, of course, but it does mean that much of the existing writing about devising tends to make it sound easier and more uniformly joyful than it often is. Conversely, I would hate to imply, by my focus on tensions within devising processes, that it is usually or largely an unhappy experience; on the contrary, it is an activity I deeply enjoy. My key point is that a creative process based around human interaction should take account of the full scope of human emotions that feed into it.

Emotion and cognition: A summary

Neuroscientist Joseph LeDoux states, 'Minds without emotions are not really minds at all'.[3] From the middle of the twentieth century neuroscientists began to challenge the Cartesian dualism which had previously framed scientific understanding of human thought and feeling. Rather than these two aspects of human nature existing independently of one another, neuroscientists argued that they were profoundly interlinked. While this area of research is relatively recent and thus various points of disagreement remain, the central theory of the interdependence of cognition and emotion is now widely accepted. In essence, this theory proposes that the basic emotions of joy, distress, anger and fear[4] are primary, which is to say not only that they precede cognitive responses, but that they mould *how* we think. The theory draws on a supposition that emotions are ancient in evolutionary terms: they exist to help us survive, thrive and procreate; they protect us from danger by alerting us to threat and encourage useful behaviour with the reward of pleasure. Beyond these basic functions, emotions also form an essential part of our interpretation and evaluation of situations and events. One way they do this is by directing our attention to particular aspects of an environment or situation, sharpening the outlines of those aspects that have emotional relevance for us and blurring those that don't. Emotional relevance is determined by our emotional memories, the records our brains hold of how we have felt about previous experiences, on the basis of which we make decisions about how to act and what to avoid, in the present and the future. All of this happens with the speed of a reflex at an unconscious level meaning that, initially at least, we have neither conscious awareness of what stimulus is prompting our feelings, nor conscious control over them. The fact that the unconscious nature of much of our emotional experience puts it beyond our will or control is a key point made LeDoux in *The Emotional Brain* (1999), which is one of my major reference points for this chapter. Before I proceed further in exploring the relevance of LeDoux's insights for devising dramaturgy, though, I will briefly contextualize this exploration with reference to how other performance scholars have drawn on theories of emotion and cognition.

Although there is, as yet, no work which is directly concerned with devising processes, a range of scholars have engaged with a variety of neuroscientific and psychological theories and approaches in analysing creativity, acting and actor-training, applied theatre and spectatorship. Of these, essays by John Lutterbie on creativity in the rehearsal process and by Rhonda Blair on actor training (both in Bruce McConachie and F. Elizabeth Hart's 2006 edited volume, *Performance and Cognition*) offer insights relevant to devising processes. McConachie's monograph, *Engaging Audiences* (2008), focuses on how the emotion-cognition relationship functions with regard to performance spectatorship. James Thompson's *Performance Affects* (originally published in 2009) and Nicola Shaughnessy's *Applying Performance* (2012) deal with applied and socially engaged performance, employing what they call 'the affective turn' as a means of challenging received ideas about the purpose, impact and evaluation of such theatre forms. This use of the word 'affective' brings me to a necessary clarification as regards terminology. There is some slippage between the use of the words 'emotion', 'affect' and 'feeling' within performance-based writing in this field. Thompson uses 'affect'; his field of reference includes neuroscientific research but is largely indebted to cultural and aesthetic theory. At the risk of oversimplifying his quite complex interrogation of the term, he and Shaughnessy both use 'affect' to describe the physical, visceral sensations experienced within the body as a consequence of our emotional engagement with objects, people and experiences. Rhonda Blair prefers to use the terms 'emotion' and 'feeling', basing her definitions of them on the distinction offered by the neuroscientist Antonio Damasio: 'emotions are basically biological responses, while feelings are conscious mental formulations of the former'.[5] Although Damasio does not himself distinguish between 'emotion' and 'affect', his 'somatic marker hypothesis' (see Damasio, *Descartes' Error*, 2006) offers us a connection between the three terms through his principle of 'homeostasis', which is the body's need to maintain a stable state. Emotions are part of the body's constant, unconscious tendency to regulate itself, manifested as somatic 'affects'. As Blair, citing Damasio, puts it, 'when emotions rise to consciousness, feelings result … [and] "translate the ongoing life state in the language of the mind"'.[6] In this chapter, because I am concerned more with internal than external states, I will refer mainly to emotions and feelings rather than to 'affects'.

How people feel about ideas

'Emotions', writes LeDoux, 'are things that happen to us rather than things we will to occur'.[7] He argues that the capacity of our emotions to 'flood' our consciousness is much stronger than that of our conscious mind to control our emotions. 'This is so', he tells us, 'because the wiring of the brain at this point in our evolutionary history is such that connections from the emotional systems to the cognitive systems are stronger than connections from the cognitive systems to the emotional systems'.[8] LeDoux's proposition is that the basic emotions trigger a 'quick and dirty' processing route (associated with the amygdala), which bypasses the areas dealing with conscious mental processing (associated with the hippocampus), thus creating emotional responses that we 'feel' but cannot explain. This 'automatic' activation of emotions 'means that their presence in the mind and their influence on thoughts and behaviour are not questioned. They are trusted the way we would trust any other kind of perception'.[9]

The implications of LeDoux's insights that interest me concern the particular tension between the open, spontaneous creative responses devising tends to encourage in its initial stages and the dramaturgical manipulations these will inevitably undergo later. The desire to create in the actor a state of 'unthinking' response is not specific to devising. Lutterbie opens his chapter with a metaphor of the actor 'suspending certain aspects of the self so she can be surprised by the discoveries made in improvisational, creative play'.[10] Actors, he explains, at certain stages of their creative work, seek to 'switch off' the conscious mind, the implication being that this will allow them access to some other sort of 'mind' which is usually hidden beneath consciousness. This desire to access a level of response beneath or beyond conscious thought is common throughout the creative arts. Educational psychologist Guy Claxton writes:

> A creative project, whether it be scientific, artistic or practical, often starts from a small seed. And the less rational mind enters here, right at the beginning, for such 'seeds' are often, at the time, inexplicably poignant.[11]

Claxton's 'inexplicable poignancy' is revealing. Spontaneous responses, where the actor or deviser is asked to respond immediately to an object, environment, person, piece of music or text, are likely to be of LeDoux's 'quick and dirty' kind, rooted in emotional memories of which we may not be consciously aware. Their direct connection to internal emotional sources can mean they have powerful resonances for their creators, although those creators may not be able to articulate clearly what those resonances are and they might seem strange, even incomprehensible, to others. One of the frustrations of a devising process can be the failure of an attempt to explain an inspiration or interpretation that matters a lot to you but seems merely to perplex those to whom you are trying to articulate it. Claxton notes that the timing of discussing 'inklings' is important, explaining that some artists feel early exposure of 'the small shoot of an idea to a frost that might nip it in the bud' is threatening or that the requirement to articulate it calls for 'a degree of clarity or fixity that would inhibit or skew its subsequent development'.[12]

One of the contradictions of devising is that, while it is seen as essential to generate a sense of investment and ownership of ideas within the group, participants must also be willing to give up on individual ideas, or to see them edited, adapted, altered or even handed over to someone else in the service of the 'overall' idea, which often means the one emerging in the director's head. It is usually the director who selects and presents the original stimulus material (although she might ask devisers to then gather and share their own additional materials) and this will be something that is already meaningful to her. In my own case, I am aware that this predetermined 'meaning', which I might only recognize as a feeling, can become a filter through which I watch and respond to what is going on in the room, honing in on what seems to fit it and often missing (or, worse, dismissing) what does not. In other words, the operation of the director's emotional spotlight could have the effect of filtering out the very multiplicity of personal response which gives devising its richness and complexity, its defining quality of openness to interpretation as opposed to the 'closed' meaning of the single-authored text.

For me, this is both a dramaturgical problem and an ethical one. In a collaborative devising process there will be many different ideas and perspectives about which the people in the room will feel passionately, and care needs to be taken to pay attention and accord value to the emotional investment individuals have in the creative contributions they make. Yet, if a piece is to communicate with an audience, it needs to achieve some kind of unified vision. The deliberations of a conference working group on 'Dramaturgy as/and Collaboration' frame this tension clearly. Peter Eckersall tells us that, in debates around the notion of a 'decentred dramaturgy', while people liked the notion of diversity, concerns were expressed that such a decentred approach threatened to produce 'a jumble of chaotic interactions'.[13] I do not have a magical solution to this conundrum. It is telling that devising companies which started out as collaborative collectives so often evolve into director-led shapes over time, suggesting perhaps that our need for order outweighs our desire for creative freedom. Chaos is a state many people dislike. The performer-deviser Wendy Houstoun told me that although she is able to 'hold with a lot of chaos for a long time' she knows that 'this can drive people mad'.[14] James Thompson's meditations on 'beauty', though, offer a helpful dramaturgical perspective. He uses 'beauty' not in the sense of something that has a culturally determined loveliness of form, but more as something that speaks very directly to us on an 'affective' level and which he characterizes as 'being perpetually out of reach'. '[Beauty's] elusiveness at the point of comprehension', writes Thompson 'is, perhaps, the place from which its power to stimulate engagement with the wider world starts'.[15]

The social anxieties of collaboration

As Vsevolod Meyerhold observes, 'An actor can improvise only when he feels internal joy. Without an atmosphere of creative joy, of artistic élan, an actor never completely opens up'.[16] Meyerhold's term 'élan' signifies a feeling of joyful playfulness that he suggests is generated through an atmosphere of mutual trust and creative freedom within the group. Callery goes on to point out that other influential practitioners such as Grotowski, Lecoq and Gaulier also employ the term 'élan'. Devisers know that the ability to respond openly and freely to others is based on feeling safe and confident within the group. The subtext of Meyerhold's statement, however, is that this state is not always achieved and one of the things that prevents it is anxiety. Anxiety is related to fear, one of our most deep-rooted basic emotions. On an evolutionary level, we are highly attuned towards spotting and avoiding what seems dangerous. Anxiety is characterized as 'a state of undirected arousal following the perception of threat',[17] a general wariness, in other words, rather than a direct response to a frightening stimulus.

In a review of studies of the factors provoking anxiety in human situations, one of the four common factors identified was 'fears about interpersonal events or situations [which] included fears of criticism and social interaction, rejection, conflicts and evaluation'.[18] All these things might be perceived as likely to occur within devising processes. Emma Rice, artistic director of Kneehigh, speaks in an interview of 'that sort of immediate fear "will I be accepted and am I any good"',[19] suggesting that, however experienced a deviser you are, those kinds of anxieties re-emerge each time you find yourself in a new situation or environment. It is rare, though, for such feelings to be acknowledged or discussed in the literature on creative process. The emphasis of this literature on the importance of openness, responsiveness, élan, can make us feel like failures when we experience insecurity, uncertainty or any form of negative reaction to exercises or to other group members.

While basic emotions like fear can be seen to relate in direct and relatively simple ways to the survival and success of the individual, there is another set of emotions known as 'higher cognitive emotions',[20] which are related to the fact that humans are a social species. These include complex emotions like love, guilt, embarrassment, pride and envy, which are culturally inflected. Fischer and Manstead propose that emotions contribute significantly to the establishment and maintenance of social relationships, and social positions relative to others, explaining that 'social survival is a complex endeavour because it requires a balance between cooperation on the one hand, and competition on the other'.[21] We seek both to find 'harmony, closeness and love' and to 'avoid others who pose a threat to us, to win at the expense of others, to exert control over others, or to enhance our social power or social standing'.[22] When we begin a devising process with trust games and 'getting to know' exercises, we are drawing on our instinctive knowledge and understanding of the social functions of emotion. The expression and sharing of emotions 'help[s] to increase intimacy in interpersonal relations' and 'emotions ... serve affiliation functions, because they enhance positive interactions, cooperation and trust'.[23]

Such strategies for achieving group trust and confidence are valuable and effective but I question the possibility of banishing more 'negative' emotions completely from the rehearsal room because, given the unconscious internal drivers of our emotional states, their power to flood our consciousness and influence our interpretations and judgements, we are not entirely in control of what we feel. Internal struggles related to social status, competition and control continue unconsciously, despite our best efforts, and we may not fully grasp their emotional roots. For example, Amit Lahav of devising company Gecko describes what happened during a training session with his creative partner Allel Nedjari, for a boxing match Gecko wanted to include in their show *The Arab and the Jew* (2007–8):

> [Nedjari] caught me and I reacted to being caught. ... I think it was clear to both of us that I reacted. Rather than just being in the moment, I said, 'right, you hit me, I'm going to hit you back now'.[24]

This is an overt example of the 'person' intruding into the role but there are plenty of more subtle, covert occurrences of this phenomenon. Keith

Johnstone, in his book *Impro* (originally published in 1979 and still a core text for many teachers of improvisation and devising), explicitly acknowledges the tendency of student actors to 'block' the creative 'offers' made to them by others in improvisation and the need to train them out of their resistance to giving up control and just allowing things to happen. Fear of losing control is related to fear of looking foolish which is, in turn, related to fear of being judged by others. Claxton notes 'the destructive effect on creativity of having a voice that is superficially critical and quickly dismissive',[25] while the actors cited by Lutterbie talk of judging and self-judging as 'clutter' which impedes concentration.[26]

In relation to this fear of being judged, I want to briefly mention Michael Lewis's description of the higher cognitive emotions as 'self-conscious emotions'. These, according to Lewis, emerge later in life than basic emotions and 'involve a set of standards, rules or goals (SRGs) [which] are inventions of the culture that are transmitted to children and involve their learning of, and willingness to consider, these SRGs as their own'.[27] A theatre-making process creates its own set of SRGs which apply within the rehearsal room, but the SRGs of normal life are still there, suppressed rather than eliminated. A devising process often involves the creation of a 'special' place in which the conventions of normal social behaviour are set aside in order to enable participants to act in playful, childlike, possibly exposing ways but the suspension of social rules is temporary and fragile and can only be achieved with the full agreement of everyone present. Such agreement is not arrived at by wholly conscious means. It is negotiated on an internal level, over time, as the group comes to know one another.

As an example, in a project with students, not all of whom had worked together before, I was using the artist Paula Rego's 'Dog Women' series of paintings as a stimulus. One of these, called *Baying*,[28] shows a woman squatting on a beach, her head lifted and mouth stretched open as if howling like a dog. At an early stage in the process I asked each participant to take up the 'baying' position, sticking closely to the way in which it was represented in Rego's painting; they were to do so one after another, placing themselves in the space in relation to each other, and to 'howl' as they imagined the woman in the painting might sound. Despite the fact that the woman in Rego's painting is facing diagonally forwards, all the performers except two chose to face upstage, away from those of us watching the exercise. Of the two who did not, one placed herself in a position where her face was hidden and the other played the moment for laughs. What I saw in this response to the exercise was a revealing subconscious negotiation of the competing demands upon them. They wanted to enter into the spirit of the exercise but they were still feeling their way with each other, unwilling to let go of their protective social restraints until they were sure it was okay to do so with this particular group of people. The social need not to look foolish was, at this stage, too strong to overcome. As the project continued, the group relaxed and let down their guard. The emotional rewards of 'baying' began to appeal more than their deeply embedded embarrassment-avoidance mechanisms and they began to relish the 'permission to howl'. For me, the key lesson here is how much time matters in a devising process. All groups need to go through this process of establishing a place of emotional safety before they can make themselves vulnerable. At the beginning of a process, rules and instructions might serve an emotionally protective purpose defining the boundaries within which it is alright to play. In subsequent stages, those boundaries can be progressively stretched as devisers feel more ready to step off into the unknown. It is through this sense of how the timing and structure of a devising process works that I feel understanding of social emotions impacts on the dramaturgy of process. It helps us to understand why the different stages of process (usually characterized in terms of preparation, generation/ exploration, organization, performance and reflection) matter and when various exercises and interventions are most likely to work effectively. It also helps us to distinguish between those interpersonal reactions that are relevant in terms of the content and development of the material and those that aren't.

Conclusion

I have argued that certain tensions and contradictions are intrinsic to devising processes and that these are generated in part by the impact of unconscious emotional processes on conscious cognitive operations. Our emotions are always at work, directing our attention, influencing our perceptions, framing and moulding our interpretations and judgements. Because these operations occur at a subconscious level we have little control over them. Devising as a mode of work encourages participants to respond spontaneously and impulsively to stimulus material, thereby engaging their emotions and producing a profound sense of investment in what they create, yet it also demands a willingness to relinquish 'ownership' of ideas in the service of the whole. The literature on devising recognizes the importance of generating trust and a sense of safety within the group but has paid too little attention to the anxieties of social interaction which can interfere with these processes. In this context, I suggest that the dramaturgy of a devising process needs to be an emotionally intelligent and an emotionally ethical one, which acknowledges and addresses the profound effect of emotion on devisers' ideas and responses to stimuli and their interactions and relationships with others.

References

Blair, Rhonda. 'Image and Action: Cognitive Neuroscience and Actor-training'. *Performance and Cognition: Theatre Studies and the Cognitive Turn.* Ed. Bruce McConachie and F. Elizabeth Hart. Abingdon and New York: Routledge, 2006, pp. 167–85.

Callery, Dymphna. *Through the Body: A Practical Guide to Physical Theatre.* London and New York: Nick Hern Books, 2001.

Claxton, Guy. 'Creative Glide Space'. *The Creative Process in Contemporary Performing Arts.* Ed. Christopher Bannerman. London: Middlesex University Press, 2006, pp. 58–70.

Damasio, Antonio. *Descartes' Error: Emotion, Reason and the Human Brain.* London: Vintage Books, 2006.

Eckersall, Peter. 'Notes on Dramaturgy as/and Collaboration'. *Dramaturgies: New Theatres for the 21st Century.* Ed. Peter Eckersall, Melanie Beddie and Paul Monaghan. Melbourne: Carl-Nilsson-Polias on behalf of The Dramaturgies Project, 2011, pp. 87–91.

Evans, Dylan. *Emotion: The Science of Sentiment.* Oxford: Oxford University Press, 2001.

Fischer, Agneta H. and Manstead, Antony S. R. 'Social Functions of Emotion'. *The Handbook of Emotions, Third Edition.* Ed. Michael Lewis, Jeanette M. Haviland-Jones and Lisa Feldman Barrett. New York and London: Guildford Press, 2010, pp. 456–68.

LeDoux, Joseph. *The Emotional Brain.* London: Phoenix, 1999.

Lewis, Michael. 'Self-Conscious Emotions: Embarrassment, Pride, Shame and Guilt'. *Handbook of Emotions. 3rd ed.* Ed. Michael Lewis, Jeannette M. Haviland-Jones and Lisa Feldman Barrett. London and New York: The Guilford Press, 2010, pp. 742–56.

Lutterbie, John. 'Neuroscience and Creativity in the Rehearsal Process'. *Performance and Cognition: Theatre Studies and the Cognitive Turn.* Ed. Bruce McConachie and F. Elizabeth Hart. Abingdon and New York: Routledge, 2006, pp. 149–66.

McConachie and F. Elizabeth Hart, eds. *Performance and Cognition: Theatre Studies and the Cognitive Turn.* Abingdon and New York: Routledge, 2006, pp. 149–66.

Mermikides, Alex and Smart, Jackie. *Devising in Process.* Basingstoke and New York: Palgrave Macmillan, 2010.

Öhman, Arne. 'Fear and Anxiety: overlaps and dissociations'. *The Handbook of Emotions. 3rd ed.* Ed. Michael Lewis, Jeanette M. Haviland-Jones and Lisa Feldman Barrett. New York and London: Guildford Press, 2010, pp. 709–29.

Radosavljević, Duška and Emma, Rice. 'Emma Rice in Interview with Duška Radosavljević'. *Journal of Adaptation in Film and Performance* 3.1 (Bristol: Intellect, 2010, pp. 89–98.

Rego, Paula, 'Baying'. *Paula Rego.* Ed. John McEwen. 2nd ed. London and New York: Phaidon Press Limited, 1997, p. 211.

Shaughnessy, Nicola. *Applying Performance: Live Art, Socially Engaged Theatre and Affective Practice*. Basingstoke and New York: Palgrave Macmillan, 2012.

Smart, Jackie. 'Sculpting the Territory: Gecko's *The Arab and the Jew* in Process'. *Devising in Process*. Ed. Alex Mermikides and Jackie Smart. Basingstoke and New York: Palgrave Macmillan, 2010, pp. 165–85.

Thompson, James, *Performance Affects: Applied Theatre and the End of Effect*. Basingstoke and New York: Palgrave Macmillan, 2011.

'A Way of Listening'

Interview with John Collins
(artistic director, Elevator Repair Service, New York)

Ana Pais

'Elevator repair man' was the automatically generated answer eleven-year-old John Collins received from a career-placement test that he had filled in at his aunt's office. Several years later, a friend and co-founder of a new theatre company in New York encouraged him to make the dream come true. In 1991, Elevator Repair Service *(ERS), the experimental ensemble was born. With ERS, Collins doesn't fix plays as an elevator repair man would fix elevators: he finds them.*

Collins founded the ERS ensemble two years before he started working for the Wooster Group as their sound designer (1993–2006). This period of collaboration with the Wooster Group was to prove particularly influential on both Collins and the subsequent work of the ensemble. Working collaboratively, often over extended periods of time, Collins developed a particular devising technique anchored in sophisticated dramaturgical practices. Through immersion and free association, the company combines disparate source material such as YouTube videos, court transcripts, dialogue, choreography and the unexpected of everyday life into a single performance text.

After a long period of producing purely devised work, ERS turned their attention to the adaptation of novels using the same techniques. This gave rise to ERS's internationally acclaimed trilogy: Gatz *(2005),* The Sound and the Fury *(2008) and* The Select *(The Sun Also Rises) (2010). The reception to these adaptations has cemented the reputation of ERS*

*around the world. This success has not given rise to a formulaic approach
however, with new challenges arising with each work.*

Ana Pais:
After the international success of the novel trilogy Gatz, The Sound and
the Fury *and* The Select, *can one say that there is a devised period and a
text-based period in the work of ERS?*

John Collins:
In a practical way, that is true. There are always different elements that
form a production of ours, and they come to us in various states. Text
would be one of those elements, and sometimes it comes to us as a
'found text'. Sometimes we are working from the point of view of the
structure, and we take the text and 'plug in' it. But I am not entirely
comfortable in making such a dividing line.

Just for the sake of argument, in those earlier pieces something
would determine the structure. *Cab Legs* could be a good example. We
had created a structure based on a number of dances that we had made,
devised from an idea about periods of silence and waiting interrupted
by big periods of activity. When we found the text that we eventually
used, a heavily processed and paraphrased version of a Tennessee
Williams play, we took it and we inserted it into that structure.

Now when we have novels, because of the nature of that material, they
bring their own structure, although there were structural elements – such as
the office setting in *Gatz* – imposed on of the work as well. I don't ever stop
thinking in a certain way because I am working with a certain material.

AP:
How do you see this trilogy in the history of ERS?

JC:
It helped me come to an understanding of how text can work in the
theatre I want to do. Up to that point, I have resisted writing, partly
because I wanted to make sure that I had the autonomy that the
traditional hierarchy of text-based theatre threatened. I think we've
proven to ourselves that we won't lose our identities or any of our
creative freedom by working with texts.

We try to reinvent ourselves with every new production, to reinvent what ERS is, because we want to create a body of work that is recognizable and coherent in an honest way. If there were things that we did in *Gatz* that happened out of an organic process of discovery, then I want to have that organic process again.

AP:
How do you generate the material?

JC:
We come to the material through free association or research. There is a fuzzy line between research and free association with us. In *Arguendo*, we wanted to find as much information as we could about this particular case. The starting point for *Arguendo* was the transcript from the oral argument from a Supreme Court case (that part of the Supreme Court's process where the lawyers go and make their arguments out loud to the justices, thirty minutes at a time). We started to educate ourselves about the case of these erotic dancers who were claiming free speech right to dance completely naked. It was absurd and strange and it satisfied a condition of mine which is that it was not designed for the stage. It was going to present us with a problem.

Our first dramaturgical action was to try to get inside it, to learn as much as we could about it. Ben Williams found an archival video that shows the lawyers being interviewed down on the Court House steps on the day that the argument happened. Another person got interviewed on the sidewalk that day – an erotic dancer. That became part of the show too. Some material leads us to other material. At any point something could become material for the show.

AP:
What are your resources?

JC:
As many as possible. We have always been drawn to using videos and the internet. Before the latter existed, we would look at old videotapes or watch movies. We loved watching movies together because it was a

great way of immersing ourselves in something. We like to absorb, we like to find things. There is an instant richness of material. When you are working the way we are and you are willing to free associate, anything you stumble on could be a great environment to put yourself in.

AP:

What chance brings along doesn't always fit what you already have developed. How do you deal with that?

JC:

We like things that have arguments with each other. We like things that collide, that don't belong together. We don't do it just for the sake of creating chaos. We do it because we are looking for meanings that we hadn't anticipated. We are looking for these different elements to speak to each other in some way, to tell us something we haven't already imagined. We try to put ourselves in a kind of chaos of material because we want to experience the joy of discovery. I don't like having a plan; I would rather just be there when things happen to fall together.

AP:

That reminds me of Eisenstein's concept of montage, extremely influential for Brecht's theatrical concepts. For Eisenstein, montage in cinema derives from conflict. He was influenced, in turn, by the way that in Japanese language words are written, that is, by clashing letters one to another: two things come together to create a new one.

JC:

That's a very filmic idea and we are surely influenced by film in that way. Film has this great ease with contrasting images and because it's photography, there is a kind of realism to it even if it's showing you things that you could never see side by side. Film invented a whole way of looking at the world. You are really seeing one thing and seeing another. But as it is happening in time, your brain attempts to rationalize a meaning from that. In ERS, we are allowing the conflict to play out more. It becomes multidimensional in a way. It becomes narrative.

AP:

Could you give me an example of how this comes up in your dramaturgical process?

JC:

For instance, we started off *The Sound and the Fury* with a dance that was devised before we even knew what book we were doing. We don't insist on discovering our material in any particular order. We had the idea of doing something southern or rural, something that involved country people. That was a very open idea so we narrowed it. Ben Williams brought interesting YouTube videos: a Tennessee guy selling his buckle-belt knife, the fainting goats (these goats that you startle and they get stiff and fall over) that we became obsessed with.

We are looking for as many details as we can find, no matter in what form they come to us. Sometimes it will just be someone's physicality that we will extract, like in this case: we used the physicality of these materials to devise that first choreographic moment of the piece. We were predisposed to look for dance, because dance is great to get any kind of work started. It is a kind of instant theatre.

AP:

Is that also the reason why sound has such a playful dramaturgical role in ERS shows?

JC:

Well, it goes back to the influence of the Wooster Group because even before their sound design got so complicated as it is now, sound was always a big part of what they did. Back in the 1980s, I had never seen a show before where all the actors were using microphones in the way they do there. It had such a rich sound to it and it was so layered. I had seen *Frank Dell's The Temptation of Saint Anthony* so many times, then I came back and saw *Brace Up!* It was so different and yet the first thing I noticed was, it had that same sound. I immediately got this jolt of excitement that I was back in that exciting familiar place.

AP:

The way you just said it makes me think that this was a 'sonic' place, that what was being created was an aural environment …

JC:

Yes. One of the ways I experienced that was that it defined a physical space for me. It gave another dimension to the space that felt in some ways architectural. It really affected my whole physical experience of the space that I was in. I think that led me to a new approach towards sound in my own work. What Elizabeth LeCompte inspired me to do was to be aggressive with sound but to also make sure it was absolutely integrated, that the sound spoke to what was going on, and what was going on spoke to the sound.

AP:

How do you treat the material that you generate in research or in the rehearsal room?

JC:

There is no rule that makes us use all the material. We bring things in because we want to see if they connect with each other. There is always a lot of material that sits around but we never find a use for it. But also, just having all that extra material around means that when we are trying to solve some problem or do some transition from one scene to another, or try to give somebody something to do on stage, that material provides solutions.

Their relationship is kind of arbitrary sometimes. To illuminate it with a metaphor, we throw things into a washing machine together and we spin it and try to see what comes together. One of the main ingredients always is the set of limitations that we are dealing with. For instance, with *Arguendo*, the limitations are the number of people that we have, because we decided we would do it with a smaller company. There are more characters in the transcript than actors, so we are finding ways to switch from one character to another. If it's a novel, however, things are being organized and structured for you in a way. We always try to deal with the material rigorously.

AP:

Do you consider that you are still devising when you are working with a text?

JC:

For sure. At the moment we are working with Sibyl Kempson's play.

AP:

Is this the first time you work with a playwright who writes for the company?

JC:

Yes. It's been an unusual experience, because she has been writing the play along the way. The writing process has been in many ways another way of formalizing a devising process. She is getting feedback from us, but she is also seeing things that happen in the rehearsal room by accident, and writing them in, and she is seeing our attempts to solve problems. In some ways, her writing is documenting our devised process. There was a little bit of improvisation on the material she brought in at the beginning as well. Her writing is almost more of a raw material than something that determines every move we make.

Sibyl is doing in a literary way what we have always done in a theatrical way, which is to look at different things that speak to each other, throw some things together that don't belong together and see what happens. Our rehearsal process has been a laboratory for that. We are accustomed to the text 'ignoring us', and ignoring the structure or the solutions we come up with. It maintains a rock solid integrity, and resistance that is the key. Her writing – because it is listening to us – sometimes doesn't resist as much; sometimes it absorbs what we do.

AP:

Is devising still a good word to describe your kind of dramaturgical practice?

JC:

I have trouble with the whole term because I find there is a *continuum*. The reason why I am a little uncomfortable with the term is because it suggests that there is a neat category. It suggests that you do things in that kind of work that you don't do when working with a play. I see that all sorts of processes overlap constantly. Sometimes I think labels have more to do with how productions look like when they are finished, not how they are made. Maybe the expectation is that a devised theatre piece is going to be non-linear, that we will be able to see that a whole bunch of different people contributed to it, and that all those contributions did not exactly agree with each other.

I don't think you should be able to tell the difference when something is finished. I try not to be ideological about it, but I am suspicious of some ways of making work. I am suspicious both of those situations where the actors and the director are afraid to make too many decisions on their own, and I am also suspicious of situations where it's theatre by democracy. That can be even more disastrous.

AP:

Apparently you have never had the urge to work with a dramaturg.

JC:

It's what our whole practice is: the work of dramaturgy. And everyone, to a greater or lesser extent, has the expectation that they will do that kind of work.

AP:

So everyone researches, everyone looks for material and so on?

JC:

Yes, but again some people are more comfortable working that way. Some would just rather have you given them an assignment just about performing. But this group has thrived in having a lot of performers who are dramaturgs.

AP:

How did the concept of Gatz *emerge, and how did you manage to keep the performance's coherence throughout six hours?*

JC:

We started with a simply stated but potentially complicated idea: putting a book on stage without adapting it. The way how to do that came up in a very practical way. We were dealing with the very beginning of the book and realizing that it was not especially dramatic. That would be the opportunity to establish some kind of frame or theatrical justification for the assignment that we had given ourselves: we have to hear every word of the book.

For problem solving I look for tools that are immediately available to me: the people who I have right there, the physical situation that I am in. In that case, the situation was a little office above a theatre where we rehearsed. That gave us another layer to work with. We experiment with those things. We take those elements and we try them out, see how they work. That seemed to speak to us. It's a lot about just having an intuitive response to it.

Then it became about managing the progression through the book and the progression through this other story of the guy reading the book. There were some difficult sections to get through, to figure out how to get the other characters on stage for the first time, for instance. You just look deeper and deeper into what you already have. That always seems to work the best. You want to find the play, not fix it. We are developing a language, a kind of strange vocabulary for a piece that way. Sometimes we start developing that vocabulary long before we decided what the central material will be.

AP:

If you create a new vocabulary, you will need to find a new grammar to figure out the order of the elements, the units of meaning and so on.

JC:

We try not to do that too self-consciously. It's another way of looking around and see what's available. Sometimes what's available is a dance we created a month before, or a video that we've been preoccupied with but haven't found a use for it yet. There is no order to it. It's not done in an orderly way.

It's not a method. We've perfected a way of creating an environment in which we work: it's a way of listening. It's a kind of openness. We find ourselves doing similar things over and over again but not because we are trying to. What we try to do deliberately is putting ourselves in unfamiliar places, working with unfamiliar material, even unfamiliar method. We try to frustrate any process that we've developed before, because we want to achieve a state of being. It's almost as if we want to be able to get out of the way of the play that is trying to happen. We want to be present. When the materials we have brought together find ways of speaking to each other, we want to get them together in the ways they want to. It is believing that this thing that you are trying to put together already has a kind of soul or life.

AP:

And you would be facilitating that task for it?

JC:

Yes! And it's the things that intrigue us, that we choose to bring in create that environment in some way. How it all tends to interact is what we try to facilitate. We want to experiment, not to force a result.

(The interview was made in New York, 3 July 2013.)

The Appliance of Science

Devising, Dramaturgy and the Alternative Science Play

Alex Mermikides

In their article, titled 'Science and Theatre in Open Dialogue: Biblioetica, Le Cas de Sophie K. and the Postdramatic Science Play', Campos and Shepherd-Barr assert that 'the interaction of science and the stage lends itself by its very nature to the postdramatic condition'.[1] Van Kerkhoven identifies science–art interdisciplinarity as a key factor in the shifting landscape of twenty-first century European dramaturgy.[2]

However, the practical experiments discussed in this article, in which 'postdramatic' and interdisciplinary devising strategies were employed in the theatrical realization of biomedical science, sometimes produced dramaturgies more aligned to those of the dramatic tradition. This was all the more surprising given that the project under discussion, *Bloodlines*, was otherwise representative of what Shepherd-Barr describes as the 'alternative science play'.[3]

This 'second wave of recent science plays'[4] is distinguished from its antecedents by its rejection of 'the traditional emphasis on character, and on other dramaturgical staples like linearity and causality'.[5] Rather, 'the science enters the stage not disguised as usual, but as it is, in all its asperity and difficulty'[6] and this in turn creates for the audience an 'experiential' and immersive encounter with the science, and dramaturgies that Shepherd-Barr characterizes as 'postdramatic'. The unexpected 'dramatic' orientation of some of our own experiments in devising the alternative science play suggests that dramaturgy, which is defined here as the 'dialogic relationship between what is being presented and how it is presented',[7] operates in surprising ways when 'what is being presented' is information derived from medical sciences.

Context: Dramaturgies of the alternative science plays

The critical success of the productions that Shepherd-Barr uses to illustrate this wave of science-based performance attests to its significance within avant-garde theatre, at least in the United Kingdom and on the continent. Complicite's *Mnemonic* (1999) and *A Disappearing Number* (2007) are seminal productions within the international festival circuit, and John Barrow and Luca Ronconi's *Infinities* (2002) and Jean-Francois Peyret and Alain Prochiantz's *Darwin trilogy* (2004) are acclaimed within the European avant-garde. More recent productions such as Katie Mitchell and Stephen Emmott's *Ten Billion* (2012), a co-production between the Royal Court and the Festival D'Avignon, indicate the continuing health of this area of practice at an international level. On a more local scale, British funding initiatives such as The Wellcome Trust's Arts Awards continue to seed innovative responses to biomedical science, such as Sound and Fury's *Going Dark* (2012, in collaboration with Hattie Naylor) and Melanie Wilson's *Auto-biographer* (2012).[8]

Most of these productions resist the 'dramaturgical staples' noted by Shepherd-Barr above. Although they may not do so to the point of constituting the 'death of character' described by Elinor Fuchs,[9] they variously disturb the performer-character dyad as the target of the audience's subjective identification. For example, *Ten Billion* opens with Stephen Emmott stating that he is not an actor; in *Auto-biographer*, the main character is split between several performers whose voices are at times dislocated from their bodies. To this extent they resist the Aristotelian format wherein the audience's emotional engagement with a single protagonist is entrained to their conflict against internal and external forces, and to the resulting rising action. David Mamet equates this dramaturgical model to the 'perfect' football match, one in which victory is won at the last minute against a worthy opponent,[10] giving the game (and the performance) its carefully paced turns of suspense and reward.[11]

If character and narrative arc are the key mechanism for the audience's emotional engagement in the dramatic tradition, how might this engagement be achieved in the alternative science play? Answers to this question might be found in other arts or performance disciplines such as dance, digital media and sound: the search for alternative dramaturgical strategies gives one explanation for why alternative science plays often entail interdisciplinarity beyond the obvious engagement with science.

Of these, sound seems to be offering particularly innovative solutions to the question of how to engage the audience without recourse to traditional character and narrative forms. Frances Dyson argues that sound is 'the immersive medium par excellence ... perceived in the here and now of an embodied space'.[12] The immersive quality of sound is of particular value in the depictions of medical conditions, wherein it allows the audience to experience approximations of some of the symptoms. For *Auto-biographer* evoked a sense of dementia through a structure of repetitive phrases replicating disruption to autobiographical memory; in *Going Dark* the audience, like the protagonist, becomes reliant on sound (a radiophonic sound track) as his blindness develops (the darkening lighting design). The following discussions will explicate its significance in *Bloodlines*.

Rationale: *Bloodlines*, 'BloodLines' and the search for felt form

Bloodlines has a basis in personal experience. In 2004, the sound composer (Milton Mermikides) was diagnosed with Acute Lympho-blastic Leukaemia (ALL), 'a deadly disease for which the best available therapy is only available to a fraction of patients and is itself potentially lethal'.[13] That treatment constitutes an aggressive course of chemo– and radiotherapy from which the patient is 'rescued' by the bone marrow transplant (BMT),[14] in this case donated by the author (the dramaturg, and his sister). Despite the risks of treatment-related morbidity, BMT represents the best chance of survival for adult forms of the disease (around 20% for those with a sibling as a donor, less for those with an unrelated donor – and none for those with neither).[15]

The extreme nature of our experience may seem to lend itself a performance in the dramatic tradition (indeed it could be argued that the story of siblings facing and defeating death through the gift of life blood has the makings of a melodrama). The possibility presents itself of mapping our story to the compositional arc of the dramatic tradition. By this logic, Milton's diagnosis might be seen as the 'inciting incident', the decision to go ahead with the donation (despite the risks) as the crisis point, his survival in the face of the enemy (cancer) as the 'denouement' and its happy ending.

However, despite this corollary to traditional dramaturgy, we chose not to employ 'traditional modes of drama and dramaturgical strategies'[16] in our approach to *Bloodlines*: not to have characters (however loosely based on ourselves), nor a series of causally motivated actions driven by a protagonist. Instead, we sought to engage with the subject of ALL and BMT through a focus on the physiological and medical processes taking place within the bodies of a patient and a donor.

This produces a rather paradoxical engagement with the body in the project. On the one hand, the performer's body is put under representational pressure, for example when it is required to depict non-human elements (variously in the experiments described below) or because it is absented altogether (in the 'BloodLines' track). At the same time, the human body and its intricate workings are the project's central subject.

This also prompted the project's specific dramaturgical approach. The fact that 'what is being presented' were 'structures and functions of the body at a level which eye and brain cannot straightforwardly comprehend'[17] required us to work in a metaphorical way wherein the performers' bodies (where they exist) represent abstract or unfamiliar entities. The challenge for us was to do this in a way that was somehow meaningful to the audience, whether by calling on their subjective identification as described above, or otherwise. The project thereby drew us to a type of sign usage that Sheets-Johnstone describes in her remarkable essay tracing of the evolution of symbol-making from bacteria's 'surface recognition sensitivity' to Martha Graham's *Lamentation*. Here Sheets-Johnstone describes the latter as 'not a story about grief ... but its felt form' wherein 'the movement dynamics ... are congruent with the affective dynamics of sorrow, of deep mourning'.[18]

If we replace Graham's subject matter of 'grief', with that of the biomedical science we are engaged with, the concept of a 'felt form' defines an important goal in our explorations. A similar ambition is described by Alistair Skinner in relation to his own artwork documenting his experience of terminal bowel cancer (*It's Inside* with Kate Meynell), which, he suggests, sought to generate 'equivalences to a visceral understanding of the disease'.[19]

That 'felt form' could be achieved without recourse to character or, indeed, representational sign usage, was suggested by a sound composition created by Milton in 2005 during his treatment.[20] In this, Milton used the technique of 'data-sonification',[21] translating the results of his daily blood tests into sonic form by assigning a distinct sound to each of the eleven blood cell populations and programming them to rise and fall in relation to fluctuations in blood count and composition. Here the resulting piece is described in the composer's words:

> ... the undulations in health can be heard musically as the piece progresses. In particular, the prominent microtonal swell can be heard to descend as the white blood cell count starts extremely high due to the leukaemic cells, and is massively reduced by chemotherapy until the body reaches a vulnerable neutropaenia.[22] ... The 'autobiological' nature of the work engenders an emotive response and memory of the journey through treatment.[23]

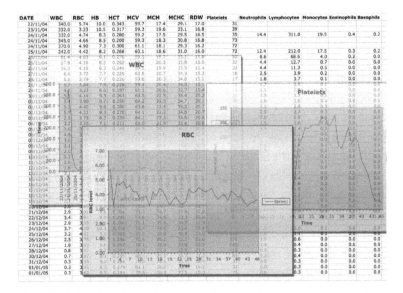

Figure 4 *BloodLines* cover art showing the composer's blood counts. Note extreme fluctuations in the white blood count (WBC). Image courtesy of Milton Mermikides.

This 'emotive response' seems to communicate with others too. For example, one listener at the research presentation at which our experiments were presented, described 'a sinking feeling', adding that 'you know it, you feel it, you don't necessarily need to understand [the science]'. These psychoacoustic effects correlate to the dramaturgy of the alternative science play: it is experiential and the 'science' is 'manifested' (through sound) rather than mediated (through text or representational sound).

A surprising effect of the 'BloodLines' track is that the piece also seems to exhibit a compositional form reminiscent of the dramatic arc: the high pitch of the 'microtonal swell' at the beginning of the track feels like an inciting incident, its sharp descent like a crisis point, which then settles by the end of the track at a level that feels like a resolution. (See Figures 4 and 5).[24]

It should be acknowledged that these interpretations may be an arbitrary effect of the particular data Milton had in hand (a different

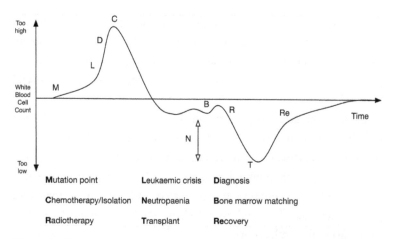

Figure 5 Charting the WBC at key points of the treatment results in something resembling a dramatic arc. Image courtesy of Milton Mermikides.

period of treatment may have produced a different arc), or indeed that they are a projection of the listener/respondents' knowledge of the work's autobiographical basis.

If not, then the emergence of something like a dramatic arc from a 'postmodern' process (i.e. one wherein authorial intention is at least partially delegated to found material, chance and automated procedures) already tests Campos and Shepherd-Barr's designation of the alternative science play as 'postdramatic'. And it points to the possibility that particular scientific disciplines may engender different dramaturgical structures when represented in performance. Could the 'arc' be attributable to the biological nature of the source material, or indeed its particular basis in disease? This is a question to which I return in the conclusion of this chapter.

Experiments: Devising with science

I turn now to an analysis of three short pieces of performance material, produced with and by dance and drama students participating in a workshop at Kingston University on the *Bloodlines* project (spring

2011). Led by the author and the sound composer, the five-week workshop addressed two research questions: 'what is the dramaturgy of disease and treatment?' and 'what creative strategies and compositional principles can be usefully shared between a composer and a theatre-maker?'

Each of the selected performances – which I entitle *HLA-Dance*, *Cell Monologue* and *Pascal's Triangle* – responded to these questions in ways that elucidate the interrelationship between form and content when dealing with biomedical material. The workshop culminated in a research presentation to an invited audience of performance practitioners, scholars and postgraduate students, whose responses form part of the evaluation.

HLA-Dance

The title of this experiment is derived from the test used to assess whether prospective bone marrow transplant donors and recipients are a 'match', that is, are sufficiently genetically compatible for a transplant to go ahead. 'Matching' donor and recipient mitigates the effects of a potentially debilitating or fatal condition called graft-versus-host-disease.

Their compatibility is determined by their having an identical portion of genetic code (on chromosome 6). There is a one-in-four chance of siblings being matched. Those without a matched sibling and therefore reliant on bone marrow registries have a much lower chance of finding a match. The results of an HLA test are expressed as a series of five numbers[25] (so comparing tests for donor and recipient might feel a little like checking a lottery ticket).

Taking the data-sonification used in the creation of 'BloodLines' as a cue, the experiment sought to test a performative equivalent of this (which we nicknamed 'data-choreography') on a dataset relating to this theme of matching (one which, we felt, might not have an inherent dramatic arc as it dealt with statistical probability as well as biological compatibility). Both data-sonification and data-choreography can be situated within a postmodern art's tradition that seeks to delegate authorial intention through the use of found material and chance, and through automated or task-based processes. For performance, this tradition encompasses contemporary British companies such as Rotozaza and Station House Opera, with historical precedents in the work of Judson Church, and Merce Cunningham and John Cage. The latter, of course, is an important precedent both in terms of performance and sound composition.[26]

The method used in this experiment might be likened to a complex game of 'snap' or 'stone, scissors, paper'. The five numbers on an HLA test were each assigned an everyday gesture, and pairs of student-devisers were asked to simultaneously execute a run of these gestures that might, or might not, 'match'. The resulting rudimentary performances had some energy, interest and, often, humour to them. The energy came from variations in the timing and speed of the actions. The interest and humour derived, in part, from asking students to represent abstract entities: there is something both disturbing and funny about people attempting to represent non-human elements, a sense of the uncanny provoked by the blurring between the familiar human, and the unfamiliar non-human.

The students automatically adopted a similar performance mode in all versions of this exercise, one that sought to eliminate the humanity or personality of the performers through a certain neutrality of facial expression, an economy of gesture and a commonality of stance and movement between individuals. As might be predicted by those familiar with task-based performance practice, the inevitable failure to sustain this attempt at automation formed a key part of the interest of the performance, and its humour.

However, unlike the 'BloodLines' track upon which the experiment was based, the performance failed to achieve a 'felt form'. We decided that a key reason for this failure was that the significance of the 'matches' between performers was not integral to the dramaturgy itself. An audience member might work out the rules of the game, and experience a moment of satisfaction with each match. However, enabling the audience to understand that our 'snap' moments correlated to the search for matching donor would require additional priming. Moreover, leaving the timing of these matches to chance rather than design also prevented the audience from attributing significance to those moments. Unless we engineered a build-up of intensity to the 'matching moment' and make the audience aware of the risks involved if a match is not found, the piece would feel underpowered.

Cell monologue

If *HLA-Dance* was an attempt to 'dehumanize' the performer's body in relation to the science, *Cell Monologue* can be seen as an attempt to humanize the science through the body. Initially created by one student, *Cell Monologue* is an apology spoken by a blood cell which/ who has inadvertently triggered the overproduction of mutant cells that categorizes ALL.[27] It is interesting that this anthropomorphic strategy was also used in the Skinner and Meynell piece previously mentioned, with Gary Stevens using his 'deadpan comic delivery' to represent a cell mutating.[28]

By anthropomorphizing the cause of the disease, the piece represents a happy compromise between the dramatic reliance on character, and the postmodern approach we took in *HLA-Dance*. Another nod to the dramatic tradition was the call made by the piece upon the audience's empathy, for example, by having the cell characterized as a factory worker who makes a mistake on the production line and is subsequently ostracized from its community of fellow workers:

> So I queued, hoping that nobody would notice my uniform and started my shift: flow, reproduce, get your bearings, nurse; flow, reproduce, ask yourself a couple of introspective questions such as 'who am I', nurse; flow, reproduce, find yourself, nurse; flow, reproduce, make a self-

assertion; nurse, flow, reproduce, get on your feet again, nurse; flow. ... Apparently, I got carried away and over-reproduced. And in such a society, this is unacceptable. ... Well, they isolated me – and you see it was useless by then, because I had already 'spread the contamination' as they shouted at me.[29]

Audience responses when this was shown at the research presentation indicated that there was 'something powerful' about the student's choice of strategy. For example, it was noted that the character of the faulty cell became a personification of cancer, a highly stigmatized and emotive disease. Representing this disease as a worker 'just doing her job' was identified as a very effective 'de-stigmatizing' device. *Cell Monologue* seemed to achieve a 'felt form'. It did so through what the student described as the blending of 'non-narrative and narrative elements' and 'operating the abstraction within a narrative structure'.

The narrative, the student argued, was necessitated by that of the disease itself – an important point to which I will return. I would suggest that this 'abstraction' was most apparent in a moment that also represented the most powerfully 'felt' moment within the *Cell Monologue* performance.[30]

Pascal's Triangle

The moment in question has the cell character struggle to explain the Pascal sequence, the 'fixed mathematic array' that happens to also describe the proliferation of blood cells:

> You have a triangle. Ok? Suppose you have 1 on top. The rule is you always have to add the numbers above ... 1 = 1, 1 = 1, 2, 1 - 1, 3, 3, 1 ... No? 1, 1 = 2; 1, 2 = 3. ... So, once you've got the triangle, if you add up the numbers in each row, you get the exponential sequence, which illustrates our reproductive scheme. ... It's like, 1, 2, 4, 8, 16, 32, 64, 128, 256, 512 and so on ...[31]

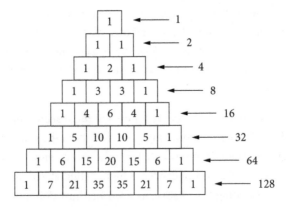

Figure 6 Pascal's Triangle. Image courtesy of Rod Pierce.

The students who were developing this piece in rehearsal noticed that the brick pattern on the wall of the rehearsal studio coincided with the diagram used to illustrate the (see Figure 6) and decided to incorporate this 'triangle' into the piece. Given the postdramatic emphasis on chance and found material, it is significant that the moment in question came about as a result of a chance discovery in the architectural features of the room in which we were working. In the final performance, the performer assigned a number to each of the bricks forming the triangle on the wall through a touch of her hand.

The triangle itself was barely distinguishable from the surrounding bricks and the difficulty of discerning the triangle, and of grasping the 'maths', became an important factor in what we saw as the success of this performance moment. The analogy between cell growth and the series of numbers had a nice logic to it, especially as the brick pattern seems congruent with the way in which cells are commonly visualized.

However, what seemed to be more significant to the audience's experience was the way in which this moment drew an analogy between a performative situation in which someone tried to explain and others tried and for the most part failed to understand, and the experience of disease that the (thankfully cancer-free) audience could also sense. Featuring the maths (itself an explanation of the science of cell reproduction) 'in all its asperity and difficulty' evoked something of the unknowability of disease, the unsettling realization that our health and life depend on the mathematically ordered functions of bodily entities that are normally unavailable to our view and grasp.

Conclusion: The devised/alternative science play as postdramatic dramaturgy?

As experiments, the explorations above are somewhat lacking in scientific rigour particularly as their results are measured and interpreted through our audience's and our own personal responses to the resulting material. However, one point that can be made quite conclusively is that Shepherd-Barr's characterization of the alternative science play as essentially postdramatic merits further examination.

As we noted above, Shepherd-Barr distinguishes the alternative science play from the 'traditional' one by its 'unmediated' conveyance of scientific ideas. This, she suggests, results in dramaturgies which are best categorized in terms of Lehmann's postdramatic theatre, which he in turn describes as employing: 'a type of sign usage ... [that] becomes more presence than representation, more shared than communicated experience ... more manifestation than signification, more energetic impulse than information.'[32]

Of our experiments, the 'BloodLines' track and *Cell Monologue* most successfully achieved this sense of 'presence', 'shared ... experience', 'manifestation ... energetic impulse' (i.e. what we called a 'felt form'). And they did so through the unexpected ('BloodLines') or strategic (*Cell Monologue*) deployment of two interrelated cornerstones of the dramatic tradition: the dramatic arc and character. *Cell Monologue* in fact used both as the Cell describes the story of her mutation and her guilt in the face of its cataclysmic results (the Aristotelian fatal flaw and anagnorisis perhaps). The most successful moment within *Cell Monologue* (*Pascal's Triangle*) presented a character in a very live 'conflict' with the audience: seeking to explain the maths despite her own inability to communicate clearly and the audience's inability to grasp it.

The least successful experiment, *HLA-Dance*, failed, we felt, because it lacked something that might have been achieved through these elements: a sense of risk or danger perhaps, or the disturbing thought that people's lives are dependent on statistically rare genetic matches. Discussions with workshop participants almost resulted in our rigging the improvisation so as to delay the 'matching moment' to the end of the piece (creating a sense of build and eventual climax). Whether or not this would have succeeded, the desire to do so attests to the readiness with which we as devisers are drawn to this particular dramaturgical shape, which in turn may reflect the readiness with which we as audience members respond to it on a 'felt' level.

If this is the case, then an interesting implication is that the historical pervasiveness of the dramatic arc might be regarded as a manifestation of our embodied experience; the particular subjective response that it produces (as described by Mamet's ball game above) as a result of our recognizing in it the pervasive but unconsciously perceived biological patterns of our body's life-support systems.[33] Perhaps this is what one respondent to the 'BloodLines' track meant when they said 'you know it'.

In pointing out the dramatic devices which operate within the 'abstraction' (as Mauro puts it) of these otherwise postdramatic or postmodern pieces, I am not arguing for the superiority of one tradition over the other in terms of eliciting a felt response. I am, however, suggesting that, in some cases at least, devising with science results in dramaturgies that interestingly intertwine the dramatic and the postdramatic. That such intertwinings should exist is not controversial: Lehmann himself does not propose these as completely discreet forms, denying that the latter is 'an abstract negation or a mere looking away from' the former.[34] Likewise Shepherd-Barr sees the alternative (postdramatic) and traditional (dramatic) science plays as 'a complementarity' rather than in 'opposition'.[35] However, what I would like to propose in concluding this chapter is that this post/dramatic intertwining can be characterized as a manifestation of – and arguably a result of – the interdisciplinarity of the devised/alternative science play.

Bringing together distinct disciplines invites unexpected innovation into the process as our assumptions are challenged by new knowledge, perspectives or representational strategies, thus drawing us to newer dramaturgical forms.[36] At the same time, this interdisciplinarity can also provoke a simultaneous pull towards the familiar and the universal in search for common ground. While the latter statement might imply a degree of conservatism (and recourse to the established dramatic tradition), what can be more interesting is where the 'lowest common denominator' is found as a point of thematic intersection in terms of 'what is being presented'.

For biomedical science an obvious point of connection is its engagement with the human body and, by implication, with the ultimate 'arc' that is our struggle for life. Thus, as Ede points out, 'the mystery of death may lie at the heart of artists' obsession with the sentient body but it is a curiosity shared with biomedical researchers and clinicians'.[37] If it is indeed the 'mystery of death' which provides the common ground between devising practitioners, medical science (and in some cases, scientists) and with the audiences of the performances that are created as a result of such collaborations, this intertwining between postdramatic and traditional dramaturgies raises yet wider, and more philosophical, questions.

And if, as Shepherd-Barr suggests, alternative science plays share a 'concern with essentialism' and the human condition[38] then it is not so surprising that emergent dramaturgies dealing with this monumental theme might intertwine existing forms, and indeed, reach beyond them.

(The project described in this article was subsequently developed into a production, performed at London's Science Museum and the Rose Theatre Kingston in 2013. This formed part of a research project exploring intersections and collaborations between performance and science (the Chimera Network).

The Chimera Network was supported by the Arts and Humanities Research Council UK.)

References

Bettelheim, Bruno. *The Uses of Enchantment: The Meaning and Importance of Fairy Tales*. London: Penguin, 2012 (originally published 1975).

Campbell, Joseph. *The Hero with a Thousand Faces*. California: New World Library, 2012 (originally published 1968).

Campos, Liliane and Shepherd-Barr, Kirsten. 'Science and Theatre in Open Dialogue: Biblioetica, Le Cas de Sophie K. and the Postdramatic Science Play'. *Interdisciplinary Science Reviews* 31.3 (2006), pp. 245–53.

Dyson, Frances. *Sounding New Media: Immersion and Embodiment in the Arts and Culture*. Berkeley and Los Angeles: University of California Press, 2009.

Ede, Sian. *Art & Science*. London and New York: Taurus Books, 2010.

Edgar, David. *How Plays Work*. London: Nick Hern Books, 2009.

Edwards, Barry. *Artscience: Creativity in the Post-Google Generation*. Massachusetts and London: University of Harvard, 2008.

Fielding, Adele. 'Current treatment of Philadelphia chromosome-positive acute lymphoblastic leukemia'. *Haematologica* 95.1 (2010), pp. 8–12.

Fielding, Adele and Goldstone, Anthony. 'Allogeneic haematopoietic stem cell transplant in Philadelphia-positive acute lymphoblastic leukaemia'. *Bone Marrow Transplantation* 41 (2008), pp. 447–53.

Fuchs, Eleanor. *The Death of Character: Perspectives on Theater after Modernism*. Bloomington and Indianapolis: Indiana University Press, 1996.

Haskin, Rob. *John Cage*. London: Reaktion books, 2012.

Hunt, Andy, Hermann, Thomas and Neuhoff, John, eds. *The Sonification Handbook*. Berlin: Logos Verlag, 2011.

Larson, Kay. *Where the Heart Beats: John Cage, Zen Buddhism and the Inner Lives of Artists*. London: Penguin, 2012.

Lehmann, Hans-Thies. *Postdramatic Theatre*. Trans. Jürs-Munby, Karen. Oxford and New York: Routledge, 2006.

Mamet, David. *Three Uses of the Knife*. London: Methuen, 1998.

Mauro, Margherita. Performance transcript and supporting statement submitted for assessment at Kingston University, 2011.

McKee, Robert. *Story: Substance, Structure, Style and the Principles of Screenwriting*. London: Methuen, 1999.

Mermikides, Milton. *Changes Over Time: Theory and Practice*. PhD thesis, University of Surrey, 2010.

Meynell, Katherine and Skinner, Alistair. *It's Inside: The Story of a Cancer*. London and New York: Marion Boyars, 2005.

Nyman, Michael. *Experimental Music: John Cage and Beyond*. Cambridge: Cambridge University Press, 1999.

Sheets-Johnstone, Maxine. *The Corporeal Turn: An Interdisciplinary Reader*. Exeter and Charlottesville: Imprint Academic Press, 2009.

Shepherd-Barr, Kirsten. *Science on Stage: From Doctor Faustus to Copenhagen*. Princeton and Oxford: Princeton University Press, 2006.

Shepherd-Barr and Bartleet, Carina. 'New Directions in Theatre and Science'. *Interdisciplinary Science Reviews* (special issues 2013 and 2014).

Stein, Anthony and Forman, Stephen. 'Allogeneic Transplantation for ALL in Adults'. *Bone Marrow Transplantation* 41 (2008), pp. 439–46.

Turner, Cathy and Behrndt, Synne K. *Dramaturgy and Performance*. Basingstoke: Palgrave Macmillan, 2008.

Van Kerkhoven, Marianne. 'European Dramaturgy in the 21st Century'. *Performance Research, On Dramaturgy* 14.3 (2009), pp. 7–11.

Part Four

Dance

Time and a Mirror

Towards a Hybrid Dramaturgy for Intercultural-Indigenous Performance

Rachael Swain

This chapter will expose some of the functions of dramaturgy in the work of Marrugeku, an intercultural dance theatre company working at the nexus of Indigenous and non-Indigenous experience, knowledge and creativity in remote communities in the north of Australia. My aim is to explore some of the context surrounding the production of contemporary intercultural and Indigenous art in Australia, and by also drawing associations from Indigenous visual arts, begin to identify the possibilities of a hybrid dramaturgy for devised intercultural-Indigenous performance.

Marrugeku is based in Broome, in the far north of Western Australia. The company is co-directed by Yawuru choreographer and dancer Dalisa Pigram, together with myself, as director of the productions. Each multimedia production is developed in situ, in stages over two to three years, followed by tours to other remote communities and national and international arts festivals. The demands of speaking to remote community Indigenous audiences, as well as national and international arts festival audiences, has deeply affected the emergence of an intercultural dramaturgy in our work.

Marrugeku works in an Indigenous frame of cultural production that is also an intercultural frame, in a state of continuous negotiation. We have adopted the term 'intercultural-Indigenous' to describe the company and its work. This cosmopolitical outlook and performance idiom has been informed by the specific histories of the town of Broome from the

Figure 7 Trevor Jamieson and Yumi Umiumare in *Burning Daylight* (Marrugeku, Broome, 2009, dir: Rachael Swain). Photography: Rod Hardvigsen (2009).

turn of the last century. Broome was made exempt from the Australian Government's 1901 Immigration Restriction Act, commonly known as The White Australia Policy, which was constructed to minimize Asian immigration to Australia. The exemption was granted due to Broome's flourishing pearling industry which was serviced almost completely by indentured Asian workers. Relationships between immigrant Japanese, Chinese, Malaysian, Filipino and Indonesian workers and members of the local Aboriginal community were common, despite being illegal under the Western Australian government's cohabitation laws.

The lived experience of the Broome-based company members, direct descendants of these political histories, has led to the emergence of a dance dramaturgy developed in a multiethnic-Indigenous context. It is also a dramaturgy developed in a situation of loss and revival of cultural practices, of intergenerational hauntings by the many who were stolen due to the forced removals or deported under the stringent cohabitation laws. Navigating plural loyalties to multiple cultural backgrounds has led us to working with cross-cultural collaboration and cultural intuition as valid and important places to work from as artists.

Dramaturgy

In *Dramaturgy and Performance*, a recent critical overview of the practice, Turner and Behrndt propose that dramaturgy is concerned with the 'composition, structure or fabric'[1] of a play or performance, and that doing dramaturgical work implies 'an engagement with the actual practical process of structuring the work, combined with the reflective analysis that accompanies such a process'.[2] That this 'reflective analysis' and approach to structure necessarily abides by other logics in different cultural contexts and in the language of other, non-text-based forms, is central to the dramaturgy which has emerged in our work.

Strategies for exploring alternative 'modes of perception' and other experiences of space and time emerging from beyond the borders of dominant Western perspectives are central to new notions of a dramaturgy which is deeply connected to an artist's relationship to the world.

I am more concerned with dramaturgy than the role of the dramaturg. I propose that dramaturgy is practised by a range of collaborative artists, including the dramaturg. In the work of Marrugeku the role of the dramaturg takes on specific functions, affected by the impact of different knowledge systems and how they are operating in each production. We have only ever been able to address the dramaturgical needs of a project with a 'cluster' of practitioners and consultants addressing different areas of specialist knowledge. This has included Indigenous law men and women who consult on the work, Indigenous custodians who have contributed a specific dance or story, and invited guest artists who may have skills in writing, theatre craft or dance dramaturgy.

I acknowledge that this is a complex arena of negotiation within the company where fractured areas of knowledge are negotiated, in some senses, without resolution. As director of the work I am often functioning to process the multiple perspectives being addressed during the collaborative process, which tend to come from local, national and international frames of reference.

In discussing what it is she does as a dramaturg from a perspective of practice Van Kerkhoven notes:

> Dramaturgy is for me learning how to handle complexity. It is feeding the ongoing conversation of the work, it is taking care of the reflexive potential as well as of the poetic force of the creation. Dramaturgy is building bridges, it is being responsible for the whole, dramaturgy is above all a constant movement. Inside and outside. The readiness to dive into the work, and to withdraw from it again and again, inside, outside, trampling the leaves. A constant movement. '*Wenn ich still stehe, verstehe ich nichts*', (When I stand still I don't understand anything).[3]

In Marrugeku's dance theatre making this 'constant movement' and 'handling [of] complexity' is carried in a set of knowledges which are both intersecting and differentiated, by a small group of people who each are functioning, in part, as 'the dramaturg'.

Time and a Mirror: Dramaturgy in an Indigenous context

Tim Etchells, artistic director of *Forced Entertainment*, proposes several ideas about dramaturgy in contemporary performance practice which I find useful to re-frame into our intercultural-Indigenous contexts. He states that 'dramaturgy is doing time':

> It took us many years to realise that time, more than anything else, was what we were dealing with. The unfolding of actions over duration, the economy of events in the frame of hours, minutes, seconds and split seconds.[4]

Following this understanding, Indigenous Australian perceptions of time become central to the specific make-up of the dramaturgy we are considering, to the structure a work might take and the logic it might follow. Indigenous notions of time and conceptions of history underpin causation and effect in story structures and their place in a community's collective understanding. Patternings of occurrences interconnected with others, and intersections of the presence of creation spirits poised in the landscape with historic events can present a reality radically different from non-Indigenous understandings. A notion of time functioning in dramaturgy then, which, after Cultural Studies author Stephen Muecke, 'operates in ever tightening rhythms'.[5] Here history is ever present and story structures are not only polysemic, they are multi-temporal.

The results, in narrative terms, are built on hybrid systems of knowledge, consciously exposing gaps and ambiguities which, in themselves, are indicative of the cultural negotiation and intermediation that the function of dramaturgy in this work entails. In furthering his ideas of 'expanded dramaturgical practice' Eckersall notes:

> dramaturgy's sense of ambiguity as a practice should be greatly valued. In this regard, the 'new poetics of dramaturgy', with its sensibilities of disorientation and flow, makes for a productive site of cultural negotiation and contest.[6]

In a paper discussing dramaturgy in 2007 Etchells considers the dramaturgy of the so-called 'real' versus the so-called 'theatrical':

> As if all it were – our dramaturgy – was the positioning of information, the positioning for the most part of some things as being more proper, some things less proper, or maybe some things apparently more real, some things apparently less real than others. A matter of giving weight to information, of creating hierarchies. A matter of sequence and managed revelation arranged across time.[7]

Etchells's considerations can be helpful when applied to the way Indigenous Australian concepts of time and what is 'real', or perhaps 'alive' can be valued differently across a series of events in the structure of a live performance work. This reality, or 'aliveness', has a direct relationship to place, or to 'being in place' in an Indigenous context and therefore a dramaturgy which follows this notion would be: a matter of sequence and managed revelation arranged 'in place', but 'in' as opposed to 'across' time.

Elsewhere Etchells has suggested that the dramaturgy of *Forced Entertainment*'s early work was propelled by a desire to stand in the complexity of contemporary experience and 'for just a moment to hold the world and see it properly'.[8] If this notion is translated into an Indigenous performance-making context then this 'holding the world and seeing it properly' would of course reflect Indigenous perceptions of the world and reality.

In *The Speaking Land* anthropologists Berndt and Berndt state:

> Aboriginal mythology, for any particular group of Aboriginal people, was and is, like a huge mirror that reflected – sometimes dimly, sometimes in an exaggerated way, sometimes phantasmagorically – what was familiar to them, something they expected to see and something that they could identify. It was not necessarily a mirror reflecting reality, in the sense in which we normally use that word, but in many cases it was very close indeed to that.[9]

This notion of a mirror which has the ability to refract an Indigenous reality with a range of differing qualities – phantasmagoric, dim, exaggerated and so on – is a useful metaphor for the nature of dramaturgy in contemporary Indigenous performance. A dramaturgy which allows an audience a glimpse into a way of 'holding the world and seeing it properly', a way of seeing which is, for the local Indigenous audience, expected and familiar, yet for non-local, non-Indigenous spectators may demand a new kind of attention.

Context: Contemporary Indigenous art

The context surrounding the work of the audience practising this 'new kind of attention' is the social and political histories which affect Indigenous knowledge transference, collective remembrance and Indigenous storytelling today and in turn, how this informs the development of contemporary Indigenous art practice.

Indigenous art often exists at many levels of meaning, both revealing and actively hiding its content, or perhaps, revealing some information to some people and other information to others – those who have the knowledge or experience to perceive it. Leading an audience into a mode of perception where it can 'feel' this presence and absence of meaning, yet not be alienated by the gaps in knowledge, is one of the more subtle and complex demands of this dramaturgical practice.

In a wider Australian context this work of listening differently requires commitment and attention across a range of fields of endeavour. Marrugeku's work of 'salvaging' stories in contemporary forms and bringing them into focus in open public settings has a small part to play in this national project.

There is much to be learnt in the performing arts from considering understandings developed in Indigenous visual arts, particularly concerning the relationship between artist, story and the way an Indigenous artist's own country is 'seen' and represented. The place paintings of the western and central desert artists frequently depict country, songline, story and actions undertaken in both human and spirit worlds simultaneously through intricate designs which can symbolize single or multiple meanings. Art historian Howard Morphy proposes that this:

> in part reflects the fact that paintings are connected to a revelatory system of knowledge about the world in which people learn deeper meanings as they pass through life. While some elements of meaning are secret, it is more the case that, as with any system of knowledge, people need to acquire information over time in order to develop a fuller understanding. In harmony with this is the belief that the surface forms of things derive from underlying structures and relationships.[10]

During the creation of Marrugeku's 2006 production *Burning Daylight* we encountered multiple cross-cultural transactions during the devising process where our investigations into 'the surface forms of things' in a choreographic sense led us to new approaches to 'underlying structures and relationships' which came to constitute the emergent dramaturgy.

During the devising process the Indigenous dancers and the two choreographers Serge Aimé Coulibaly and Dalisa Pigram began working from a place of embodied memory to develop new approaches to choreographing phrases. The dancers identified traditional dance material which was open for public viewing and that they had permission to perform. They improvised new interpretations of the material, applying their own cultural intuition and individual imagination to transform the underling rhythms, tones and textures into reflections on their contemporary experience. The results of this explorative work were in turn presented to local cultural custodians of the dance styles and permission was granted to continue our experimental approach to choreography and character development. Working closely with cultural custodians on research, conceptual development, narrative structures and choreographic investigations as an ongoing practice in our productions has enabled the work to function as a vehicle for the production of contemporary Indigenous art which is deeply connected to the specific logic of local experience and knowledge.

Arts journalist Rosemary Sorensen's review of *Burning Daylight* in the *Australian* describes Dalisa Pigram's solo as an example of the results of this process. She states: 'Her solo work and with the other heterogeneous collection of performers in *Burning Daylight* are breathtakingly good. Like every one of the cast, she seems to move in entirely her own way, a body that is both memory and future tense.'[11]

It is this embodied reclamation of memory as a place, a foundation from which to create as an artist and its projection into the future, which is the essence of the work and the company's danced search for new performance languages.

However Marrugeku's process in Broome, of creating contemporary dance in a context of 'culture loss' and 'culture gain' and as an exploration of the significance of indigeneity, is an interpretative struggle. One not easily won. As art historian Fred Myers states:

> To find common ground between the so-called traditional and the contemporary as equal instances of culture-making is not to claim a simple continuity. The point is rather to insist on interpretive struggle and ambiguity, as regimes of value are constantly brought into new relationships.[12]

In intercultural live performance making the 'interpretive struggle' is both the practical and conceptual work of dramaturgy. This is precise work, ephemeral in its nature, elusive, yet painstakingly achieved through cultural negotiation, on the one hand, and through the

Figure 8 Dalisa Pigram's solo in *Burning Daylight* (Marrugeku, Broome, 2009, dir: Rachael Swain). Photo: Rod Hardvigsen (2009).

'professional cultural intuition' of artists manifested in their creative improvisational techniques, on the other. The work of contemporary Indigenous art brings into play a potent mix of biography, cultural intuition and the navigation of a shared political history. It frequently functions in a context of loss, longing and separation and can function as both radical innovation and in dialogue with the way 'traditions' are transformed in intercultural lifeworlds.

Haunting as a Way of Knowing: A dramaturgy of talking to ghosts

In the programme notes which accompanied the national tour of *Burning Daylight*, I stated that I believed that creating the production within the legacy of Broome's history of forced removal and government control 'had left us in the streets at night talking to ghosts'.[13]

Haunting is a significant knowledge trope utilized in the dramaturgy of *Burning Daylight*, where there are three modes of place and time structured into the narrative of the work. Each character on stage had a ghost or a double on screen, and the structure of the work utilizes linked and reflective micro-narratives across each mode of storytelling to weave backwards and forwards between the understandings of place and time, cause and effect.

Early in the creation process my friend and collaborator André Lepecki had given me a copy of *Ghostly Matters: Haunting and the Sociological Imagination* by Avery F. Gordon. Gordon's book started to resonate in multiple ways as we developed *Burning Daylight* in Broome as a site of multiple losses, multiple histories and multiple cultural affiliations. The book contributed to my thinking about 'loss as a way of knowing' and 'understanding that comes from feeling' in Indigenous contexts.

With her considerations of unaddressed and 'disappeared' social injustices in America and Latin America, Gordon proposes haunting as a social phenomenon which asks us to redress past atrocities, but also as a way of knowing which draws us into another reality, into a 'structure of feeling':

> If haunting describes how that which appears to be not there is often a seething presence, acting on and often meddling with the taken-for-granted realities, the ghost is just the sign or the empirical evidence if you like, that tells you a haunting is taking place. The ghost is not simply a dead or missing person, but a social figure, and investigating it can lead to the dense site where history and subjectivity make social life. The ghost or the apparition is one form by which something lost, or barely visible, or seemingly not there to our supposedly well-trained eyes, makes itself known or apparent to us, in its own way, of course. The way of the ghost is haunting, and haunting is a very particular way of knowing what has happened or is happening. Being haunted draws

us affectively, sometimes against our will and always a bit magically, into the structure of feeling of a reality we come to experience, not as cold knowledge, but as a transformative recognition.[14]

Remembrance haunts us, as the stories we tell are never an exact truth. Rather they are a truth that enables us to live in the here and now. The Broome peninsular is indeed touched by many ghosts with histories of massacres, Indigenous relatives remembered but stolen, or Asian relatives who lived there for a time but were deported. Ghosts can tell us of that which a society, any one family or a government has rendered invisible, and that the invisible can actually be a seething presence, moving between us affecting our lives, our dreams, our desires. For the production *Burning Daylight*, 'haunting' came to be understood as a very particular way of knowing and 'being with' the past of a certain place, and the act of remembering and of telling ghost stories became an action, a 'work to be done'. Gordon talks of haunting, unlike trauma, as distinctive for producing 'something-to-be-done', the moment of disturbance indicating when:

> things are not in their assigned places, when the cracks and rigging are exposed, when people who are meant to be invisible show up without any sign of leaving, when disturbed feelings cannot be put away, when something else, something different from before, seems like it must be done.[15]

I propose (after curator Hetti Perkins and art historian Fred Myers) that it is perhaps a shared political history which is the only thing which could be claimed to identify a unifying principle to Indigenous art in Australia. The *Bringing Them Home* report into the forced removal of Aboriginal children from their families estimates that between one in three and one in ten Indigenous children had been removed between the years of 1910 and 1970 and that not one Indigenous family in Australia remains untouched. This denotes that Indigenous theatre and dance created in Australia is united by a politics of the present as disturbed by the ghosts of the past. Dramaturgy in this context must be a dramaturgy which engages with this disturbance, with the 'something-to-be-done'. It is a dramaturgy which engages with 'the structure of feeling of a reality we come to experience, not as cold knowledge, but as a transformative recognition'.[16]

The function of collective memory and the way it has been abused by forcible breakdown of families and communities under Australian government policy, and, as Gordon points out, 'the conditions under which memory is produced in the first place',[17] all come into play in a consideration of 'haunting as a way of knowing' in an intercultural and Indigenous dramaturgy in Australia. Remembrance as a practice in this multifaceted application functions as a counter-memory and brings us into the terrain of justice and reconciliation.

It is this role of memory, given form in devised performance work, and its possibility of offering counter-memory towards a 'restorative truth' (South African Truth and Reconciliation Commission) and placing it in the context of the national imagination which makes haunting a knowledge trope central to Indigenous dramaturgy in Australia.

In the dramaturgical structure of *Burning Daylight* ghosts are stirred, danced with, but not laid to rest; there is no fantasy of reconciliation as closure, or of ghosts pacified and silenced. In the final scene of the show, *Ikebana Tango*, Yumi Umiumare dances as the ghost of her on-screen character, alongside Trevor Jamieson's Aboriginal cowboy who has come to town, stirring up the ghosts of the past. Together they haunt the young rapper, Dazastah, singing as their descendent. We see the rapper who has given voice to the young people roaming the streets in previous scenes. In a slow, incanted rap, Dazastah sings of his memory of his grandmother crying in the night, removed under the cohabitation laws and to his experience of today:

> Poor balla me, mix breed me,
> I am a brother and stranger on the streets,
> I'm a stray mongrel sensing the scent,
> of black flowers wen I walk in the darkness,
> I'm your little mongrel, a seed's seed of the blossoms,

Blown with the winds of time, weathered by the seasons of problems,
Knocked unconscious by stolen cultures, I dream of my history,
Robbed by Lawful Vultures, my past is such a mystery,

The Aboriginal cowboy appears as a ghost upstage laying flowers at a
Japanese grave, the young man walks through the back of the space in a
pool of blue light singing the chorus:

How come me, the past come to haunt my soul
How come me, the past come to taunt my soul
How come me, the past come to haunt my soul
Wanna take me home won't let me go.
Dazastah[18]

The cowboy steps into the space and a tango begins between the two
ghosts centre stage, juxtaposed with the young rapper singing, sitting
on an empty bench in the streets.

Here a dramaturgy which engages in social and political worlds,
considering reactivating memory as 'work to be done', is evident.
Such a dramaturgy brings us to the work of justice and restitution,
where knowing the full extent of past atrocities is always in itself, an
impossibility, as with the nature of trauma. Bringing other ways of
knowing to the surface is required. Gordon states:

Following the ghosts is about making a contact that changes you and
refashions the social relations in which you are located. It is about
putting life back in where only a vague memory or bare trace was
visible to those who bothered to look. It is sometimes about writing
ghost stories, stories that not only repair representation mistakes, but
also strive to understand the conditions under which a memory was
produced in the first place, towards a counter memory for the future.[19]

One of Australia's most well-known creators of ghost stories is the visual
artist Tracey Moffatt. In the following section, which explores narrative
and dramaturgy in the contemporary photographic and filmic work of
Moffatt, I will outline her notion of 'dreaming with our eyes open'.[20]

Figure 9 Trevor Jamieson as a ghost in mourning in *Burning Daylight* (Marrugeku, Broome, 2009, dir: Rachael Swain). Photography: Rod Hardvigsen.

Fantasy and Biography: A dramaturgy of 'dreaming with our eyes open'

Considering the work of the Australian-born, internationally acclaimed visual artist Tracey Moffatt is one of the important connections for my practice. Her narrative-driven photographic series, which she calls 'photodramas', and her cultural subversion of genre in her short and feature film work have been a source of inspiration for various scenes in several of my productions.

Tracey Moffatt is an international artist, now based in New York, who grew up in Brisbane, Australia. She was born to an Aboriginal mother and along with three siblings was fostered with an Anglo-Irish family where there were several other children. She acknowledges both mothers as strong influences in her life and her experience of her childhood and teenage years growing up in a working-class suburb of Brisbane in tropical Queensland, has significantly informed her work. She literally places herself, her own body, in much of her work and as such she often blurs the lines between performance art, art and cinema. As author Catherine Summerhayes notes, her public performance of self 'becomes for us an interpretation of her own memories'.[21]

Her highly theatrical, staged photographs and films, often in supersaturated colour evoke the power of history, myths, popular culture as well as the supernatural and operate on many levels of meaning as 'performed remembrance', and an experience of secrets, never fully known. Multiple perspectives pervade her work which is peopled by protagonists from a range of Indigenous and immigrant Australian cultural backgrounds, often on the margins of a multicultural society. There is a strong sense of inferred theatrical narrative frequently with alternative scenarios suggested or unresolved outcomes in both her photographic and film series. In some works such as her feature film, *beDevil* (1993), this can evoke what I would call a productive confusion or lack of resolution in her work.

In a discussion of Moffatt's work Régis Durand states:

> One of the most remarkable things in her work is the condensation between the various temporal strata brought into play by memories, dreams and fantasies, between which she shifts back and forth with no respect for chronology. The work is anachronous, floating between memories of different times and natures; memories of lived experience, whether physical or cultural ... imaginary memories of adopted or appropriated identities.[22]

The description of 'the various temporal strata' and alternative chronologies echo some of my ideas of how narrative functions in Indigenous storytelling which has a direct relationship to country, but here with Moffatt's work we introduce both biography and fantasy in the storytelling palate. In an interview with curator Gerald Matt, Moffatt states:

> I think all my imagery comes from my subconscious, from dreams. I am not talking about when I dream at night (these are far too weird and sick) but the dreams I have when I am awake. We can dream with our eyes open. This is why I have been hesitant to be written about as a social commentator. I think my work is very dream like.[23]

Here I will take a leap across disciplines and extend an application of Moffatt's considerations in her practice into the emerging possibilities of a contemporary intercultural-Indigenous dramaturgy. If we accept this dramaturgy to encompass a listening for stories which are never fully told, where meaning is both hidden and revealed, or perhaps will never be fully known and if we understand that the logic comes from a perception of several parallel times and realities, grounded in experience of place and memory, then we begin to identify key elements informing a 'fantasy' and an ability to 'dream with our eyes open' as a creative and culturally intuitive process in a contemporary Indigenous art-making context.

If we accept multiplicity of readings and uncertainty of resolution as the nature of this project, we may begin to define intercultural-Indigenous dramaturgy as enigmatic, exploring a fluctuating contemporary reality that forfeits closure and a refusal to nominate a single meaning for the work. To this end Durand says: 'I have spoken of enigma. But the enigma implies something hidden, in Tracey Moffatt's work, as indeed in many supposedly enigmatic situations or representations one must nonetheless accept the idea that everything is there, visible'.[24]

If we apply the notion that 'everything is there visible', yet hidden, at least to some sections of the audience, to notions of contemporary Indigenous dramaturgy we come once again to an approach to meaning that is deliberately multi-vocal, and it is precisely this floating and 'feelingful' approach which accounts for its enigma and its richness.

With *beDevil*, Moffatt examines secrets which are involved with the many and varied experiences of being an Indigenous person in Australian settler society. Summerhayes states:

'They are stories of ghosts and memories of secrets which, in Foucault's sense, are not so much "repressed" as nurtured in the form of carefully controlled discourses where silence and secrecy are a shelter for power, anchoring its prohibitions; but they also loosen its holds and provide for relatively obscure areas of tolerance'.[25]

Here I would propose that the creation of contemporary intercultural-Indigenous performance which 'listens for secrets' and which 'dreams with its eyes open' actively takes on the-work-to-be-done of 'nurturing' this silence and secrecy in contemporary Indigenous narratives. As such, this work of providing a space for 'obscure areas of tolerance' speaks of a reconciliation, which is not about resolution, but embracing dislocation, transgression and enigma.

This is a dramaturgy of incompleteness; an incomplete experience that demands of audiences a kind of reckoning with the context of the intercultural nature of Indigenous lifeworlds. It is compelling, it evokes a curiosity in the spectator, a need to listen for meaning as it emerges between what is seen and what is unseen. This is a dramaturgy which destabilizes dominant perspectives on how the power of knowledge might function.

In this way the dramaturgy we are speaking of has paradoxical requirements of its spectators. Initially it requires a surrender, or openness to enter into an experience of displacement and uncertainty, to accept that the signs are both familiar and unfamiliar, where a fragmented logic, part documentary, part fantasy is orchestrating events. This coexists, I would argue, with an active need for scholarship, for knowledge that is earned as a requirement of participation in the experience of being in Australia and knowing our country's stories, its art and its history.

This dual passive/active mode of attention I identify as 'ways of listening' required of the spectator in his or her participation as audience in contemporary Indigenous art. This new kind of attention significantly influences a 'dramaturgy of the spectator' and how it functions in Indigenous contexts, revealing in itself the 'work to be done' by audiences and artists alike in our country.

Taken together, these points are an account of the artistic, intercultural and deeply political processes that emerged in making *Burning Daylight* and other devised works by Marrugeku. They identify the main features of a dramaturgical process that I have called 'ways of listening', encompassing a devised rehearsal practice of remembrance and the role of intercultural dramaturgy in creating counter-memories for the future.

References

Berndt, Ronald M. and Berndt, Catherine H. *The Speaking Land: Myth and Story in Aboriginal Australia*. Ringwood, Vic.: Penguin, 1989.

Durand, Régis. *Specific Climates*, L.F.L.C.d. Barcelona, Editor La Fundacion La Caixia de Barcelona, 1999, pp. 103–5.

Eckersall, Peter. 'Towards an Expanded Dramaturgical Practice: A Report on "The Dramaturgy and Cultural Intervention Project"'. *Theatre Research International* 31.3 (2006), pp. 283–97.

Etchells, Tim. 'Addicted to Real Time'. *Entropy* 3.3 (1997), p. 204.

—'Doing Time'. *Performance Research* 14.3 (2009), pp. 71–80.

Gordon, Avery. *Ghostly Matters: Haunting and the Sociological Imagination*. Minneapolis: University of Minnesota Press, 1997.

Marrugeku. *Burning Daylight*, R. Swain, director. 2006.

—*Burning Daylight* Programme Notes, Marrugeku, 2009.

Moffatt, Tracey and Matt, Gerald. 'An interview with Tracey Moffatt' in *Tracey Moffatt*, M Snelling (ed), IMA/Asialink, Brisbane 1999, pp. 65–8.

Morphy, Howard. *Becoming Art: Exploring Cross-Cultural Categories*. Sydney: University of New South Wales Press, 2008.

Muecke, Stephen. *Ancient & Modern: Time, Culture and Indigenous Philosophy*. Sydney: UNSW Press, 2004.

Myers, Fred R. 'Unsettled Business: Acrylic Painting, Tradition and Indigenous Being'. *The Power of Knowledge: The Resonance of Tradition*. Ed. L. Taylor. Canberra: Aboriginal Studies Press, 2005.

Sorensen, Rosemary, 'Revelation found in broad daylight', *Australian* (30 October 2009), available http://www.theaustralian.com.au/arts/ revelation-found-in-broad-daylight/story-e6frg8n6-1225792599690, (Accessed: 1 December 2013).

Summerhayes, Catherine. *The Moving Images of Tracey Moffatt*. Milan: Charta, 2007.

Turner, Cathy and Behrndt, Synne K. *Dramaturgy and Performance*. Basingstoke: Palgrave Macmillan, 2008.

Van Kerkhoven, Marianne. 'European Dramaturgy in the 21st Century'. *Performance Research, On Dramaturgy* 14.3 (2009), pp. 7–11.

Going '*Au-delà*': A Journey into the Unknown

Reflections of a Choreographer and a Dramaturg

Lou Cope and Koen Augustijnen with
contributions from Annie Pui Ling Lok

Les ballets C de la B *is synonymous with what is now recognized as Belgian dance theatre. Known for staging 'anarchic, eclectic, committed*[1] *shows that are created by a choreographer creating material with, rather than on their international cast of dancers, rehearsals are often lengthy processes (normally four months, or longer for Platel's large-scale productions) that involve the dancers exploring tasks inspired by a given theme. As Platel states, 'the result of what you make is a condensation of what you have lived over the previous months'.*[2] *All* les ballets' *choreographers work closely with a dramaturg.*

Lou Cope:
I got a call one day in March 2010, completely out of the blue, from choreographer Koen Augustijnen asking me if I would be interested in meeting up to talk about becoming his dramaturg for his next show, *Au-delà*. It's unusual for work to come this way – normally it comes through meeting people on jobs.

It was like Koen was saying, 'Hi. Will you temporarily join my family, become incredibly intimate with me and accompany me on a very private, potentially painful, journey, with extremely public results?' It is an extraordinary thing to ask a stranger.

But I had been recommended through a mutual colleague,[3] so we met to talk things over. During our two-hour meeting, Koen told me about his ideas for the show and I talked about myself, my previous work and what I consider myself to be 'for'. He explained that his relationship with his previous dramaturg had come to a natural close after many years, and that he was looking for someone new to work with. Possibly someone who looks from a different perspective, is clear about their own opinions and is able to give him and the cast very direct feedback about how they are working and what they are making – particularly important as Koen was also dancing in the show.[4] He also said that he was interested in changing his methods of generating material.

Shortly after our meeting I signed a contract that made me Koen's dramaturg for the next seven months. There was no specification of days to be worked, but I was to receive a set fee plus all travel and research costs.

A few years previous to this, I had worked with a choreographer who had never worked with a dramaturg before, and I had written a document to try to explain, not what dramaturgs are for (I would never dare do that!), but what I considered *myself* to be for. I now use it in all my new processes and in my teaching. I ask directors and choreographers to go through it and tell me what they want, don't want or need that isn't mentioned. I sent this document to Koen and he said he was very happy with it ALL – which I found very exciting.

The lines between being a dramaturg, a coach and a mentor are sometimes clearly drawn. In this case, they weren't. It was immediately clear that Koen was very open, and very keen to engage in a dialogue not only about the work but also about his personal journey and his practice too.

For me, the unspoken, the feared, the assumed and the worried-about are the enemies of my work. It helps me enormously to try to get as much clarity as we can before we start so that we can all rid ourselves of insecurity, second-guessing and uncertainty. This way I try to clear my own mind of the fear and paranoia that can come with living on the murky outside of the inside.

Koen Augustijnen:

My previous collaborations with dramaturgs had always come out of working with people beforehand. One I met while I was performing for another choreographer; another had worked for me previously as a musical director. With Lou it was different. I trusted the opinion of our mutual colleague as well as my intuition after our first long meeting. She had a straightforward way of communicating, a lot of experience in directing theatre (which was different for me) and appeared capable of keeping a certain distance. She was also very interested in being involved with the dancers' issues. Last but not least, we were new to each other, which felt positive and fresh.

I appreciated the document Lou had written and felt it demonstrated that she had a very analytical side, which I thought would be a good balance to my more intuitive way of working.

To my mind, working with a dramaturg is not a luxury. At some moments I am so busy working on the material in a detailed and technical way, as a craftsman, that there is not enough distance between me and the work. It is then important to me to hear a second opinion. This often generates ideas to make the material better and clearer. A dramaturg is also somebody who looks after the original concept and tells me when I go off track. Articulating my ideas, thoughts and choices forces them to evolve and gain clarity.

A dramaturg brings a table full of documentation and information to the rehearsal space. He or she is a good listener and a sharp third eye, at times taking distance to give the right feedback. They ask essential and critical questions without blocking the process, with the goal of defining the artistic proposal.

LC:

Koen wanted to make a piece set in the after life, danced to the music of Keith Jarrett and called *Au-delà*. Au-delà is taken from the French *l'au-delà* meaning the hereafter, which without the 'l' means 'beyond'. And that was where he wanted to go: beyond his previous work, beyond this life and far into the 'Great Beyond'.

Koen was in his mid-forties, he had lost his father not long before, and he was naturally turning his attention to what might come next. He declared himself to be an agnostic confronted by some unanswerable questions that had never troubled him before. He wanted to work with older dancers, partly because he thought they would relate to the subject more than younger ones, and partly because he wanted to develop movement material that might be influenced by the changes, limitations and opportunities of an ageing body. He also wanted to make a piece of hope.

These were some quite big, and quite personal issues, and in our early meetings, I wanted to spend time getting to know Koen and delve deeper into why he wanted to make this show. We both felt clear from the start that it would be easy to allow the show to end up as a vague meandering about something unknowable, and I tried to focus on moving it from the general to the specific. To Koen's ideas, fears and expectations, and later to those of the dancers.

Koen is a gentle man and he was never particularly comfortable with my attempts to place him at the centre of his work. Of course *les ballets* are known for creating work with rather than on dancers, so we all knew that most of the movement material would come from the dancers themselves. But Koen was one of those dancers, as well being the choreographer, and I was convinced that unless we could really get into him and his own feelings about death and grief, then we could not expect the piece to do that either.

KA:
As I was one of the dancers I had to answer and improvise my own tasks. Often I showed my material last so as not to influence the other dancers too much. After a while, it became clear that my proposals often represented some kind of tormented struggle, and one of the dancers asked me why this motif kept recurring. I guess this was a key moment where I told them about the very intimate difficulty I have accepting the loss of my father. There was such a sadness coming out of me that the dancers seemed to immediately understand where this piece was coming from and where it was going. This certainly helped.

LC:

We also talked about Koen's past work. I watched all his previous productions on film, one of which, *Ashes*, we watched together – discussing in detail what we thought was successful and in what ways he wanted this piece to be different. I asked him general questions like 'What are/aren't you good at?', and 'What do you want to give your audience?' We talked about the process – namely how Koen wanted to evolve his practice, and how I might help with that; and we mused over the literary and philosophical roots of the piece.

Koen had become interested in the bardo – the Buddhist idea of an in-between moment of heightened consciousness, a moment of choice and of transition between the past and the future, between confusion and wisdom. I set about researching this; and trying to understand how it could be used in terms of developing dramaturgies, movements or tasks. The Buddhist texts also gave us something else vital to framing our understanding of what we hoped the show might be for.[5] Their belief that 'in learning about dying we learn about living' reminded us throughout that this was what we wanted: to make a show about death that was about life.

I also read a number of works of fiction (which I would often summarize and give to Koen) – notably *Sum* by David Eagleman, *Nothing To Be Frightened Of* by Julian Barnes and Milan Kundera's *Immortality*. I was drawn to the concepts of legacy and immortality – which went on to underpin much of the text written by myself and the performer who delivered it – Claudio Girard. In addition to this, Koen was fascinated by Near Death Experiencers (NDErs), and we used some published personal testimonies to inform tasks, text, choreography and dramaturgical structure.

I, unlike some other dramaturgs, do not consider myself to be a theoretician, an academic or an intellectual. I consider myself to be an artist, a practitioner, a collaborator in performance-making processes – there to support the work, and those who are making it.

Nevertheless the reading and research process is vital to what I do. It gives focus to my attempts to climb into the brain and soul of the person/people I am working with, and it arms me with ideas, contexts and resonances that I draw upon throughout the process.

It is my job, as she who sits on the outside of the inside looking in, to also look outwards and see ways in which the material being developed speaks, and is linked to, the growing worlds around it – the world of the piece, but also the world outside the cosy rehearsal room.

KA:

It is a dramaturg's job to know, as much as possible, where I want to go with my work and, at times, to confront me with the fact that the work is either representing or not representing these ideas, and whether it is communicating what it means to.

A new thing for me was that Lou was willing to bring in texts that could be performed. She brought in some which were good additional information but, to my mind, not usable in the piece. Until one day she came up with some text by Milan Kundera about two famous people in the hereafter complaining that the world keeps talking about their private lives and not about their achievements. So, still no peace in the hereafter. We took this idea and improvised on it and it became a monologue for Claudio Girard. Before Lou brought the text in, I had tried to generate material with Claudio but hadn't found anything I wanted to use. Then Lou came with this text and the two ideas mixed into one monologue.

So, a dramaturg can have a profound influence on the creation, and it would have certainly been another piece, as well as process, without her.

LC:

Often, as the process went on, Koen and I would discuss tasks before rehearsals. Some were related to the concept of the piece: 'You arrive in the void – what do you do?', or 'Embrace the clouds' (the results of which went on to become the huge final group sequence). Others were purely physical: 'Take off your skin', or 'Move together like a flock of birds'. Still more related to the performers and/or potential characters: 'Make something starting from a strong memory' or 'Travel fast through your past'.

In retrospect, I feel that I, and therefore we, could have done a better job of interrogating the specific value of each task. Of course, you don't want to over-talk something before it has been tried, you have to allow space for surprises, and this was a great concern for me. But in truth I do feel that more careful tailoring of tasks towards what Koen was really looking for could have helped in terms of efficiency, clarity and character/movement development.

In the early phases I often say very little while actually in the space. My job is to 'bear witness' to the people, the ideas and the material. Koen and I talked on the phone almost every night. We discussed what we thought was exciting, and then we made a plan for the following day.

(Planning is certainly not always a part of my job, but with Koen it was important. We talked a lot about how he would want to focus each day, and we would meet or talk every Sunday evening to discuss what he wanted to have achieved by the end of the following week.)

As a dramaturg I like to work in collaborative processes, where the choreographer leads without being in control and where the work is both authored and created by those who perform it. It is in these processes where the choreographer can be necessarily blinded by their own proximity to the work, (and in this case their presence in it), that I find myself to be most useful.

And when I'm allowed, (it isn't always appropriate or required), I choose to position myself in the spaces not only between the director/choreographer and the piece, and of course the piece and the audience, but also in the spaces between the performers, the creative team and their relationships with each other.

Of course not all dancers, or collaborators, want this. There are always those who look appalled, and avoid eye contact at all cost – so as not to be forced into a thinking that, for some, has a negative impact on creativity, spontaneity and thinking through the body.

(One rehearsal diary entry – after I had not been in rehearsal for several days read: '*I see that it can be so good for them that the "Queen of Meaning" isn't always here! Movement just needs to exist as movement, before it is greedily seized upon by the likes of me.*')

But there are other performers who gradually drift my way, and I see it as part of my job to try to help them. Working with them to make connections between the material they are creating and the conceptual ideas for the piece, or helping them with ideas of 'character' that either represent them as authentic individuals or that speak of mini-narratives expanding from and adding to the theme of the work.

I know that some dramaturgs don't like to get involved with the performers, seeing themselves as there to serve the choreographer. But as someone who nearly always works in devised processes where the product is multiply authored, (even if singularly signed), and who believes that the process is always entirely present in the product, I think it is crucial to pay attention to the detail of the making process to try to ensure that the best possible piece gets made in the best possible circumstances. Needless to say, there are varying degrees of success here.

KA:

Lou's interest in the needs and problems of a performer particularly caught my attention in her original introductory document, and it makes her a constructive bridge between the choreographer and the dancers. My previous dramaturg had another approach: he was close to me but much more distant from the dancers.

To give an example, there was a difficult moment when Lou and I had almost decided the structure of the piece and I knew that I wanted the last scene to be a solo by Gil Ho Yang. But Gil Ho had lost confidence in his technical skills for this scene and no longer wanted to perform it, and had gone to Lou to tell her he wanted to withdraw it. The three of us then had a long talk and we were thankfully able to bring him back on track and convince him that there was still time and space to assure the quality of the material.

LC:

Because Koen was performing in the piece, the issue of having someone on the outside looking in was even more important than usual in this production.

Often, when Koen set a task and they improvised a response I was the only one who had seen it. So they would emerge blinkingly from the inward intensity of the improvisation to turn to me, and say 'Well…?' At times and in the early phases especially, this felt a bit much to me, and I was concerned that my role was sometimes being confused with that of the assistant director. But that was what was required for this job, so that was how it went. It was clear to all that I could only speak for myself and that Koen would watch the footage later and make his own decisions, but I felt close enough to Koen's intentions, and trusted enough by the other performers, to be able to speak with honesty about both my reading and valued judgement of what I was seeing.

Koen would, of course, sometimes feedback immediately on improvisations and rehearsal he was in. He could base his response on either how he felt as a dancer, or what he had managed to perceive by peeking out of his own activity to see what everyone else was doing. This is difficult of course, and inevitably had impact on the space Koen was given to immerse himself in his own performance. I worried for him about this, and occasionally we would set aside a few days when he would 'only' be a choreographer, or a few hours when he would 'only' be a dancer.

The fact that Koen had to watch the rehearsal footage each evening brought its own problems too. Obviously, it slowed the process down enormously. Not only was it incredibly time consuming and exhausting for Koen, but the dancers would also want more immediate feedback about whether they were on the right track or not. I felt their need for decisive feedback from me grew as both time and patience began to run out.

KA:
Lou did a great job of giving feedback on improvisations by describing what she had seen during the session. It was also good that it was not only me who was giving the feedback but somebody else with another way of speaking and seeing, coming more from theatre. The dancers often welcomed this.

Having said that, although at some moments it was tiring to look at the videos in the evening, it also had the advantage of giving me time to review sessions and proposals until I was clear about my opinion.

And yes it worked better for me to occasionally 'stop' directing, or 'stop' dancing. Switching from dancer to director and back in the same hour was sometimes too much. And when I felt I was being only half of each I decided to make clear choices about which to be. It helped us all I think.

LC:

Added to this, Koen, by his own admission, does not work very quickly. Though the décor, the music and some key scenes were chosen from the outset, other material was developed by intuitively ploughing through task after task, with Koen waiting for ideas to jump out or make associations. He is used to having a longer rehearsal process than the three months we had, and he struggled at times to adapt to this time frame.

I felt it was often my job, in our meetings after rehearsals, to encourage him to make decisions in order to speed things up. He would often resist this, preferring to wait longer before making commitments. That is, of course, his right!

KA:

For most other creations I have had four months: two months of improvising and experimenting, with only a few actual scenes being developed, and two months of gradually evolving selected material. With 'Au-delà' I felt that I needed a few more weeks to generate more material and a few more weeks to work it out.

In terms of decision-making, Lou and I often had different opinions and rhythms. I tend to wait quite long before taking a decision. Sometimes my patience was an advantage because something better occurred, sometimes it was a disadvantage because it made the dancers impatient and nervous. It is important to find the right balance. After six weeks, I was planning to do one more week of improvising hoping to discover even more new things. But in an after-rehearsal meeting Lou woke me up saying it was time to work things out. After discussing it for an hour!, I agreed that it was the right thing to do.

LC:
After-rehearsal meetings were not always just for Koen and I. Annie Pui Ling Lok, the movement advisor who was also there two or three days a week, would often join us.

A three-way conversation between choreographer, dramaturg and movement advisor could potentially be dizzying and unhelpful, but I hope that Annie and I used our different perspectives in a way that made Koen feel both challenged and supported.

I would talk about the meaning and the reading of the material in terms of relationships between dancers, dancers and material, material and audience etc. Annie would talk about the movement in a much more detailed and physiological plane. Where I talked about meaning as painted by a thick brush, she would use a finer brush to talk about, for example – a release in the shoulder or an energy in the arm swing. Also, really importantly, she would dance much of the material too, so she would then be able to give feedback 'from the inside'. On more than one occasion, she usefully stated that what I was imposing on the material felt counter to what was actually happening inside the body of the dancer.

Annie Pui Ling Lok:
It was a close-knit process between Lou, Koen and I, as much in rehearsal as in the conversations that went on in car journeys, Skype sessions, emails and after work in bars, restaurants and at Koen's home.

I was working with the dancers on the close-ups, while Koen was working on the close-up, the mid and the wide shot simultaneously. This was made possible because of Lou's presence and skill in framing the 'whole'. I could zoom in and in because Lou was always bringing the piece out and further out; negotiating and testing the relevance of movement that would in time become a phrase, a scene, a section and so on.

The work done by Lou, with Koen, therefore, was to constantly refine, define and polish the shape, size and colour of the piece from a place that meant I could get on and do my job.

KA:

There were a few moments when I felt I was saturated by the feedback and opinions of Annie and Lou. But they sensed that themselves, and sometimes Annie would take the train alone in the morning instead of coming with me in my car. They were a great help, especially with me being in the piece. Annie talked about the movement qualities and was able to describe them to the dancers in a technical way, where Lou would use more poetic vocabulary. The triangle team definitely worked for me. Annie also gave warm-ups – one of which inspired me to make the big and important group dance in the middle of the piece.

LC:

When it came to the dramaturgical structuring of the piece, I got out my laminator and made colour-coded pieces of card (red for solo, blue for group sequence, grey for text etc.) that were then placed on a big board in the space. I love doing this – you can tell my mother is a teacher! And Koen and I spent many hours jiggling them around.

The beginning of the show had been clear in Koen's mind from the earliest inception of the idea. He wanted to show a YouTube film about a young guy marvelling at the wonder of a 'double rainbow' before the characters appeared from above and below the huge tree that was the décor.[6]

What was to come next though was undecided, and we tried placing a couple of different group scenes at the beginning. Reasonably quickly we settled on what we called 'Flocking' – a frenetic sequence of running and circling that became about the 'bardo' moment between life and death. Once it was placed there, it took on meaning that felt so defined and useful, it was hard to imagine it being placed elsewhere.

We then began to slowly introduce the 'characters' with solos and combined solos that were created in response to various tasks.

Figure 10 The 'Flocking' scene in *Au-delà*. (les ballets C de la B, Ghent, 2012, choreography: Koen Augustijnen). Dancers: Fatou Traoré (half pictured), Koen Augustijnen, Claudio Girard, Florence Augendre, Gil Ho Yang. Photography: Chris Van der Burght.

Koen was always clear that he wanted the overall arc of the piece to go from restlessness to peace, chaos to calm, resistance to acceptance. This in itself represented a bardo-like transition, and this is where the hope he sought to express, found its place. Another of the *fils rouges* in the piece was the idea that as it progresses the characters move further and further away from their corporeal forms. The longer they are in the after-life, and the more they are forgotten by those they left behind, the more they shift from being their human selves into being just memories – mere 'particles in the wind'. The movement vocabulary, accordingly, would become more abstract and less rooted in the quotidian.

And here, dramaturgically, we encountered a problem. In traditional terms you might look for situation, conflict and resolution, and it was clear we had no conflict or perhaps it had been at the beginning of the piece. We had no catalyst for change and we struggled to find either a conceptual reason or a shift in dynamic that could make a transition allowing the characters to pass through a bardo, come to terms with their journey and in so doing move us further into the abstraction of the latter part of the piece.

We tried a number of different possibilities: some inspired by amalgamated religious beliefs (you pass from a waiting room, through judgement, into 'the realm of possibilities' before being reborn or released). Others influenced by Julian Barnes's version of the phases we go through in bereavement (which was how we saw our characters – removed from their loved ones and thus bereaved). We even flirted with a lovely medieval image Barnes had brought to our attention – that of the bird flying from dark through a lighted room to darkness again. None of which fully ignited, explained or earned the transition we needed.

Koen then had the idea that a sort of decomposition would take place. That they would go to a darker, less familiar and more frightening place – where they would clash against themselves, each other and their environment abandoning their sense of 'self' to the chaos of nothingness.

What follows is a much shortened extract from some words I wrote at this idea, in the hope of pinning it down and, frankly, selling it to the dancers.

> This scene could try to express Jean-Paul Sartre's idea 'that hell is other people'. Ignited by the entrance of Koen's character a kind of panic takes hold, where darkness and selfishness are allowed to prevail. Instead of working together they fight: humanity leaves humanity.
>
> In much the same way as London recently rioted, these people riot. It is about anger, pain, bitterness, disappointment, envy, sadness, loss. But as they reach the climax, they realise that they have a 'global responsibility' to do better. That they have to accept the situation as it is and take their place in the community to do what is needed.
>
> It can be a metaphor for global politics – if we want it to be …
>
> Hell is not other people. Heaven is other people. Each other is all that we have.

These words, and more significantly, these ideas had limited success. I'm not sure we ever cracked that middle section. Perhaps the deconstruction didn't go far enough, and maybe the cause was never fully decided upon. Perhaps we were imposing a shift in energy that the piece needed, but hadn't earned. I suspect it is something that Koen and I will wonder about for years to come.

Having said that, on tour it seems to have found its place more, and certainly the dancers seem more comfortable with it.

KA:
The whole explanation above still makes a lot of sense to me but I think it is more important for us than the public. They will never exactly see our reference but they will hopefully feel or imagine something related. That's what happens with this type of work, and that's what I hear in after-show discussions. But actually as I read Lou's text now and as I write this, I have a new idea that might make it stronger. I will try it. The work is never finished and we keep evolving and finding new things as we continue to tour. It is an ongoing process; that's why I love it.

LC:
No, a piece isn't finished even when it's on tour – though my work on it is. It's always strange for me to think of shows touring away, and I rarely know when or where they are on. I envy the camaraderie of the cast and crew, and I envy the piece 'growing old' with them. Movements become easier, more familiar and more owned, while ideas and relationships evolve, change and blossom.

It is then that I am forced to remember that I am not really on the inside of this family. That I never can be. That I am paid not to be. But lucky me I get to pack my bags and move on, ready to peer privilegedly in at the next family who will give life to, nurture and set free a whole new bunch of ideas. Can't wait.

(With thanks to the cast and crew of *Au-delà* and all at *les ballets C de la B*.)

Au-delà production credits:
Direction and choreography: Koen Augustijnen
Created and performed by: Claudio Girard, Fatou Traoré, Florence Augendre, Gil Ho Yang, Koen Augustijnen
Music: Keith Jarrett, Walter Augustijnen

Dramaturg: Lou Cope
Movement advice: Annie Pui Ling Lok
Set design: Wim Van de Cappelle
Light design: Kurt Lefevre
Sound design: Sam Serruys
Costume design: Dorothée Catry

Production: *les ballets C de la B*
Coproduction: Théâtre National de Chaillot (Paris), Grand Théâtre de Luxembourg, Guimarães 2012 Cultural Capital, TorinoDanza

Re-Membering *Zero Degrees*

Guy Cools

Introduction

The title of this essay is a reference and pays tribute to the book *ReMembering the Body* (edited by Gabriella Brandstetter and Hortensia Volckers), that accompanied the exhibition STRESS at the MAK in Vienna in 2000. In its opening chapters, Aleida and Jan Assmann discuss in detail the history and symbolism of the *Membra disiecta*: the rituals of embalmment which put the body central as the individual's biographical memory bank;[1] and the myth of Osiris whose dismemberment and his consecutive re-collection, that is the collection of his dispersed body parts and their reassembling by Isis, are a symbolic representation for the collective, cultural memory of a country or community.[2]

> This act of searching, collecting and assembling together ... in which the Egyptians continuously assure themselves of the endangered identity and integrity of their culture – is something which one is compelled to link with the English concepts 're-collection' and 're-membering' ... which, in their basic etymological meaning, signify nothing other than 'collecting together again' and 'assembling together again'.[3]

From the above it becomes clear that the act of re-membering is always one of deconstruction and transformation. Our memory is always subjective. It takes apart the factual experience, already in the moment of experiencing it through the senses, and reassembles it by stressing certain parts and forgetting others; by reordering them in a logic that seems appropriate and makes sense to the self that re-members.

In what follows, I will recollect my own subjective memory of the creation process of *zero degrees*, the epic, artistic dialogue between Akram Khan and Sidi Larbi Cherkaoui, Antony Gormley and Nitin Sawhney, seven years after it took place. Depending on my quotidian experiences of living in London while creating the work or being a privileged witness and contributing to the creation as its production dramaturg, my re-membering has at least two clearly distinctive storylines: that of the professional inside the process, collecting the traces of his memory in his notebooks; and that of the human going through the intensity of being a first-hand witness of a historical event that both colours and fixates one's memory.

Part One:
A dance dramaturg's notebooks.
A subjective memory of what I contributed

Incidentally, Anne Bogart raises the question of the dramaturg's ownership within the context where everyone else has a clear domain, and suggests that this must apply to 'archival materials and structural ideas'. ... But most interestingly, when I eventually moved on ..., my suitcases were full of 'archival materials and structural ideas' – as well as a few maps and stories.[4]

All through my professional career as a dance dramaturg, I have been a firm believer of Marianne Van Kerkhoven's dictum that as a dramaturg you should remain invisible in the final result, that you need to develop a particular kind of modesty and shouldn't aspire to be an artist yourself, at least not yet, while you are working as a dramaturg, supporting the creative process of someone else.

Dramaturgy is a limited profession. ... The work he does dissolves into the production, becomes invisible. He/she always shares the frustrations and yet does not have to appear on the photo. The dramaturg is not (perhaps: not quite or not yet) an artist. Anyone that cannot, or can no longer, handle this serving – and yet creative – aspect, is better out of it.[5]

Nevertheless there is often a clear sense of what you can and do actually contribute to the process, and by consequence also to its result, the production. But it only lives on in your own subjective memory and that of the other participants, with your notebooks as the only traces and silent witnesses.

As such this essay is an attempt to document and make public my memory of parts of my contribution to *zero degrees*. And I can only hope the other protagonists, Akram Khan, Sidi Larbi Cherkaoui, Antony Gormley and Nitin Sawhney will recognize themselves in my version of our shared history. By doing so, I will also discuss some of my insights and fundamental beliefs about dance dramaturgy as a creative and somatic practice.

How I got involved

The anecdote of how I got involved in the first place explains some key aspects of the role of the dramaturg and his relationship with the artists. Originally Akram and Larbi had decided to work without a dramaturg and in my consecutive experiences with them I can assert that both are to a large extent capable of doing so. It confirms two axiomatic notions about the role of dramaturgy/the dramaturg:

i.   Every creative process needs a dramaturgical reflection but you don't necessarily need a dramaturg for this. A lot of artists are quite capable of doing it themselves or often have other people fulfilling this role, without them being credited for it.
ii. As Hildegard De Vuyst stated once, as a dramaturg you do your work best when you are least needed.

When they did decide – quite late in the preparation – to work with a dramaturg, I was the obvious choice because I already had a personal relationship with both, having presented and co-produced all of their earlier works when I was still the dance curator at Arts Centre

Vooruit in Ghent, Belgium. I had also accidentally witnessed several crucial moments in the three-year-long incubation process of getting to know each other and further defining and clarifying their desire to co-create, that preceded the actual rehearsal process. The previous illustrates two more of my axiomatic beliefs concerning my role as a dramaturg:

iii. The necessity of having a strong personal relationship before going into a professional engagement (without becoming too dependent on each other, either).

iv. The ideal of being present as a witness as early as possible when the first creative ideas and impulses germinate.

I can only guess about their never explicitly articulated motives why they decided to invite me into their process. But the actual reality revealed from day one that they wanted and needed me most as a moderator. Which leads me to my next conviction:

v. A good moderator keeps his own voice and opinions out of the discussion (which is a further development of the principle of invisibility). But you do support and reinforce the voice in the discussion that you feel is most relevant in contributing to a solution in which everyone can eventually recognize oneself.

Another role that became very clear from day one was that I could through the public discourse that I would develop, help to defend and protect the integrity of the artistic dialogue and exchange from unrealistic expectancies from the outside world, the producers and the media in the first place. In the original programme brochure, I articulated it as such:

> By no means expect a new, perfect blend of two languages. Language does not evolve that way, neither bodily nor verbally. If it did, the result would be gobbledegook. Language evolves slowly, renews itself organically, soaks up elements from other languages, finds creative translations for 'foreign' elements. And the more two people understand

and respect the other language and culture, the more effective and interesting the translation process.[6]

vi. As a dramaturg you are there first and foremost, if not only for the choreographers; which means you always have to fight on their sight, if necessary even against the people who pay you.

From the first day, you are there to question the obvious

Because of the rigorous and long-term preparation, the material of which *zero degrees* would consist was well defined from the first day of the actual rehearsal process. Both Akram and Larbi had specific ideas and suggestions for a number of movement sections to be developed, depending on their own or shared interests, for instance, Akram exploring the spinning of kathak in a different way; Larbi learning the rhythmical kathak footwork from Akram; both being passionate about Bruce Lee and his shaolin moves. There was also a simple and clear narrative storyline: Akram's first journey to India at the age of twenty and the questions this posed to him about his identity 'in-between'. All this was too good to be true, so one of your main contributions as a dramaturg is to question the obvious all through the process.

Since Larbi and me were both guests in London, we shared the same apartment, and I remember asking him on one of the first nights after rehearsal: 'We know Akram's story, but what is yours?' I didn't accept his first, evasive answer: 'I tell my story through the stories of others', and kept insisting. And eventually he confessed that the story he wanted to tell himself was a Yiddish song, *Jerusalem of gold, copper and light*, the semi-official anthem of the state of Israel, which for him being half Arabic was a way to reach out to the other. On a more personal level it related also to the difficult relationship with his dead father, and finally it supported also his beliefs in a non-hierarchical coexistence of culture and traditions since we discovered the Yiddish version went back to a Basque one.

vii.   If you have a voice as a dramaturg, it is in the way you question things and by doing so help the artists to find their own answers.

For most of the rehearsal process, these remained my principal roles:

–   That of the silent witness[7] in the studio playing creatively and intuitively with the physical proximity or distance (for instance by changing the angle of watching or actually disappearing for some time) and by doing so, influencing the process somatically and energetically.

–   That of the moderator between the different participants. At one point for instance, I had to interfere discretely with Antony Gormley. Antony is an extremely intelligent and generous artist and a passionate dance lover as well, but it was his first experience with the slow and collaborative process of a contemporary dance creation. His trained eye often saw the still-existing flaws in the creation, long before Akram and Larbi were physically ready to address them, and his constructive criticism threatened to undermine their confidence because it often came too early. So I had to suggest him to consider a different timing for his well-meant and relevant remarks.

–   That of questioning not so much the 'what', but the 'why' and the 'how'.

viii. The older I get (and hopefully the more experienced), the more I train myself in being patient, in holding back from comments. When things resolve without my interference, it will always contribute more to the growth of both the work and the artist.

Let me at this point add a couple of literary quotes from my original notebooks:

Questions to ask Akram and Larbi at the beginning of the process:

- Meaning for them of the title?
- Meaning of Antony's dummies?
- Any idea about a possible structure?
- How do you intend to work together?

When two people want to meet, they both have to move in each other's direction. If only one moves, there will be a short moment that they will seem to linger at the same spot, but then they will separate again, one still moving, away this time and the other still standing still.

How many sections do you need to tell a story? Contemporary dance often imitates the attention span of a song or video clip by creating sections of three to five minutes. A full length piece has then on average ten to fifteen sections.

ix.   Contrary to the above, I believe each section or performance should have the length or duration it needs to have.

Re-membering always involves editing. Editing always involves re-membering

Let me now jump to the final days of the creation process, the first days of July 2005. If I do contribute as a dramaturg in a more explicit way to the creation process, it is similar to the role of an editor in film. When I read for the first time the book *The Conversations, Walter Murch and the Art of Editing Film* by Michael Ondaatje, I immediately recognized myself as a dramaturg in the role of the film editor. In its introduction to the book, Michael Ondaatje references another older book, *Portrait of an Invisible Man* by Dai Vaughan on the British film editor Stewart McAllister. The title of the latter echoes my own beliefs expressed above of the necessity for the dramaturg to stay invisible.

The editing is probably the most creative aspect of the role of the dramaturg. It consists in supporting the choreographers to order the material in such a way that the individual sections are most powerful and the whole seems coherent and follows its own inner logic. Dramaturgy as 'the weaving together' in the classical definition of Eugenio Barba.[8] Or the way Haruki Murakami beautifully defines it in *Kafka on the shore* as 'relationality'.[9]

I am a firm believer in the form of 'open dramaturgy' which again has been best defined by Marianne Van Kerkhoven:

> The type of dramaturgy I am familiar with, is miles away from the 'concept dramaturgy' that has been highly fashionable in German theatre since Brecht. ... The type of dramaturgy I relate to, and which I try to apply both in theatre and dance, follows a certain 'process': we consciously choose material from various origins (texts, movements, film images, objects, ideas, etc ...); the 'human material' (actors/ dancers) clearly prevails over the rest; the performers' personalities and not their technical capacities is the creation's foundation. The director or choreographer starts off with those materials: in the course of the rehearsal process he/she observes how the materials behave and develop; only at the end of this entire process do we gradually distinguish a concept, a structure, a more or less clearly outlined form; this structure is by no means known at the start.[10]

The form of open dramaturgy I adhere to and practise acknowledges the fact that the work of art is only finalized in its public reception. The French philosopher and dance lover Daniel Sibony defines in his book *Le Corps et sa Danse*, dance as a movement in between a body-memory ('corps-mémoire') and a body-being-present ('corps présent'). By remembering ('rappel') their own body memory, the dancers reach out ('appel') to the audience. The open dramaturgy guarantees that the memories of the dancer trigger the memories of the spectator without them having to be identical or coincide.

In this form of open dramaturgy, the editing process happens on the floor where by the accidents and changes of the process the material reveals itself how it is best connected. Often it is merely a matter of being attentive, recognizing the moments and acting upon them.

Let me illustrate this with a couple of examples of the editing of *zero degrees*.

Akram's narrative followed the straightforward chronology of a real journey with a clear beginning – the crossing of the border and the entering of the country; the passage way, mainly on trains and a projected arrival in Calcutta. There was no need to deconstruct this logic. So we kept it and the only discussions we had were: where and how to start and end each section of the narrative.

The movement sections which were originally developed from pure movement ideas, each found their way and connection to this narrative at different stages of the rehearsal process through a simple, associative logic: from the very obvious such as the 'kung fu' fight being linked to the argument with the guards at the border, to more abstract translations such as the twin motive in the 'spinning' section.

x. One of my personal beliefs why text fragments work well in contemporary dance performances has nothing to do with them clarifying or explaining the movement. It is a purely formal editing device that helps to rhythmically organize the material. It creates a punctuation that marks the beginning and end of different movement sections in such a way that they both stay separated and are connected.

In a similar way we spent the last week of the rehearsals developing new transitions using the 'dummies', which Antony Gormley casted from Akram's and Larbi's bodies, to create little comic, theatrical interludes that formed an emotional counterpoint for the main narrative.

Larbi and Akram had explored playing with the dummies in one of the earlier stages of the rehearsal process but the idea was never fully developed and eventually abandoned. It was only picked up again in the last week when we moved from the studio to the main stage.

As is often the case in this critical moment, the performers literally felt momentarily lost in the vastness of the stage, which was highlighted this time by Gormley's design. They only had each other and their dummies, especially in the solo moments, as reference points to situate and centre themselves on stage. Being life-size puppets, the dummies also allowed an 'uncanny' treatment[11] that the real bodies would not necessarily allow.

Other editing solutions that were found accidentally involved the emphasizing rather than the hiding of the real exhaustion after the first full run, which fitted the narrative of the relentless train journey. Or the problematic visible presence on stage of the live musicians breaking the symmetry of the twin effect finding its solution by them becoming part of the shadow world.

The main issue in the editing process had been from the beginning how to relate Akram's narrative to Larbi's, the Yiddish song he wanted to sing. Earlier in the process, there had been an intuitive sense that the song should come towards the end and when it eventually found its place, both spatially and time-wise through a lot of trial and error, it also revealed and gave an essential meaning to the whole production that was not originally intended. But that is another uncanny story, which I will briefly discuss in the second part of this essay.

As a dramaturg your role often evolves during the process from the purely receptive one of being a silent witness over that of being a dialogue partner and/or moderator to the more active one of being an editor. In all these functions and at all these stages, the subjective re-membering of the previous stages of the process is the most relevant tool at your disposal. If it is the artist's creative challenge to go into unknown territory and to find a new form or articulation, as a dramaturg you can ground that process by being a living archive (cf. the opening quote by Duška Radosavljević) of the experience.

xi. Already during the process itself, the most relevant feedback you can give the artists is to help them re-member its earlier stages and by doing so bringing them back on their original track.

Part Two:
Two distinctive ways of re-membering dance[12]

But the re-membering and archiving doesn't stay isolated within the studio space, it is extremely porous and gets also influenced and contaminated by what happens in the outside world. My whole career in the performing arts I have been fascinated by how perception and memory are interrelated in very unpredictable ways. In my personal experience certain major events or time periods can be played back as a detailed, real-time film documentary, while others, equally important, have been reduced or syn(aes)thesized to one single image or sensation. In what follows I will describe two such contrasting experiences that have been formative for my experience as a dance professional.

The principle of synchronicity

As a production dramaturg, the creation process of *zero degrees* has been my most satisfying experience until now. For everybody involved, it was the right time and place, and the result was a relatively smooth creation process with little creative tensions and no human conflict at all. A quasi-ideal world of dialogue and exchange with everybody contributing and building on each other's knowledge and experience. But that ideal microcosm got shaken and was brought to a completely other dimension by the larger political macrocosm: the London metro bombings of 7 July 2005, which happened one day before the first public performance of *zero degrees*.

Zero degrees has a simple and clear narrative structure. It tells the story of Akram Khan's first visit to India at the age of twenty, and his questions about his identity as a second-generation immigrant, growing up in-between cultures, in-between bodies. Two-thirds in the performance, this personal narrative ends with another story about being confronted the first time in his life with a dead body on a train, approaching Calcutta. From there *zero degrees* becomes a contemporary lamentation for this dead body, repeated and performed in different styles and mediums: for instance traditional abhinaya (the story element of kathak) performed by Akram, or a theatrical farce with 'dummies'. Also Larbi's 'story', the Yiddish song he sang to reach out to 'the other' and to lament a dead father, had found its place in Akram's narrative, lamenting the dead body on the train to Calcutta. While Larbi sang his song, holding his dummy pieta-like, Akram danced a distorted, contemporary dance solo around his dummie soul, being both aura and ghost, leaving the body. The very last image of the piece only revealed itself on the very last day of the process: Larbi carrying Akram offstage, leaving the stage empty, except for the dummies with the cello and violin of the shadow world repeating their version of the lament theme.

xii. As stated above, the form of open dramaturgy I practise implies that you trust the process to follow its own necessities and inner logic and that you accept that only at the very end the work reveals its meaning to you.

In the case of *zero degrees*, this meaning became also very determined by its first public reception. All through his career Sidi Larbi Cherkaoui's creations have had a remarkable and sometimes uncanny synchronicity with events in the real world: the second invasion of Iraq coinciding with the premiere of *Foi*; the earthquake and nuclear disaster in Japan, while rehearsing *TseZukA* there. But never was the 'coincidence' so powerful as in the case of *zero degrees*: two choreographers with a mixed identity between West European and Muslim cultures had created a lament for a dead body on a train, at exactly the same moment that fundamentalists created a massacre with many dead bodies on trains.

Both for the whole artistic team and the first London audiences, the performance became meaningful and emotionally charged in a way that we could never have anticipated. And it kept this emotional charge until its last performance three years later in New York and even when today, I look at the video capitation, I feel the original grief[13] and have to fight against my tears welling up.

I have a very detailed memory of the whole rehearsal process of *zero degrees*: where I sat in the studio, watching Akram and Larbi rehearse; my dialogues with them individually or together, inside or outside the studio; my own contributions to their creative process; the relationship I had with the other collaborators. But I have a particular, vivid memory (both image-wise and emotion-wise) of 7 July. How on my way from my residence in north London to the centre, the metro was already blocked. How I got on a bus instead. Getting off near King's Cross station where the first survivors were coming out of the emergency exits. Still not realizing what had happened. My early morning meeting at The Place which got interrupted by the bus explosion, out of sight, but less than a couple of hundred metres away. The confusion of the first hours after, being obliged to stay in, only getting flashes of contradictory news through the radio. The Place employees trying to check if everybody was safe, an improvised emergency meeting in a dance studio. Walking hours later through the completely deserted streets of central London from The Place to Sadler's Wells. The discussion we had with the artistic team on whether we should go ahead with our first public try-out the next day. If I would give myself the time and the effort, I could probably write out a detailed account of the whole experience in a substantial volume.

The above account also resonates strongly with another iconic text by Marianne Van Kerkhoven. At the annual Dutch-Flemish Theatre Festival in 1994, she gave the 'State of the Union' in which she pleaded for a theatre that was again in touch with the social and political reality of the world around us and in which the coexistence of cultures with a Christian and Islamic heritage has become a major issue. Her 'State of the Union' concluded: 'The theatre today dwells in the world ... it has walls of skin, that are porous, that breathe.'[14]

Memory as a somatic experience

The other memory that marks my career is as meaningful, but of a very different nature. What remains of it is just one general sensation and it would take a lot of research to actually remember more detail, including when it took place and the actual title of the piece. What I do remember is that it was one of William Forsythe's epic pieces that he continued to rework over a long period and that I saw it in deSingel in Antwerp.

Through my career as a dance critic, there was a growing consciousness that next to my rational understanding of the work and my trained perception as a professional spectator, I got easily energetically influenced, both negatively and positively, just by watching dance.

Certain works gave me literally an energy boost, while others could drain me completely, sometimes already after five minutes into the performance. The highlight of any such energetic experience was the above-mentioned Forsythe performance, which gave me all through its duration an amazing, soothing energetic massage of the whole spinal column. Something I only occasionally and never so intensely had experienced before, after a particular good yoga class. The latter is closely related to Christel Stalpaert's plead for an embodied corporeal dramaturgy, 'that moves away from a cognitively based dramaturgical method'[15] with the dramaturg as an 'outside body' rather than an 'outside eye'.

In my personal assessment and evaluation of the work, the energetic quality became a more and more important evaluation criteria, which I relate to the way the work has been created; and whether there is a genuine generous intention behind it: to give and share with the audience as opposed to an egocentric asking for attention.

xiii. Restating the claim of my earlier text on dance dramaturgy,[16] my choices of whom to collaborate with are more determined by ethical than by aesthetical criteria and the above principle of generosity for both one's collaborators, one's environment and eventually one's audience is a very important one.

Conclusion

Both memories – the detailed one of *zero degrees* and the vague but profound one of the Forsythe piece are strongly connected in the way they have both become part of my experience and my beliefs as a dance dramaturg. This process of re-membering is both somatic, in the way it involves the whole body, and creative. It also means that, as illustrated in the above, it fictionalizes and transforms the past experience in whatever way is necessary and relevant to nurture the present. But this essential subjective nature of the act of re-membering doesn't devaluate it. On the contrary, it is one of the main contributions of your invisible voice as a dramaturg.

References

Assmann, Jan. 'Re-Membering Osiris: From the Death Cult to Cultural Memory'. *ReMembering the Body*. Ed. Gabriella Brandstetter and Hortensia Volckers. Ostfildern-Ruit: Hatje Cantz Publishers, 2000, pp. 42–78.

Barba, Eugenio and Savarese, Nicola. *A Dictionary of Theatre Anthropology*. London: Routledge, 1991.

Brandstetter, Gabriella and Volckers, Hortensia. *ReMembering the Body*. Ostfildern-Ruit: Hatje Cantz Publishers, 2000.

Cools, Guy. 'De la dramaturgie du corps en danse'. *Cahiers de theatre Jeu* 116 (2005a), pp. 89–95.

—programme note, Sadler's Wells, *zero degrees*, 2005b.

—'Giving a Voice to Mourning'. *Receptions of Antiquity*. Ed. Jan Nelis. Ghent: Academia Press, 2011, pp. 145–52.

Gross, Kenneth. *Puppet, an Essay on Uncanny Life*. Chicago: The University of Chicago Press, 2011.

Murakami, Haruki. *Kafka on the Shore*. London: Vintage, 2005.

Ondaatje, Michael. *The Conversations, Walter Murch and the Art of Editing Film*. Canada: Vintage, 2002.

Radosavljević, Duška. 'The Need to Keep Moving, Remarks on the place of a dramaturg in twenty-first century England'. *Performance Research, On Dramaturgy* 14.3 (2009), pp. 45–51.

Sibony, Daniel. *Le corps et sa danse*. Paris: Editions du Seuil, 1995.

Stalpaert, Christel. 'A Dramaturgy of the Body'. *Performance Research, On Dramaturgy* 14.3 (2009), pp. 121–5.

Van Kerkhoven, Marianne. 'Looking without pencil in the hand'. *Theaterschrift, On dramaturgy* 5–6, (1994a) pp. 142–4.

—'Het theater ligt in de stad en de stad ligt in de wereld en de wanden zijn van huid: State of the Union voor het Theaterfestival 1994'. *Etcetera* nr. 46 (1994b), pp. 7–9.

—'Le processus dramaturgique'. *Nouvelles de Danse, Dossier Danse et Dramaturgie* nr. 31 (1997), L Contredanse, pp. 18–25.

Part Five

Spectatorship

Porous Dramaturgy and the Pedestrian

Cathy Turner

In the early decades of the twenty-first century, there seems to be little decline in the recent enthusiasm for performance that takes place outside a theatre or gallery. Taking place in 'found' spaces, built installations or on the street, a range of performance dramaturgies has developed in response to site. In particular, theatre and performance taking place on the street is necessarily forced to consider its encounter with quotidian movements and expectations, where the audience member, as pedestrian, will encounter serendipitous events and objects, unanticipated by the artist. Heidi Taylor has outlined principles for a 'deep dramaturgy' of site-specific practice, in which she implies a need to 'embrace' accidents, contradictions and signs in the performance space that offer independent meanings, all of which may 'contribute to the complexity of the work'.[1]

This need to 'embrace' suggests an encircling movement, opening to and then holding such accidental, coincidental or tangential meanings. An attention to the relationship between inside and outside. The possibility of reciprocal movement or resistance. A structure that is porous.

I am one of four founder members of a company that creates site-based work, with its roots in performance. The other three members of Wrights & Sites (1997–) are Stephen Hodge, Simon Persighetti and Phil Smith. We have all used the word 'porous' to describe this work. For instance, it is described as such on our website (in text written by Hodge and Smith and approved by myself and Persighetti):

> Our work, like walking, is intended to be porous; for others to read into it and connect from it and for the specificities and temporalities of sites to fracture, erode and distress it.[2]

I have also used the word 'porous' to attempt to articulate an understanding of a range of approaches to dramaturgy. When Duška Radosavljević and I began to consider the notion of a 'porous' dramaturgy in 2012, we drew on Kully Thiarai's use of the term when artistic director at Leicester Haymarket:

> As a team we talked a lot about how you might create a 'porous', 'transparent' theatre organisation; how you might integrate the diverse arts practices of the communities of Leicester into a physical space that revealed and celebrated the craft of theatre-making and performance. How could you create a theatre that supported and retained the traditions of Western theatre forms and integrated the performance traditions of the East and Caribbean? How could you realign the stages with the street and create an environment where a performance could happen around you and not just on a formal stage?[3]

Radosavljević and I used the term as a way to think about the way that the dramaturgy of the theatre event might be similarly inclusive, might negotiate and produce communities,[4] and perhaps, as Taylor implies, embrace and include 'the stages of the street'. We defined it as follows:

> In using the term 'Porous Dramaturgy' we imply work that attempts to engage the audience in co-creation through its underpinning concepts and formal structures, including interactivity, immersion and site-specificity.[5]

This notion of the 'porous' is, like the suggestion of an 'embrace', expressive of theatre/performance that creates a space, or spaces for what is beyond itself and is brought to it by an audience. Its association with Thiarai's use of the term is significant because of its political implications: it might be considered in relationship to a civic need for that encircling 'embrace' (space and holding) of what is incidental, frictive, contradictory, or of that which produces meaning in unforeseeable ways. We can, of course, argue about what kinds of 'space and holding' serve which politics, and whose needs are being acknowledged.

These three uses of the term 'porous' are related, but not identical. Wrights & Sites' use of the term is defined by the company's work;

Thiarai's use of the term is applicable to the underpinning ideals of a theatre institution and its architecture; whereas the broader application of the word 'porous' demands that we recognize the different degrees, types and politics of porosity.

This chapter constitutes a first attempt at considering this notion of 'porosity' a little more critically, specifically in relation to performance in 'public space'.[6] I will identify some of the nuances and implications of the metaphor, before exploring some of the questions this raises. While I do not discuss the role directly, the chapter suggests concerns for the dramaturg. My understanding of 'dramaturgy', as a time-space structure, always in process and performative, is already implicit in the description of a work as a porous structure open to occupation. At certain points, however, I need to describe particular aspects of dramaturgy rather than the process of curating or composing the whole.

While I do not pretend to be a geologist, and while the word has accrued a range of meanings that are not scientifically precise, I want to draw attention to, and then to discuss five aspects of geological porosity, and questions that arise from these:

1. A measurement of porosity does not describe interactivity.
2. Porous structures may be changed by, contain and/or produce changes in the occupying substance(s).
3. Porosity is closely related to permeability.
4. The greater the porosity, the greater the structure's vulnerability when unoccupied.[7]
5. Porosity is a description of a spatial structure.

1. In geological terms, porosity is a measurement of the proportion of voids within sediments or rock. The greater the proportion of void spaces, the greater the porosity. Porosity can exist due to the material's composition, or due to fracturing, or to dissolution of rock grains, or to a combination of these.[8] Porosity might imply interaction, but it is not in itself a *measure* of interactivity or exchange, nor does it describe what kinds of exchanges might occur. It merely suggests that the structure contains space within it available for occupation. If the dramaturgy of a work is described as 'porous' this implies that it is structured so

that it contains space for intervention, habitation or contribution by audience, passers-by or other aspects of the space itself. There might be differing levels of porosity across different kinds of dramaturgical structure. However, this raises the question as to what, in performance terms, constitutes a 'void space'? Is all work 'porous' and what defines different degrees of porosity? Given that interactivity is not specified, how do we need to nuance the description of work as 'porous'?

2. Although 'porosity' is not a measure of interactivity, Radosavljević and I defined 'porous dramaturgy' as inviting co-creativity. It must be acknowledged that in terms of both geology and performance, some level of interactivity between a structure and its 'guests' is always present. However, one might describe our initial conception of the 'porous' work as being analogous to the porosity of carbonate limestone which is partly dissolved by the carbon dioxide in rain water as it percolates the joints and fissures, or hits exposed surfaces. This reaction produces and is produced by porosity (or more strictly, permeability), resulting in a range of unpredictable features such as underground caves and chambers, or formations such as stalactites.[9] On the other hand, not all work that offers a 'porous' structure allows itself to be so self-evidently redefined by its audience. It might be more analogous to sandstone, which may possess a fine grain that acts as a filter.[10] We might use this notion (very loosely) to describe an event that seeks to produce a reaction in its audience, while retaining a repeatable, strong and fairly independent structure. Alternatively, the relationship between porous structure and its 'guests' might be one of relative mutual independence. Departing from the geological metaphor, we might designate the relationships within these three forms of dramaturgical porosity as 'co-creative', 'independent' and 'directive'. Reference to actual examples will tend to complicate and move across these categories, since in practice most work combines types of porosity.

However, whether the work is co-creative or not, the concept of 'porosity' cannot tell us whether the audience members are addressed as individuals or as a group, which may be politically crucial – particularly if we recall the reference to civic needs, and public spaces. This raises the question as to whether it is appropriate to consider the audience as a single fluid body, as the metaphor of 'porosity' might tend to propose.[11]

3. Porosity has a close relationship to permeability: 'effective porosity' describes the proportion of the connected pore volume, which allows water, for instance, to flow through the rock.[12] In terms of performance, this could be variously interpreted. In this instance, I will relate it to the possibility of disengagement, of 'flowing' out of the artwork. It might be expected that some work taking place in the street will need to be highly permeable in order to allow passers-by to drop in and out again at their will. However, on other occasions, site-based performance does demand our full attention and 'entrap' the movement of the spectator, however willingly. The emotive and coercive implications in the idea of 'entrapment' might suggest the desirability of returning to the differently emotive idea of the 'embrace' or perhaps to the psychoanalytic idea of the 'holding environment'.[13]

4. The larger the voids, the greater the fragility of the structure when unoccupied. This might suggest why the 'porous' work risks its identity as artwork by creating space for occupation and intervention by others. Is this fragility problematic, or an important aspect of its politics?

5. Related to this, if porosity describes a spatial structure, what implications does it have for our occupation of, or construction of city space?

What, in performance terms, constitutes a 'void space'?

It is evident that all kinds of performance contain some level of porosity, since all performances make an appeal to the imagination of the spectator. While it is possible to give examples of high porosity, it may be difficult to identify a point at which work ceases to be porous. A few examples may help to clarify the types of porosity I am considering here.

When we first set out to create site-specific performance, Wrights & Sites found ourselves consciously creating voids in the performance event, in order to facilitate interaction between the audience members and the 'host' site.[14] To give one example, our first performance, taking place on and alongside a boat on the canal, was structured so that on the return journey, the audience members were given time in order to enjoy the sunset and to create 'landscapes' by holding small wooden frames up to compose the view.[15] These represented, quite literally, spaces/times which audience members were invited to fill, responding playfully to the environment around them, in the context of an audio- and installation-based performance about the landscape (and ideas of landscape).

This moment of porosity was contained and if it modified the experience of other aspects of the boat journey, it had no implications for its structure, but functioned relatively independently. An alternative example might be found in Pearson/Brookes' work, *Polis* (2001), in which audience members were taken in small groups to a range of Cardiff locations, where they were invited to document their surroundings and encounters with performers. Returning to Chapter Arts with this material, each group would also be given time to observe material brought back by other groups and in this way a shared understanding of a city and characters lost within it (a kind of Cardiff Odyssey), gradually emerged: 'The polis is an aggregate of many members'.[16] The audience also shared and filmed some individual narratives, thus contributing to the interweaving stories and creating a sense of temporary community, albeit one with multiple perspectives. All shared a moment of live performance in a space at Chapter Arts in the conclusion of this event. As in the previous example, the audience members were offered ways of 'framing' the event, but in this case, the audience's role was decisively co-creative and shaped the experience of the work quite substantially. On the other hand, there were limits to the audience's creative freedom and aspects that were 'directive' – my companion, attempting to film incidental features of our surroundings, was politely directed to focus on the performer who was speaking.

Another example can be provided from Wrights & Sites' work. After our initial season of site-specific theatre, we found ourselves seeking to increase the porosity of our work. Our 'Mis-Guides',[17] alternative guidebooks which offer the reader/walker a series of suggestions for ways of exploring and reimagining the spaces they walk through, essentially hand any form of performance over to the responsibility of the reader/walker. In this sense, the work is intrinsically porous, since each Mis-Guide page offers nothing more than a loose framework for walking. While a 'Guide' tends to be 'directive', the 'Mis-Guide' deliberately avoids this,[18] and the experience of the artwork is co-creative, in that it is different on every occasion; all that remains constant is the written page, which acts as a performance 'score', but which also explicitly invites its own reinvention or modification. Clearly the Mis-Guide owes a debt to the Fluxus event-score, which proposes encounters with everyday objects, but which is re-made and interpreted on every occasion. However, both these examples give rise to questions as to whether the 'performance' itself is porous, since the porosity of a 'score' or 'script' is fixed in each moment of enactment, and will not necessarily appear 'porous' to any secondary audience which remains external to it. However, where the primary audience is the performer or participant themselves, it still seems appropriate to describe the work as 'porous'.[19]

A further example might be German company LIGNA's *Radio Ballet* (2002–3). Pre-recorded for the radio and directive, it addresses each audience member through their headphones, though in the context of a wider group experiencing the same instructions. It proposes both a series of simple actions and a commentary on those actions within a 'public space' (a station or a mall). Each audience member is invited to experience the tensions inherent in performing (or refusing to perform or reinterpreting) actions that belong to 'a grey area' between acceptable and forbidden.[20] The porosity of LIGNA's work is suggested by their assertion that they 'regard their audience as a collective of producers'.[21]

The site-specific work always mediates the relationship between site and audience. However, 'voids' within this kind of performance might represent the moments when the work steps back from mediation and allows or prompts the audience member to become the mediator and lead explorer of site, and to experience it in a sensory, embodied way, particular to themselves. This might sometimes be important in facilitating a thoughtful and active engagement with place and group and avoiding a tendency for the artwork to impose its own dominant narratives of place, obscuring or suppressing what is already present and overlooking the audience member as a body in space.

Is it appropriate to consider the audience as a single body?

The metaphor of 'porosity' could provoke the assumption that an audience responds as a single, fluid body. However, as implied above, audience members may have widely different experiences and perspectives. It may be important to know in what sense an artwork addresses an audience as a group, as a dual body (participants and spectators), as clusters or as individuals. This is a bigger debate than can be dealt with fully in this chapter.

The Mis-Guides, as suggested above, tend to address small groups and individuals and generally assume that there will be no conscious adoption of the perspective of secondary observer of that reader/walker's performance. However, they have occasionally been used by larger groups and they could produce a secondary audience on occasion. It could be argued, moreover, that our first Mis-Guide, *An Exeter Mis-Guide* (2003), implicitly addresses an imagined 'community' of Exeter citizens. Although the book can be used, and has been used by visitors, and even by those who are exploring other cities, elements of the text explicitly address the local inhabitants: 'Make an A–Z of your street', for example, pre-supposes an Exeter location, while other pages propose visiting spots in the city that have previously had importance for you, or rely on an extensive knowledge of the city. Perhaps it is not surprising to note that the work, which addresses the individual occupation of space, simultaneously invokes the possibility of occupying a role as citizen of a city.

But what is a city? Even if, as with *An Exeter Mis-Guide*, there is no attempt to define 'community' in any systematic way, one might argue that this is disingenuous and that there remains a conceptualization of 'Exeter' that results in a form of unconscious mapping of a city – and if city (something more than buildings and spaces between them), then implicitly 'community' of a kind. As Exeter citizens ourselves, we did not propose that our experiences would necessarily be shared by all; however, our being-in-the-city, and the choices we make in walking it, produce an impression of a presumed, if leaky whole. If the guidebook is implicitly a map, the Mis-Guide is an anti-map: nevertheless, in Kris Darby's evocative phrase, it inevitably 'remaps the map', even if it suggests a continuous, not a final re-mapping.[22]

When we worked with Tanzquartier Wien and the Wiener Festwochen[23] to curate a mini-season of walks and tours by and involving Viennese citizens, the idea of a shared or, in our case, not-shared, geographical experience consciously shaped some of the choices made. For example, it was important that although we had a role as curators and, in a sense, as dramaturgs to the contributors, the walks and tours were led by those who came from the city, whether they were artists or not. Secondly, it felt politically important to include diverse experience of the city. In many ways, this amounted to a negation of the idea of a single, united 'community': however, to some degree, I think the choices were again informed by a 'leaky' perception of the city and its history as a conceptual whole, which required that certain elements should not be left out. For example, it was felt important to acknowledge Black Austrian history through the *First Listen Up! Decolonizing Vienna Tour* by Pamoja/Research Group on Black Austrian History and Present. Other problematic lacunas in Viennese memory were gently proposed through Georg Blaschke's *Lehmann's Addresses*, which invited an engagement with a 1935 Vienna address book. Some tours explicitly dealt with edgelands, suburbs and in one case, with a rubbish dump – to some extent mapping disparate and/or difficult parts of the city and related experience, albeit in order to propose the existence of further multiplicity.

When we responded to a recent commission for Weston-super-Mare,[24] we found ourselves again dealing consciously, but differently, with the idea of a 'community', this time imposed by civic authorities. Here, in the context of a regeneration programme, designed to increase economic prosperity, we were anxious that our own work should not unproblematically assume consensus on the priorities and needs of the town. The work we produced, *Everything you need to build a town is here*, comprised a series of textual signs, placed in locations around the town and beyond; these signs addressed both visitor and inhabitant (but were designed primarily for the latter) and proposed a co-creative relationship between architecture and the individual walker, through a range of comments and proposals:

TAKE TO THE TREES.

FORGET ARCHITECTURAL TRAINING.
DRAW ON THE DEN-MAKING OF YOUR
CHILDHOOD. EVERYTHING YOU NEED
TO BUILD A TOWN IS HERE.[25]

The aim here was to question the limited notion of 'community' (with shared interests) implicit in the idea of economic regeneration. However, this might also imply a differently understood idea of 'community', one that included the drug rehabilitation centres as well as the hoteliers.

In each of these examples, there is a tendency to 'remap the map', and then to remap it again. These porous works address small groups, or address the individual, but invariably, even if inadvertently, place individuals in relation to group structures, ranging from those of their immediate companions to a wider 'community', geographically, politically or aesthetically defined. These group structures are, I suggest, simultaneously reconfigured and problematized. By integrating the audience member into the flow and structure of the work, especially when this work takes place in a public space, the invitation to negotiate a relationship with group, city or 'community' is implicit and ongoing.

On the other hand, the metaphor of porosity tends to suggest a frictive relationship between the work and those who I continue to call, awkwardly, the 'audience members'. It provides images of erosion, filtering, dissolution, fracture, contamination and stress. This draws our attention to the power relations inherent in particular examples and these inherent tensions may be as important as any cohesion.

When is permeability important and when might we want to think about porosity as a 'holding environment' or embrace?

Our fear of rigidity (theorized by Bauman, for instance)[26] might lead us to worry about artwork that potentially 'entraps' an audience within its structures. However, I began with the idea of 'embrace', which suggests quite a different relationship to the event, and one that might suggest care and even tenderness. A related, but less emotional term might be the idea of the 'holding environment' which psychoanalyst D. W. Winnicott proposes as a way to describe the safe space provided by a parent for their developing child.[27] The 'holding environment' is essentially a space of play, in which a child is not required to differentiate between itself and the objects that surround it, but can negotiate creatively between them.

I have previously used this idea to describe the Mis-Guide pages as 'holding environments', inviting the walker to play at the edges of the safe space, as a child swings on a gate: 'The *Mis-Guide* hopes to enable a potential space between the walker and the city, but not one that is sealed off from the possibility of challenge.'[28] It could be argued that this description implicitly infantilizes the audience, but Winnicott suggests that this negotiation between self and other is necessary as a life-long practice.

As suggested above, the structure offered by the public artwork may be a way to enable unexpected relationships to a place (authorized and facilitated by the rules of the game), or it may be a way to direct and bring together an audience in a shared experience. However, whether the work is experienced as offering 'entrapment', 'embrace' or 'holding' by its audience is likely to depend partly on the individual audience member and partly on the particular qualities of engagement that the work offers. Permeability, or the ability to disengage might be ethically important, however, even where the work proposes an embrace,[29] or even where a sense of 'entrapment' is part of its game.[30]

What is the importance of fragility and strength in artistic structure?

Bauman suggests that we only trust very provisional structures now:

> Fully 'biodegradable' structures, starting to disintegrate the moment they have been assembled, are nowadays the ideal, and most, if not all structures, must struggle to measure up to this standard.[31]

Bauman's description of the 'biodegradable' structure is close, though not scientifically identical to the soluble 'limestone' porosity. This desire for a temporary or fragile structure may be a response to the historically rooted fear of rigidity. It is difficult to know whether the dissolving, mutating, porous structure is complicit with the unequal power relationships of a 'liquid' modernity, in which the liquidation of foundational beliefs, ideologies and systems is closely identified with the interests of an economic elite – or whether, alternatively, it models new kinds of structure that might be needed. Indeed, it may be that both of these are possible effects and that just as a porous structure could be seen as symptomatic of a decline into formlessness, it could also offer a necessary negotiation between fluidity and structure. It may therefore be, as a recent panel suggested, that the curator of such artworks, or indeed the dramaturg or artist is 'an architect of sorts, producing places of exchange and mediation'.[32]

Wrights & Sites' shift, in Weston-super-Mare, towards work that became a material feature (metal, paint and fixings) within the architectural environment, was a move to commit to a degree of fixity and structure in the work's engagement with place, while still preserving the possibility of multiple responses and interpretative possibilities (porous occupation). We saw this as a way of owning our own town-planning (as opposed to town-dwelling) potential and aspirations. However, our intervention whispered its subversion, blended into the aesthetic environment and was minimally directive. While this diffident quality within the work is part of its politics, it is possible that this limits its accessibility and impact. The managerial tone of these words, however, starts to make me wonder whether this is not also part of its meaning, and whether the work paradoxically claims a space for those retreating qualities of the enigmatic, elusive, slow, gentle and unobtrusive.

Conclusion: Porosity as a spatial structure

In our contribution to Heddon and Klein's *Histories of Live Art*, Stephen Hodge and I proposed that site-specific performance has frequently oscillated between the form-dissolving possibilities of critiquing and rendering fluid the dominant 'rules' of place, and reconstituting that place for or with new bodies, new activities and new, if provisional, architectures, suggesting 'a tendency to invite the audience, bodily, into that evolving and undecided place, which might also be conceived as a 'ghost' architecture built on a 'host' site. Or might we rather suggest a 'host' architecture on a 'ghost' site?'[33]

Porosity is not an essential term within a field littered with related terms: 'collaborative', 'participatory', 'socially engaged', 'littoral', 'dialogic', 'relational' ... [34] Nor is dramaturgy always a useful term, where work does not recognize a relationship with drama. However, the notion of 'porous dramaturgy' draws our attention to the specific relationship between the architectonics of the artwork and the way these invite and respond to occupation.

Walking art and site-specific work is often discussed in terms of its expression of the fluid and mobile activity of the urban dweller, as opposed to the urban planner. However, the questions raised and explored above suggest that it might also be important as a form of constructive effort upon the city or town – or indeed, the rural – and that it provides an attempt at an 'architecture of adventure'.[35] By 'remapping the map' it allows us to experience some of the tensions and negotiations between the fluid and the fixed, the dweller and the dwelling, the passer-by and the artist, the audience and the dramaturgy.

References

Anderson, Benedict. *Imagined Communities*. London: Verso, 1983.

Anon. *Anatomy of the Earth*. Vol. 3, *Joy of Knowledge*. London: Mitchell Beazley, 1980.

Bauman, Zigmunt. *Liquid Modernity*. Cambridge: Polity, 2012.

Beech, Dave, 'Include Me Out! Dave Beech on Participation in Art', *Art Monthly*, Issue 315, April 2008, p. 28.

Bhagwat, S. B. *Foundations of Geology*. New Delhi: Global Vision, 2009.

Boym, Svetlana. *Architecture of the Off-Modern*. Princeton: Princeton Architectural Press, 2008.

Crick, Bernard. 'Politics'. *Introductory Readings in Government and Politics*. Ed. Mark O. Dickerson, Thomas Flanagan and Neil Nevitte. Ontario: Methuen, 1983, pp. 5–15.

Darby, Kris. *Remap the map*, 2012. http://remapthemap.wordpress.com (Accessed: 22 March 2013).

Hodge, Stephen and Smith, Phil. 2012. 'About Wrights & Sites', found at http://www.mis-guide.com/ws/about.html (Accessed: 22 March 2013).

LIGNA, *Radio Ballet – Leipzig, Part 1*, 2008. http://www.youtube.com/ watch?v = qI3pfa5QNZI (Accessed: 22 March 2013).

—'About LIGNA/Über LIGNA', 2012. http://ligna.blogspot.co.uk/2007/11/die-gruppe-ligna-existiert-seit-1995.html (Accessed: 22 March 2013).

Pearson, Mike. 'Special Worlds, Secret Maps: A Poetics of Performance'. *Staging Wales: Welsh Theatre 1979–1997*. Ed. Anna Marie Taylor. Cardiff: University of Wales, 1997, pp. 85–99.

Pearson/Brookes (Mike Pearson and Mike Brookes). *Polis*. Cardiff: Chapter Arts, 2001.

Radosavljević, Duška. *Theatre-making: Interplay Between Text and Performance in the 21st Century*. Basingstoke: Palgrave Macmillan, 2013.

Shunt. *The Architects*, Live Performance, The Biscuit Factory. London, 2 February 2013.

Taylor, Heidi. 'Deep Dramaturgy: Excavating the Architecture of the Site-Specific Performance'. *Canadian Theatre Review* 119 (Summer 2004), pp. 16–19.

Theatrum Mundi/Global Street. 'Between Curatorial and Urban Practice', 2013. http://theatrum-mundi.org/projects/between-curatorial-and-urban-practice (Accessed: 22 March 2013).

Thiarai, Kully. 'Cultural diversity and the ecology of dramaturgy in making vibrant theatre practice'. *Dramaturgies: New Theatres for the 21st Century*. Ed. Peter Eckersall, Melanie Beddie and Paul Monaghan. Melbourne: The Dramaturgies Project, 2011, pp. 11–19.

Turner, Cathy. 'Palimpsest or Potential Space? Finding a Vocabulary for Site-Specific Performance'. *New Theatre Quarterly* 20.4 (2004), pp. 373–90.

Turner, Cathy, and Hodge, Stephen. 'Site: Between Ground and Groundlessness'. *Histories and Practices of Live Art*. Ed. Deirdre Heddon and Jennie Klein. Basingstoke: Palgrave, 2012, pp. 90–120.

Turner, Cathy, and Radosavljević, Duška. *Porous Dramaturgy: 'Togetherness' and Community in the Structure of the Artwork*, 2012. http://expandeddramaturgies.com/?p=687 (Accessed: 15 March 2013).

Winnicott, D. W. 'The Theory of the Parent-Infant Relationship'. *International Journal of Psycho-Analysis* 41 (1960), pp. 585–95.

Wrights & Sites. *The Quay Thing – Pilot: Navigation*. Exeter Canal, 1997.

—*An Exeter Mis-Guide*. Exeter: Wrights & Sites, 2003.

—*A Mis-Guide to Anywhere*. Exeter: Wrights & Sites, 2006.

—*Stadverführungen in Wien*, Vienna. A mini-season of work curated by us, in conjunction with Tanzquartier Wien and Wiener Festwochen. 2007.

—*Everything you need to Build a Town is here*. Weston-super-Mare: Situations/Field Arts/CABE 'Sea Change' Programme, 2010.

—'About' Company website, 2012. http://www.mis-guide.com/ws/about.html (Accessed: 11 March 2013).

Dialectical Theatre and Devising

Dramaturgy as a Dialogue between the
Author and the Audience

Pedro Ilgenfritz

Introduction

This chapter researches the development of devised theatre through an active dialogue with the audience. In 2010, *LAB Theatre* from Auckland, New Zealand, engaged in a process of including the public's response in the process of analysing the dramaturgy of their show *Alfonsina*, a tragicomic story of an Argentinean cleaner migrating to New Zealand.

Alfonsina was performed in three different locations in New Zealand (Auckland, Wellington and Dunedin) and at Vértice Brasil – Magdalena Network Festival in Florianopolis, Brazil, between March and September 2010. In all four cities, a focus group was conducted with audience members after the show, where they expressed their reading of the spectacle, including their response to the structure of the story, the characters, the social, cultural, economic and political implications of the situation presented on stage, the theatre language used by the company and how they – the audience – were personally affected by the play.

Each group interviewed represented a different demographic. In Wellington, the group comprised local university students; in Dunedin, South American immigrants; in Florianopolis, individuals who had lived overseas and returned to Brazil; and finally in Auckland, members of the Food and Service Workers Union. All groups had immigrants, a mix of male and female participants and a diverse array of social classes and cultural backgrounds. Exceptions were in Wellington where the group was predominantly of European descent, and in Auckland where they were predominantly Polynesian.

The result was the inclusion of the public as an active participant in the process of analysing the narrative, extending the process of creating theatre work to the audience, their voice becoming an essential part of the narrative development. The stage became a place of beginning a dialogue, instead of a monological relationship with a passive audience. The performance assumed a position within the process of dialogue rather than at the end of it. Because the audience was invited to participate in the analysis of the narrative, the relationship between performers and audience changed, and so the role of dramaturg has evolved as a result of this collaboration.

The dialogue with the audience effectively shifts the power that was normally limited to the dramaturg. The work is open in a public forum and there is a distribution of power among the focus group participants. Susan Bennett affirms in her analysis of the audience's role in theatre that traditionally the audience enters a 'social contract' in which spectators agree to be passive in their behaviour but open, eager and active in their acceptance of a role in decoding the signs presented to them.[1] During the focus group the social contract's main proposition is no longer required. Passivity is not a prerequisite to safeguard the power of the author, and to a greater degree, the continuity of the dialogue outside the performance space demands the dissolution of their passivity. The focus group proposes the extension of the discussion on stage with a renewed contract with the audience. This method of collaboration used by LAB Theatre is a new trend in dramaturgy that examines the dialogues and relationships between the dramaturg and the spectator.

In this way, the dialogue with the audience is structured as follows:

1. The author/director proposes the skeleton of the story and coordinates the development of the spectacle in collaboration with the actors/authors.

2. The work is presented to an audience who receives/reads/interprets the work according to their own experience/knowledge/worldview.
3. Two days after the performance the audience share their response with the author/director, in a forum, during which they are totally free to express any impression/thought/opinion in relation to the work.
4. The author/director returns to the rehearsal room and makes changes and adjustments to the work according to the feedback given in the focus group.
5. The cycle repeats by showing the next draft of the work to another audience and conducting another focus group meeting where the findings inform more adjustments to the next draft/showing and so on.

These steps show a circular movement and as the procedure progresses the audience voice is included more and more in the process of analysing the dramaturgical structure of the piece. Every time a focus group discussed the choices of the creators, they were also discussing the choices of the previous focus groups. In this way, the last focus group confronted the choices of the company and all the previous participants of the process.

Alfonsina, the plot and perverted logic

The play is a comedy with a tragic outcome. Alfonsina, performed by Argentinean actress Andrea Ariel, is the heroine clown of the story, a young, working-class, single mother from Argentina who moves to New Zealand in search of a better living. The opening scene shows Alfonsina saying goodbye to her entire family at Buenos Aires International Airport and kissing her little son Manolito.

Alfonsina is a cleaner and her first contact with a New Zealander is with her neighbour Hera – performed by New Zealand actress Katie Burson – a Maori cleaner who works for the Sparkle and Shine

Cleaning Company owned by Tracy, performed by New Zealand actress Genevieve Cohen. Hera introduces Alfonsina to Tracy and she starts working immediately. The conflict begins when she is asked to show her work visa. Alfonsina lies to both Hera and Tracy, only to be discovered by her new best friend to have no work permit. Hera tries to help Alfonsina and takes her to the immigration department where they discover that Alfonsina is not eligible for any visa. Tracy discovers the truth and Alfonsina is fired from her job, and in her desperation she ends up buying a fake visa in the 'black-market' of Auckland.

Hera is suspicious of how fast she managed to get a visa, and Alfonsina reveals the truth. Events begin to go downhill when the 'unknown man' who sold the fake visa to Alfonsina comes back and threatens to blackmail her. Hera gives all her savings to help her friend but he wants more and the two cleaners end up stealing money from Tracy.

The climax approaches when Tracy challenges the duo, finds out the entire situation and fires both employees. Alfonsina assumes responsibility for the situation, returns the money to Tracy and manages to save Hera's job. The play ends with Tracy examining her actions and going to Alfonsina's home to help. However, when she gets there she finds Hera sitting in an empty apartment. Alfonsina was deported early that morning. The 'man-who-sold-the-passport' had informed immigration and she was arrested. Tracy is convinced she can resolve the situation, but it is too late. The final scene is a mirror of the first one – Alfonsina returns to Buenos Aires humiliated and defeated, and is reunited with her little boy.

The dialectics of the situation are based on a fundamental question: Who is Alfonsina? Seen from one angle, her actions are motivated by desperation and her only way to survive is to embark on an absurd adventure in another country. From another angle, she is a streetwise young woman who is ready to do whatever is necessary to achieve her goal. Alfonsina must quickly find a job and get a visa to bring her son Manolito to New Zealand. Unfortunately reality is as hard in Auckland as it is in Buenos Aires. The audience is on her side, the empathy is immediate; she is charming, energetic, positive and hardworking, but in order to stay in New Zealand she lies, buys a fake visa and steals money.

Alfonsina has multiple identities: she is a clown and represents the negative, the darkness, the corrupt, the grotesque, the animal, the irrational; she is also the trickster, the clever individual who uses her intelligence to survive in a world where values have collapsed; and she is positive too: the naïve, romantic, idealist who believes the world is a fair place to live.

The contradictions of Alfonsina's actions manifest what Joel Schechter explains as the 'Vertrackte Dialektik' or perverted logic.[2] A kind of humour derived from the perspective of the lower classes, where the author blatantly assumes the side of the socially exploited. According to Schechter there is nothing inherently funny about misery, but when misery is portrayed dialectically, as a reflection of class conflict, the 'Vertrackte Dialektik' can become a source of humour. In this way, there is nothing funny in relation to what the Argentinean cleaner goes through in her short stay in Auckland. However, her unfortunate stay in New Zealand is hilarious.

Alfonsina's identity swings between the working class victim of socio-economic crisis and the swindler who takes advantage of the situation. The contradictions of the historical context expose the insufficiency of the character. Alfonsina can be whatever she wants and her identity changes from honest to corrupt according to what is necessary. In this way, Alfonsina's actions are justified in both her excessive idealism and the social and economic reality. As a character, she is close to Bertolt Brecht's Puntila.[3] The landowner of Brecht's comedy is empathetic with human suffering when he is drunk, but an implacable capitalist when sober. The juxtaposition of both identities constitutes the destruction of the continuity of a single, fixed identity. The comedy emerges on the surface as a struggle against the resistance to change and the insistence of ego.[4] For Alfonsina, the social and economic conditions represent an unrealistic, unpreservable ideal. She is honest and dishonest at the same time.

Figure 11 *Alfonsina* by (LAB Theatre, Auckland, 2010, dir: Pedro Ilgenfritz). Photography: Cleide Oliveira.

Dialogue with the audience

According to Mark Fortier there are two general tendencies in understanding reception theory, and they explain a variety of theoretical approaches to reading works of art. The prescriptive tendency seeks to say that there is a right and wrong way to interpret artistic objects; it suggests that there is a faithful reading engaged in revealing a singular hidden truth. Alternatively, the descriptive tendency attempts to understand the way reception works without advocating one particular approach to reading works of art, embracing the notion of iterability without hierarchy between the author and the reader.[5] The descriptive tendency matches the idea of perverted logic and the multiple identities of Alfonsina.

The reading of Alfonsina's actions remained open with the realization that, in her case, neither honesty nor dishonesty will serve as a way to change the world; as with Puntila – his drunkenness did not resolve the situation. This was particularly challenging for viewers who demanded an answer to the dilemma. According to theatre scholar Elizabeth Wright, Brecht wanted his dialectical theatre to disturb the gaze[6] of the spectator by estranging the natural and not offering any moral lesson to the audience.

The ethical discussion of Alfonsina's identity and how she should act was heavily debated in all focus group meetings. The Wellington group was empathetic with Tracy as they believed she was right in protecting her business. In their opinion Alfonsina was stupid and naïve, and they were frustrated with her ignorance, not understanding why she came to New Zealand without a visa. The Auckland group wanted Tracy to be destroyed and saw Alfonsina and Hera as rebel and revolutionary respectively. The Dunedin group saw Alfonsina and Hera as martyrs and as social victims, impotent when facing social and economic crisis. Thus, the cleaner's actions were completely justified by the backdrop of historical exploitation. The Florianopolis group saw the cleaners as corrupt individuals moved by desperation. In their opinion the cleaners lacked moral qualities because the world is corrupt and their only defence mechanism was to behave in the same way. All these identities are distinct and manifest the insufficiency of the characters' singular identity.

The Wellington group was not aware of the historical context of *Alfonsina*. This group wanted more exposition and a clear explanation of her social and economic background. Their limitation in terms of general knowledge beyond their own cultural, social and political context was a clear barrier to their reading of the play. They felt no empathy for Alfonsina when she was deported.

This group examined the play and the predicament of Alfonsina from the perspective of their social class and struggled to negotiate a more dialectical approach to the play. However, this group was empathetic with Tracy and thought her actions made complete sense ('Tracy is faultless')[7] and supported her actions as the common attitude of any boss. At the end, they identified a lack of weight in the story in the last scenes and were disappointed with Tracy's softness, seeing it as incomprehensible.

The Dunedin focus group was completely different. They responded emotionally, and their empathy towards the characters and the play was complete. This group used the play to talk about their own struggles as immigrants in New Zealand; seeing the performance was a mirror reflecting their personal stories. They explained the rationale behind migrating to another country, the idealization of moving to a better place and the dream of finding happiness in starting again. In addition, this group discussed cultural shock, language barriers, difficulty making friends, the daunting experience of finding work and the slowness of immigration services. This group saw Alfonsina as a simpleton with no education – stubborn, naïve, isolated and fearful. They identified a problem in one of the scenes in which Alfonsina is alone at home and speaks in English to the portrait of her son. They argued that when Alfonsina is on her own in other scenes she speaks only in Spanish. 'She makes the English speaking audience disorientated when she speaks in Spanish, and that's the way we feel everyday.'[8] We changed the scene and Andrea Ariel delivered most of the scene in Spanish. We didn't change the scene in which Tracy tries to help Alfonsina at the end, as we were suspicious of the point of view presented by the Wellington group. The next focus group, the Dunedin group repeated the same comment regarding Tracy's character; they didn't believe the boss could suddenly turn into a generous type with no explanation.

The Florianopolis group was similar to the Dunedin group. People who lived overseas and returned to Brazil mainly composed this group. They were also very emotional and identified family expectation as the main source of anxiety in the migrant experience. They spoke about the shame of having a family member return, and the trauma and humiliation of deportation. This group suggested that the intention of the scene when Alfonsina arrives in her apartment was not clear.

In response, we made a small change in the script, cutting the part where Tracy begins to change by showing remorse for her actions, and we kept the part where she goes to Alfonsina's apartment to offer support. At the end of the focus group meeting, they stated that Tracy could not turn into a good person and try to help Alfonsina. It was too romantic according to one member of the group – 'Tracy doesn't have emotional intelligence.'[9]

The performance in Auckland happened a week after the company returned from Brazil and we didn't have time to process all the changes suggested by the meeting in Florianopolis. We managed to adjust the scene when Alfonsina arrives for the first time in her apartment, simplifying it by altering the shape of the scene, and this was achieved without altering the script. They interpreted the play as a comedy with deep cathartic power. This group felt the play was no fiction; all that was presented was pure reality. They were amused by all the scenes in which Tracy is mocked and fooled by the cleaners and obviously were not happy when Tracy turned into a good person. They severely questioned the verisimilitude of Tracy's character before knowing that Alfonsina was deported. They were opposed to the idea that the manager would examine her actions, regret her attitude, and help Alfonsina after firing her. In their opinion it was too idealistic. To them, Tracy's generosity at the end of the play made no sense – 'Bosses don't help the workers at all.'[10]

In general, all focus groups suggested small changes and minor adjustments in the script. They talked about passages of the text, nuances of scenes and details of composition, and we promptly adapted. The analysis shared in all meetings diagnosed very few problems in terms of dramaturgy, except the end of the show.

The first version of the script depicted Tracy gradually becoming guilty after firing Alfonsina and going to her house to offer support. All four groups posed the same question – 'Why does Tracy change her identity so quickly?' Precisely, we felt – Tracy should not change at all.

As a result, the final scene was altered and the show presented a completely different resolution. Tracy in the last draft of the show remains completely selfish and insensitive. We cut the part that showed her realizing her employee's struggle, and the following scene now shows Tracy going to Alfonsina's apartment only to pick up Alfonsina's employee uniform, to reaffirm her authority and to carry on with the humiliation inflicted on the protagonist. Hera tells her that the Argentinean cleaner was taken that morning. Tracy now feels the weight of her guilt and the impulse to be altruistic is merely a mechanism for self-healing, making her actions even more cynical. This new end finds its own irony and shows, with both humour and lightness, a brutal reality. The perverted logic works for Tracy in an upside-down fashion. She tries to change her own identity but what comes across is exactly the opposite. Tracy exposes the insistence of ego and her empathy for Alfonsina is just a manifestation of fear at having her own identity questioned.

Alfonsina was performed with the new ending in Auckland for the last time in September 2010. A focus group was not conducted at this time; instead there was an informal panel discussion after the show. The audience commented on various aspects of the play with emphasis on Tracy's character. They identified how she was pathetic, disgusting and funny. The change suggested in the previous focus groups helped to clarify the grotesque side of Tracy as a clown. The new ending of the story did not give any possibility for didacticism; it kept the integrity of the work by avoiding sentimentalism and moral teaching.

Conclusion

The method of sharing the dramaturgical analysis of the play with the audience allowed the company to exercise what Susan Bennett urges as the ultimate goal of reception theory: the emancipation of spectator.[11] Devising a method in which the public can express their own response towards the work and using it as a tool towards the dramaturgical construction of the play revealed itself as a liberating process. Both sides were able to engage in an egalitarian relationship creating an opportunity to gain experience and knowledge. For the audience, it was an extension of the debate around the themes proposed by the play, a conversation about aesthetics, about theatre and above all, about themselves. For the company, the concept of performance space has had to be extended with current practices such as the ones employed by LAB Theatre. Analysing and developing the play in conjunction with the audience was a way to learn that the complexity of an audience's response is the fundamental issue in the work of the dramaturg.

References

Bennett, Susan. *Theatre Audiences: A Theory of Production and Reception.* London: Routledge, 1990.

Brecht, Bertolt. *Collected Plays: Six – Mr. Puntilla and His Man Matti.* London: Methuen Publishing Limited, 1998.

Fortier, Mark. *Theory/Theatre: An Introduction.* London: Routledge, 2002.

Schechter, Joel. *Durov's Pig.* New York: Theatre Communications Group, 1985.

Wright, Elizabeth. *Postmodern Brecht: A Re-Presentation.* London: Routledge, 1989.

Acts of Spectating

The Dramaturgy of the Audience's Experience in Contemporary Theatre

Peter M. Boenisch

The emergence of relational dramaturgy

It is a truism to maintain that theatre has always paid particular attention to its audiences and spectators, whether in contemporary performance, the theatre avant-garde from a century ago, or virtually any other time we may randomly pick from theatre history. The audience is inevitably theatre's *raison d'être*: without spectators, there simply is no theatrical event. More recently, however, this central place of the spectators in theatre has become the focus of new critical interrogations and academic debates. New forms of so-called participatory theatre sought to 'liberate' the spectators from their role as (allegedly) passive consumers, while the very power of the spectatorial gaze has come under theoretical scrutiny in the wake of Laura Mulvey's seminal 1975 essay on the 'male gaze' and visual pleasure in cinema, which had its repercussions in debates on the performing arts, too, especially in the field of dance.[1] Peggy Phelan went on to dissect, in her 1993 classic study *Unmarked*, the spectator's gaze and the audience's desire within the context of her proposed ontology of performance in its irrevocable presence and the present.[2] Phelan's study influentially tackled some of the inner contradictions of feminist and postmodern critique, which at the time dominated academia and certainly the then-still-emerging discipline of Performance Studies. Analysing her selection of contemporary, primarily physically driven performance work and dance productions along an argument informed by Barthes, Austin and Lacan, she investigated the potential for the spectatorial gaze to get deflected from its habitual voyeuristic consumption of representations, and instead to obtain a different potential as a source of action and site of agency.

Such issues had become particularly pertinent with the ever-growing technical, and in particular, the emerging digital reproducibility of images facilitated by mass media. The more recent advent of new types of digital media, which stylize themselves as 'social', has even further pressed issues of spectating, media consumption and agency into the foreground of our interrogations. It may therefore have been no coincidence that recent years have seen a renewed manifest engagement with the audience from new, post-semiotic perspectives.[3] This crucial trajectory in the stance that the discipline of theatre and performance studies has taken towards the role of the audience is further mirrored by the passage of German theatre scholar Erika Fishcer-Lichte. Departing from her pioneering work on the semiotics of theatre during the 1980s, she arrived via a sustained engagement with phenomenology throughout the 1990s at her 'aesthetics of performativity'. Maintaining a central focus on the performance as the principal object of enquiry, her emphasis has now, however, shifted from an analysis of the (semiotic) structure of the *work* to the (largely phenomenal) *event* of the performance itself, or in German terms: from a structural dissection of the *Inszenierung* towards an experiential recording of the individual *Aufführung*. The latter became, not only for Fischer-Lichte, the core aspect that signifies theatre as an art form. She firmly locates the characteristic of theatre's specific mediality in what she describes as the 'bodily co-presence of actors and spectators'. The classic semiotic investigation of the production, communication and reception of meaning is hence transferred to what Fischer-Lichte calls the 'emergence' of a meaning localized directly within spectating considered as active participation in the process of making meaning, stimulated by an 'exchange of energies' and 'bodily sensing' (*leibliches Spüren*).[4] In place of the traditional idea of a unidirectional transfer of meaning from a single 'sender' (in our case, the playwright or director) to many receivers, Fischer-Lichte now posits a dynamic 'auto-poietic feedback loop' that connects the stage with the auditorium, and the performers with the spectators. Summarizing the challenge of neo-avant-garde performance art of the 1960s and 1970s (Marina Abramović, Joseph Beuys and Fluxus), which are her central examples, she argues that it

> redefined two relationships of fundamental importance to herme-
> neutic as well as semiotic aesthetics: first, the relationship between
> subject and object, observer and observed, spectator and actor;
> second, the relationship between the materiality and the semioticity of
> the performance's elements, between signifier and signified.[5]

This emphasis on redefined relationships indeed touches the core of contemporary dramaturgic challenges. Where Fischer-Lichte makes an important case for a shift, among others, in the central role of the relation between actor and spectator, we should still note that her list of altered relationships expressed in the above quotation still continues to think in dualities and binary oppositions. I propose to further push this thought and to introduce a properly *relational* perspective on dramaturgy. What we witness in contemporary theatre performance is less a mere shift of power between some binary poles, from one point to its other, opposite end. Instead, today's dramaturgic strategies activate the full interplay between the highlighted borders, as for example *between* materiality *and* semioticity. It is precisely no longer a matter of 'from' one end 'to' the other, of 'either / or'. These processes of playful negotiations (in the full Schillerian sense of *Spiel*) are at the heart of what I term relational dramaturgy. I take up prompts both from Nicolas Bourriaud's influential 'relational aesthetics' and from the lesser-known thoughts by Leo Bersani to suggest an understanding of dramaturgy as a relational aesthetic practice.[6] It forges relations, changes relationships and calibrates a dynamic interplay. Far beyond referring to a production's specific interpretative reading of a text, to procedures of adapting or translating a text 'from page to stage' (in a more conventional conception of dramaturgy), and equally far beyond 'reaching out' to audiences not traditionally part of art circles (as in Bourriaud's understanding), relational dramaturgy 'acts' in the full sense alluded to in Eugenio Barba's seminal definition of dramaturgy as a 'weaving of actions'. For him, too, an 'action' is situated on a level beyond the action of the plot or narrative; explicitly, he includes *anything* that affected and impacted, thus: *acts* on the spectator, in his understanding.[7] It is this 'action' which engenders theatre's original 'politicity' (to use a term coined by French philosopher Jacques Rancière) within our present global digital media economy. The relational mode of dramaturgy draws on and particularly highlights a production's spectatorial relations, its fluid shifting between materiality and semioticity. Let us develop these considerations that take us from an 'aesthetics of performativity' towards a concept of 'relational (dramaturgic) action' by turning to three recent theatre productions.

Instance One: *Roman Tragedies*, Toneelgroep Amsterdam

In 2007, Flemish director Ivo van Hove created for Toneelgroep Amsterdam, the principal theatre in the Dutch capital which he has been leading as artistic director since 2001, the *Romeinse tragedies*: a six-hour long compilation of Shakespeare's Roman tragedies (*Coriolanus, Julius Caesar* and *Antony and Cleopatra*), which presented the three plays non-stop, without an interval, with the audience free to roam around the theatre – and the stage. After about half an hour – we had just witnessed Caius Martius's return from his successful battle against the Volsci – neon working lights were switched on for the first scene change. While some stagehands started resetting the scene, we heard some 'muzak' from the loudspeakers, like in a department store, and a female voice welcomed us to today's performance: 'the stage is now open', we were told, and we were invited to cross that fourth wall. On stage, we were able to sit on sofas that made the set reminiscent of some hotel lobby or airport waiting lounge. Also on stage, a bar and a food stall waited for us, even a computer corner where we could access the internet, and a table with the latest newspapers and magazines.

The action of the plays would simply unfold around us in this setting. During the hours that followed, we were able to move between stage and auditorium and to change our position within the theatre space, hence also our positioning – our relation – to the performance. We were able to follow the action from very close sitting on stage or from the distance in our usual theatre chair in the auditorium. We could watch the live action in front of us, but we could instead also 'watch live' from the auditorium on a huge screen mounted above the proscenium, or on one of the many TV monitors that were scattered not only across the stage space but also outside in the theatre foyer, near the bars and toilets. Additionally, an electronic text display between the stage and the mounted screen above provided to those in the auditorium further information on the historic background of the plays (on the Volsci, Coriolanus, the wars, etc.), as well as details on the production ('three hours to Caesar's murder'), while also displaying the actual latest news headlines of the very day and even some live football results.

Instance Two: *Money*, Shunt

With their production *Money*, staged at an abandoned factory in London in October 2009, the British performance collective Shunt presented its version of Emile Zola's 1891 novel *L'Argent* which of course offers some resonances of the current financial crisis. In the spirit of 'devised performance', the original plot around the corrupt stock market speculator Aristide Saccard delivered mere prompts and a rough narrative outline for a highly visual and sensory audience experience. Already as we entered the warehouse space, a gigantic machine in the middle of the space roared, clattered, puffed and rattled. Following a prelude during which we remained seated in front of the machine, we were then asked to climb up the metal staircase, enter the machine and were led into a pitch-black space, amidst ear-spitting noise and wind. The door was closed behind us. Soon the wind and noise stopped, the lights went up and we found ourselves standing within a stunning interior space with classy wooden panelling and some benches on either side, where we eventually settled down. After another while, a kind of foreman entered from another door with some paperwork in his hand. He read out a name. We may therefore have wondered whether he had the list of audience members in front of him, as we of course had to phone in and sign up just to find out the exact location of the factory space to attend the performance. For sure, however, no hand went up. It was only on the third attempt that eventually someone identified himself and was led out of the room. As became obvious very soon, this was of course no 'real' audience member but the play's main character, that future bankruptcy cheat from the novel.

The disjointed sequence of scenes and impressions that followed over the next ninety minutes took place within this interior site, including the floors above and beneath the room as the actual floors became semi-transparent in proper lighting. At some point, we were then also directed to the upper floor to join a party at the height of the financial speculation craze in the plot. Not only the characters but also the audience members got their glass of champagne to sip, and we also soon engaged in some silly ballgame across the huge table (the transparent floor to our seating room downstairs), throwing the little plastic balls that had fallen from above at each other and at the performers. Later, we were once again ushered downstairs. Towards the end, of course, there was the big crash, where Zola's main character reaps his investors' money and flees abroad. In Shunt's version, he also took every single golden door handle with him, so that when – after some turbulent and again noisy final minutes – the light went off, and on again, we found ourselves locked into the space. There was a key on the floor in the centre of the space. We applauded. No one entered. No door was opened. We couldn't get out – until one audience member finally got up, picked up the key and unlocked the door.

Instance Three: *Hotel Medea*, Zecora Ura/ParaActive

The Brazilian-English co-production of the classical *Medea* myth (directed by Persis Jade Maravala and Jorge Lopes Ramos) has been performed since 2007 in several site-specific incarnations in Brazil, the United Kingdom and elsewhere, including during the 2012 London Cultural Olympiad. *Hotel Medea*, which I saw in its 2010 version staged in the London Docklands, starts shortly before midnight and lasts until dawn. The audience gathered at a pier on the Thames. Around midnight, little boats took small groups to the other side of the river. Off the boat, we passed some stations where we got instructions – on dance moves, some chants and how to behave in the 'Zero Hour Market', the first part of the performance. This carnivalesque happening was staged in a warehouse. We interacted with some obscure vendors, card players and jugglers, before Jason's troupes burst in (in an actual car) and made an end to this illustrious and illicit going-on. Jason here was a typical British politician of the easily portrayable Camerblair-type. He went out on his 'peace mission' to yet another foreign country where he would meet Medea and her family. They were in this transatlantic co-production played by the Brazilian cast members. During the first part, we as audience took part in Jason's pursuit and courtship, before we were divided into male and female audience members and assisted the bride or groom's respective pre-wedding rituals, and eventually performed celebratory dances during the wedding. And Medea gave, right among us, the treacherous kiss of death to her family to then follow Jason.

Later on, in Parts 2 and 3 of this night-long production, we were courted ourselves by Jason as potential electors, were photographed with him, and some of us even got his autograph. In another scene, we were brought to bed by our personal nannies who had a mug of cocoa for us, put us into pyjamas, brought us to bed and read us a good-night story – here from a comic book of the *Medea*-myth. Those who did not immediately doze off (some loudly snoring away as the lady in the bunk bed beneath me, of course it must have been around 3 a.m. by then) could bear witness, with our eyes closed, to Jason's (or is it: our fathers?) betrayal and the first argument of the couple. Later again, with dawn beginning to set in, we were led out of the building, following in small groups one of the performers, to escape the furious revenge of

Medea, hiding across the Dockland area. The performers left us behind, and after a while, per mobile phone, we were directed back to the main warehouse, where – together with Jason – we eventually discovered the massacre: we found, indeed, two of the audience members whom we had met and chatted to before in the intervals, lying there in state, surrounded by candles, and we threw flowers onto their 'dead' bodies, before following the eventual witch hunt against Medea, not the least orchestrated here by the media who played a prominent aspect throughout this contemporary take on the old story.

Sensing the 'Mise en Event': Shaking up the spectating relations

These three examples, selected from recent theatre productions, map out a panorama of dramaturgic relations that oscillate between the material performance event and its semiotic meaning. They connect, in different ways, texts, performance (*Aufführung*) and spectators. In a way that is in an additional way exemplary for a trend in current theatre practice in Europe, all three productions staged (more or less) canonical texts, by Shakespeare, Zola and Euripides/Heiner Müller. The principal 'meaning' of these productions, however, was no longer primarily located in their interpretation of the text. The relational components of dramaturgy, which we encounter here, instead exploit the interdependence of representation and theatral presentation, the interplay between the performance as actualized texture of a *mise-en-scène* and the actual event and experience. The *mise-en-scène*, in all three cases, revealed itself as first and foremost a 'mise en event'. The dramatic text and its (dramatic and narrative) textures function as an indispensible dramaturgic mediator that energizes these relations. As a result, the focus shifts from the representation of meaning to the 'sense' generated, or in Fischer-Lichte's term: 'emerging' from the very action of presenting this text in performance. This 'sense' – to be perceived by all of the spectators' senses – reveals the dramaturgic relations as its very trigger. It frames the audience's encounter with the dramatic text and establishes coordinates for our experience of the situation of watching theatre.

Relational forms of dramaturgy are, as our examples have also shown, not at all confined to new, experimental genres of so-called 'devised performance'. In fact, the conventional opposition that pitches the drama of staged text *against* an alternative mode of performance no longer suffices. The dramaturgic strategy of putting relations in play marries, as all three productions demonstrate rather effortlessly, forms and strategies of contemporary theatre-making attributed to 'performance theatre' with the staging of a literary text. We have here seen strategies of site-specific theatre, of physical theatre, or collective improvisation as creative rehearsal strategy applied in the context of staging dramatic texts. As a result, the above instances remind us not to simply assume that the core aesthetic innovations and analytic challenges arise at the very obvious surface, for example through the 'fall of the fourth wall', the suspension of conventional spatial separations or the outright escape from traditional theatre spaces, nor even *per se* in the 'active involvement' of the spectators. Ivo van Hove's production, like all of his works created for a traditional proscenium space at the Amsterdam Stadsschouwburg with one of the leading Dutch ensemble companies, is a particularly apt reminder. The actual, true shift in the relational arrangement does not happen on the very surface, by abandoning one end of the assumed opposition (the 'consuming' spectators gazing from the distance; the dramatic semioticity) and accommodating us, as spectators, on the other (the 'active' spectator participating on his feet; the event of the material performance conditions). Such a crude shift achieves nothing but to reaffirm the spectating relations and underlying ideological hierarchies *ex negativo*. Jacques Rancière challenged, in his widely debated essay 'The Emancipated Spectator', very rightly the fetish of 'audience participation'. In many cases, such productions only create even more 'stultifying' theatre experiences, as he terms it: they may blur boundaries and confuse roles, yet without challenging the underlying (ideological) principles of the hegemonic 'partition of the sensible', as

Rancière calls the dominant ways of perceiving, sensing and making sense of the world.[8]

Consequently, he determinedly argues against idolizing 'interactive' performances where the audience may no longer be seated in conventional arrangements but where still, in effect, 'what the spectator *must see* is what the director *makes her see*'.[9] True emancipation of the spectator for him necessitates shaking up the underlying spectating relations and its implicit hierarchies: it is, we may add, an essentially dramaturgic operation, indeed. It is achieved where the individual intelligence of the spectator *as spectator* in their irreducible distance as thinking interpreters is affirmed without any reservations:

> [In] a theatre, in front of a performance, just as in a museum, school or street, there are only ever individuals plotting their own paths in the forest of things, acts, and signs that confront or surround them. The collective power shared by spectators does not stem from the fact that they are members of a collective body or from some specific form of interactivity. It is the power each of them has to translate what she perceives in her own way, to link it to the unique intellectual adventure that makes her similar to all the rest in as much as this adventure is not like any other.[10]

Van Hove appeals to this very intelligence of the individual 'interpreter' where he employs – in the *Roman Tragedies* and elsewhere – a range of minute realignments and refractions of the theatre space and of conventional viewing arrangements. In their very subtlety, they disclose a relational dramaturgy at work that even in the architectural setting of the traditional late-nineteenth-century building of the Amsterdam Stadsschouwburg achieves to position the spectators no longer outside and opposite of the theatral situation, but that instead aims for a spectating situation which reaffirms the spectator *as spectators* instead of patronizing them as somewhat interactivated pseudo-participants. The director's insistence on the conventional proscenium setting discloses how we on the one hand continue, in his productions, to take our position as spectators *opposite* the production – but on the other hand, we are at the very same time placed right in the middle of a relational dramaturgic framework.

We may be at times directly addressed as friends, Romans and countrymen, and elsewhere, in the *Hotel Medea*-performance, as electorate, wedding guests or Medea's children. Above all, however, these productions acknowledge in their very dramaturgic structure our own very real, 'individual' needs: In the *Roman Tragedies*, we are allowed to come and go, to take a spectating position we *choose*, to zoom in and out again, as it were, to eat and drink. We may browse the newspaper, update our Facebook profile, or check our emails even while Caesar gets slaughtered right next to us. Or, we can make the choice of remaining in the auditorium: yet, even if we decide never to enter the stage during these six hours, we still participate in the changed relational dramaturgy. The very presence of the other spectators on stage is a constant reminder; they become the vicarious spectators that we spectate, a reminder that reaffirms our own 'real' position, too (Figure 12). Similarly careful and caring is the dramaturgic relation that

Figure 12 Watching ourselves watching Hans Kesting as Mark Antony in the *Roman Tragedies*, (Toneelgroep Amsterdam, 2007, dir: Ivo van Hove). Photography: Jan Versweyveld.

shapes *Hotel Medea*: We are taken seriously in our needs as an audience, including the acknowledgement of our tiredness in the middle of the night. We have the opportunity to *really* take a nap, and the opportunity to share the concluding communal breakfast. The production of course also engages our enjoyment of participating in play, in playing roles, and above all in participating in ways that are precisely different from the clichéd 'participatory performances' where no one wanted to sit in the front row.

Here, we were instead invited to enter protected environments of a Schillerian *play* of sense and senses, which I consider as an important factor contributing to the genuine audience emancipation that Rancière himself does not sufficiently take into account, as he privileges rational processes of 'translation' and interpreting. Let us remember that we had received some guidelines and instructions on a leaflet as we entered *Hotel Medea*'s 'Zero Hour Market' around midnight, as well as being instructed in the dance steps – a group dance which allowed us to participate while not being oddly and never carelessly exposed. This contrasts notably with another 'participatory' performance I recently attended (and which shall remain unnamed here) where the audience was invited, not to say coerced, into joining a waltz that mixed performers and spectators. This situation not only uncomfortably, and entirely unnecessarily and in disservice of the production's dramaturgic aim, exposed those who had not brushed up their ballroom skills recently, it was also forgotten to make sure there was an equal number of sexes and participants. Of all people it was me who uncomfortably remained excluded, not finding any partner, not being able to participate, and hence left to have my engagement with the production taken over by anger about an unconsidered relationing that remained utterly stultifying, superficially spectacular, and nothing but an empty gesture. In contrast, the relational dramaturgies we exemplarily encountered with Ivo van Hove and in *Hotel Medea*, acknowledged us fully as spectating subjects – in our needs, but also in our fears and anxieties. They took care of us, and in that sense the 'hotel' metaphor in the very title of *Hotel Medea* confirms the site of meaning in the relational dramaturgy: the 'Hotel' had nothing to do with the interpretation and representation of the Medea-myth here, yet everything to do with our own engagement as spectators staying overnight.

Double exposure: The 'I' of the spectator

In each of the three performances, our 'gaze' and our 'spectating' was in different ways always already inscribed within the field of the production. They require from the spectator a relation to the (re)presented drama that is different from the standard mode of engagement, which is based on identification with whom and what we see. We are no longer the 'recipients' of the classic dramatic dramaturgic paradigm, or in psychoanalytic terms: no longer 'the other' who necessarily complements the stage and gains a position and role (and hence identity) as spectating subject on precisely this ground of being the receiver, of being on 'the other' side of theatre. An explicitly relational dramaturgy hence, at its very core, opens up and prominently highlights a certain 'gap' within the spectator which puts us in an ambiguous distance towards our own 'acting' as spectators. We find here interesting echoes of the famous psychoanalytic account of the logic of signification as proposed by Jacques Lacan. He insisted on the ever gaping hole, the distance between the 'subject of the enounced' and the 'subject of enunciation': between the 'speaking I' and the 'I being spoken'. The symbolic order requires us to ignore, to erase, and to disavow this gap. In a most interesting way, the medium of theatre makes this fundamental structure of signification palpable in an even more highlighted manner. There *always* remains an irreducible, necessary distance between the 'spectating I' and the 'I of the spectator'. We are offered ways of relating, modes of sensing, spectating and engaging. It is this double experience of spectating that blurs the clear separation between representation, presentation, and the very presence and present, between materiality and semioticity. This is exactly where we find the seeds of the (political) 'act' of spectating, and/or of spectating as an act.

The interesting question to be asked is how any specific theatre production negotiates this very rift. To enable, or even assert spectating as an 'act' in the Lacanian sense, or similarly, as 'emancipation' in the Rancièrian terminology, this peculiar 'double experience' needs to be acknowledged in its ultimate incompatibility. Whether in van Hove's leather sofas or in the chequered comfy cushions and blankets in which our maids wrapped us up in *Hotel Medea*: while we were 'participating actively' in the performance, as the usual description and reading goes, our very individual subjectivity as spectators remained acknowledged precisely because the production never suggested that this fundamental experiential gap could be bridged or synchronized. In fact, in some of the cases discussed here, the opposite was true. Then, as an effect, the very process and activity of spectating loses its usual transparency – and the *activity* of spectating gains the momentum of an *act*. Activity as act means not only any response or intervention in the performance, but it is a direct assertion, even provocation of our individual 'response-ability', as Hans-Thies Lehmann famously termed it: we are at once enabled to respond, yet also cannot get away from this response – we need to take the responsibility for our act and our actions as spectators.[11] This responsibility of the spectator is the very moment that makes us abandon the (also relational) attitude of consumption which is so characteristic of our global digital economy of goods and services, including the performative service spectacles provided by our entertainment industries.

But there is also another, and equally political option. The gap in our subjective position may just as well be covered over in performance, and we as spectators are reassured (Rancière would say: stultified) by being allowed to perform an action in accordance with a script. We should here once more revisit Shunt's *Money*, since it discloses a significant difference in its relational structure compared to the other two performances referred to in this essay. The spectators in *Money* have, precisely, *not* been asked nor been allowed to take responsibility for their action beyond some token gestures of 'interactivity'. The distinction becomes very clear: if someone raised their hand in the early moment of the play, thus acting playfully, they already disturbed the play's carefully plotted machinery. At the end, one of the spectators simply *has got to* pick up the key and unlock the door. Our actions of spectating remain organized throughout; they have at all times been administered or carefully managed *for us*. We become 'subjects supposed to watch', to paraphrase Lacan once more: locked into a dramaturgy of audience relationing whose machinery would just as well function without our physical presence. This could not be said about either of the other productions alluded to. As spectators we had been in the midst of things and even literally locked in, yet we remained, as far as our own spectatorial agency and 'response-ability' was concerned, still opposite and excluded: literally locked in yet thereby at the same time left out. Shunt, hence, despite their surface appearance as a devised performance company, at the dramaturgic core of their production confine themselves to the parameters of the 'well made spectacle'.

Action as (scripted) re-action, and in opposition to an 'act', is perfectly exemplified in the forced gesture in the (in a very literal sense) 'key scene' from Shunt's *Money*, where the choice for the spectators is merely illusory and from the start only one predetermined 'choice' can be made – it is thereby that this relational arrangement exactly replicates the dominant dramaturgy of our global liberal society, with its reassuring illusory foundation of a subject position that makes safe the gap of subjectivity and prevents us from falling into the open hole that is the subject. Of course, taking such a more conservative dramaturgic option should not be outright discredited. It remains, above all, another option of relational dramaturgy. Artists as well as audiences have the space to navigate. They can (but also: *must*) take a decision as to whether, and to what degree, we participate, 'act', and – again in a Rancièrian term – 'par(t)-take' in the world, or allow such part-taking and participation. The curious double-bind of a simultaneous, yet incongruent, even contradictory perspective is at the heart of these spectating relations: relational dramaturgies revolve around the very gap between the spectating 'I' which the performance addresses and the perceiving I (or maybe better: 'eye') of the spectator. This gap may be opened or it may be glanced over. Relational dramaturgies stage theatre situations that 'put in play' this very relation: they inescapably expose us to, and hence also gamble with and put on the very line, our ultimately 'real' role as spectators, our own experience of subjective agency. Here, a relational understanding of dramaturgy makes clear that true acts of spectating are not just a matter of explicitly 'political' performances. All the time we find the singular viewing perspective threatened by the blurred sense of being at the same time opposite and still within, even right in the middle of the performance. Whether the dramaturgic relations offer moments of contingent action where spectators are prompted to 'actually act', as in *Roman Tragedies* or *Hotel Medea*, or whether 'superfluous' gestures of action effectively make a perfectly economic framework of a cause-effect logic transparent, as in *Money*, we find acts of spectating emerging where the contingent, incongruous and inconsistent gap between the 'I' as spectator and the spectating 'I' forces us to confront ourselves *as spectators*. Dramaturgic relations prompt us, in fact throw us back, onto our own actions: they force us, the audience, to take ultimate responsibility as 'acting agents', for our own agency, for our actions *as spectators* in this world.

(This essay was first published in *Critical Stages/Scènes critiques*, IATC Webjournal | Revue web de l'AICT, December 2012, Issue No. 7. It is reprinted with kind permission of the issue editor, Patrice Pavis.)

References

Barba, Eugenio. 'Dramaturgy'. *A Dictionary of Theatre Anthropology: The Secret Art of the Performer*. Ed. Eugenio Barba and Nicola Savarese. London and New York: Routledge, 1991, pp. 68–73.

Bersani, Leo. *Is the Rectum a Grave? And Other Essays*. Chicago: University of Chicago Press, 2010.

Bleeker, Maaike. *Visuality in the Theatre: The Locus of Looking*. Basingstoke and New York: Palgrave Macmillan, 2008.

Bourriaud, Nicolas. *Relational Aesthetics*. Trans. Simon Pleasance and Fronza Woods. Paris: Les Presses du Réel, 2002.

Fensham, Rachel. *To Watch Theatre: Essays on Genre and Corporeality*.
Brussels: P.I.E. Peter Lang, 2009.

Fischer-Lichte, Erika. *The Transformative Power of Performance: A New Aesthetics*. Trans. Saskya Iris Jain. Abingdon and New York: Routledge, 2008.

Kennedy, Dennis. *The Spectator and the Spectacle: Audiences in Modernity and Postmodernity*. Cambridge: Cambridge University Press, 2009.

Lehmann, Hans-Thies. *Postdramatic Theatre*. Trans. Karen Jürs-Munby. Abingdon and New York: Routledge, 2006.

Mulvey, Laura. 'Visual Pleasure and Narrative Cinema'. *Screen* 16.3 (1975), pp. 6–18.

Phelan, Peggy. *Unmarked: The Politics of Performance*. London: Routledge, 1993.

Rancière, Jacques. *The Emancipated Spectator*. Trans. Gregory Elliott. London and New York: Verso, 2009.

Read, Alan. *Theatre, Intimacy and Engagement: The Last Human Venue*. Basingstoke and New York: Palgrave Macmillan, 2008.

Afterword

In lieu of a conclusion

Katalin Trencsényi and Bernadette Cochrane

New Dramaturgy: International Perspectives on Theory and Practice was conceived as part of a larger conversation. It sought to identify understandings of the term 'new dramaturgy' a generation after its emergence. It questioned the relationship between new dramaturgy and the dramaturg in different geo-cultural regions – its capacity to empower, or even to alienate the figure of the dramaturg. It queried whether new dramaturgy was the instigator or the reflection of change. The contributors were requested to reflect on current trends, ideas and practices, and to question what the future of dramaturgy might be. These questions, either explicitly addressed, or implied, suffuse the collection.

There was no expectation that any one viewpoint would dominate or that it would be possible to synthesize a unified description for new dramaturgy. The disciplinary diversity of the contributors would seem to have excluded the possibility of consensus but the very nature of the investigation, the multifaceted nature of the subject, demanded commentary from across the world of performance.

Whether science becoming art, chaos becoming theatre, or memory becoming dance, what becomes evident is that interculturalism has a particular valency in a post-mimetic world. However, the essays, musings, case studies, interviews and interrogations supplied by the diverse ensemble of contributors suggested a loosely intersecting conceptualization of the term. All other considerations notwithstanding, new dramaturgy emerged as a commitment to a *total theatre* where every participant, from inception to reception and beyond, shares in the reality of the experience. The one sure commonality between the contributing voices resides in the scrupulous consideration of contemporary dramaturgical practice undertaken by all, in both the particular and the general.

Van Kerkhoven's comments regarding her realization that there was no terminology available to describe those paradigms in all their aspects to a large extent remains true.[1] All of the contributors have developed their own vocabulary and terminology to suit their individual needs and it has not been possible to fuse these disparate views into a coherent singularity. Indeed, to attempt to do so would be to impose an artificial order on the plurality of new dramaturgy.

While the collection has widened the dramaturgical discourse to include voices from (western) Europe, Australia, New Zealand, North America and Israel, the conversation is not over and nor should it be so. We recognize that there are absent voices from the collection. Asia, South America, Africa and the Arabic world have sophisticated and varied dramaturgical traditions. These traditions can expand and invigorate the potential for a pluralism in new dramaturgy perhaps still lacking in current articulations.

But it is not just geo-cultural voices that are absent. Other voices should also be heard, other questions asked – for instance, is there a 'queer' new dramaturgy? What is the role of new media in this transformed but still evolving dramaturgical landscape? Does new dramaturgy have a role to play in either musical theatre or children's theatre? And if so, how might such a dramaturgy be shaped and articulated? What has also become evident is that a history of new dramaturgy is well overdue.

New Dramaturgy: International Perspectives on Theory and Practice sought to question the parameters, the diversity and the understandings of this changed dramaturgical field. We look forward to the new dramaturgical discourse being widened and deepened, and to the inclusion of new voices within this conversation. We look forward to a dramaturgy of constant reassessment and renewal and never the fate of that that once was new.

Reference

Van Kerkhoven, Marianne. 'Introduction', *Theaterschrift, On dramaturgy* 5–6 (1994), pp. 8–34.

Notes

Foreword

1 Van Kerkhoven 1997, pp. 18–25.

2 Eckersall 2006, pp. 283–97.

3 Lehmann and Primavesi 2009, pp. 3–6.

4 Eckersall and Paterson 2011.

5 Turner, 'Porous Dramaturgy: "Togetherness" and Community in the Structure of the Artwork', http://expandeddramaturgies.com/porous - dramaturgy - togetherness – and community – in – the – structure – of – the – artwork (Accessed: 25 June 2013).

6 Lehmann 2006.

7 Van Kerkhoven 1994, p. 12.

8 *Context 01: Active Pooling, the New Theatre's Word-Perfect*, 25–29 August 1993, Amsterdam.

9 Van Kerkhoven 1994, pp. 5–6.

10 Staudohar 1994, p. 187.

11 Van Kerkhoven 1994, pp. 18–20.

12 Gritzner, Primavesi and Roms 2009, p. 1.

13 From the conference call. http://www.dance-tech.net/events/ international-seminar-on-new (Accessed: 18 July 2013).

14 From the conference documentation of the Society of Dance History Scholars. https://sdhs.org/conference2011-welcome (Accessed: 18 July 2013).

15 Conference call. http://www.geisteswissenschaften.fu-berlin.de/en/v/ interweaving-performance-cultures/events/symposia/symposium_ dumb_type.html (Accessed: 29 May 2013).

16 Gritzner, Primavesi and Roms 2009, p. 3.

17 Turner and Behrndt 2010, p. 2.

18 Turner and Behrndt 2010, p. 146.

19　Turner and Behrndt 2010, p. 148.

20　Turner and Behrndt 2010, p. 145.

21　Abirached, R., and Bougnioux D., quoted by J. Danan, p. 13.

22　J. Danan, p. 5.

23　Eckersall, Monaghan and Beddie, excerpt from their *Abstract*.

24　Smart, excerpt from her *Abstract*.

25　Cools, excerpt from his *Abstract*.

26　Turner, excerpt from her *Abstract*.

Chapter 1

1　Lehmann 2006.

2　Abramović in Ayres 2010.

3　Chevallier 2004 and 2006.

4　Handke 1971, pp. 15–16.

5　Biet and Frantz, eds. 2005.

6　Festival d'Avignon 2008.

7　About this moment and about the show, cf. Danan 2011.

8　Maeterlinck, Maurice, in Huret 1982, p. 123. English translation of the quote: Carole-Anne Upton.

9　Artaud 1974, p. 5.

10　Cf. Barbéris 2010, who places the contemporary scene under the double sign of the 'myth of the real' and of the 'myth of the alive'.

11　Cf. Gouhier 1989.

12　Artaud 2010, p. 66.

13　About the two meanings of the word 'dramaturgy', cf. Danan 2010.

14　Dante 2004.

15　Dort 1986, p. 8.

16　About the distinction between playscript and 'text-material', cf. Danan 2010.

17　Cf. Nancy 1993, p. 195.

18　*When We Dead Awaken*, Petit-Quevilly 2005.

19 Cf. Danan 1999.

20 Maeterlinck quoted in Sarrazac 2012, p. 66. The English translation comes from: Alfred Sutro in Maeterlinck, Maurice 1897.

21 Danan, in Corneille/Danan 2006, p. 192.

22 Berlin 2005.

23 Pommerat 2007, p. 15. The quote was translated by Carole-Anne Upton.

24 Cf. Cousin 2012.

25 Cf. Abirached 1978 and Bougnioux 2006.

26 Viripaev 2010. The quote was translated by Carole-Anne Upton.

27 Théâtre National de la Colline's programme, 2011, p. 6. The quote was translated by Carole-Anne Upton.

28 Théâtre National de la Colline's programme, 2011, p. 22. The quote was translated by Carole-Anne Upton.

29 About this play and more generally about the subject of this article, cf. Danan 2013.

30 Danis 2006.

31 Srbljanović 2008.

32 Danan 2002.

Chapter 2

1 Held in Melbourne, 17–20 February 2010. A programme of this event is available at: www.dramaturgies.net.

2 Eckersall, Beddie and Monaghan 2006, p. 1.

3 Eckersall 2008, pp. 283–97.

4 Hewitt, 1979, p. 104.

5 Turner 2010, p. 152.

6 Turner 2010, pp. 149–61.

7 Chaudhuri 1994, pp. 23–31.

8 Hardt and Negri 2000, p. xii.

9 Turner 2010, p. 151.

10 Boenisch 2010, p. 163.

11   Van Kerkhoven 2009, p. 10.

12   Kershaw 2008.

13   Christie, Gough and Watt, eds. 2006.

14   Thiarai 2011, p. 15.

15   Turner and Behrndt 2008, p. 32.

16   Lehmann 2006, pp. 84, 86–7.

17   Freeman 2007, pp. 114–39.

18   Turner and Behrndt 2008, p. 170.

19   As Geertz asserts, 'art and the equipment to grasp it are made in the same shop'. Geertz 1976, p. 1497.

20   Lehmann 2006, p. 100.

21   Wiles has skilfully examined the aesthetic and philosophical implications of this relationship over the course of Western civilization. Wiles 2003.

22   Van Kerkhoven 2009, p. 10.

Chapter 3

1   Van Kerkhoven 1994, p. 8.

2   Devin 1997, p. 219.

3   Van Kerkhoven 1994, pp. 10–12.

4   '. . . que la musique soit un langage . . . à la fois intelligible et intraduisible' Levi-Strauss 1964, p. 26.

5   Devin 1997, p. 219.

6   Proehl 2008, p. 20.

7   Turner and Behrndt 2010, p. 148.

8   Devin 1997, p. 209.

9   See Proehl 2008, p. 86; Shepherd-Barr 2006, p. 210; and Katz 2012, p. 2, among others.

10   Eckersall 2006, p. 285.

11   The English writer and critic, Sir Neville Cardus (1888–1975), contributed numerous reviews and opinion pieces on music to many publications, notably to the *Guardian* and the *Sydney Morning Herald*,

throughout his long career. As accomplished a writer as he was, often amusing, frequently strident in his opinions (both virtues in my opinion), his musical orientation was far removed from my own. He was hostile to a great deal of twentieth-century music, particularly of the atonal variety, which he found 'boring, ungracious, un-humorous, and unimaginative' (Cardus 1957, p. 237). Such works exist but his choice of words suggests an unmistakably negative bias.

12 Cardus 1957, p. 170.
13 Cardus 1957, p. 170.
14 Van Kerkhoven 1994, p. 8.
15 Van Kerkhoven 1994, p. 12.

Chapter 5

1 Jackson 2004, pp. 8–9.
2 I have dealt with this issue in greater detail in Radosavljević *Theatre-Making* (2013).
3 Blažević 2011, p. 18. Manuscript version, the author's translation.
4 McKenzie 2001, p. 50.
5 Radosavljević 2009.
6 Schechner 1973.
7 The last line is a paraphrase of Richard Schechner in rehearsal. Radosavljević, *Dramaturgical Seminar Script*, unpublished document.
8 Schechner's *Programme Note*.
9 'Nude implies being dressed in artistic terms' (Schechner in rehearsal).
10 W. B. Worthen 1997.
11 Schechner in rehearsal.
12 Schechner 2001.
13 Hartley 2005, pp. 26–7; Luckhurst 2006, p. 2; Turner and Behrndt 2008, p. 163.
14 Hartley 2005, p. 26.
15 Hartley 2005, p. 163.

16 Blažević 2011, pp. 11–12. Manuscript version, the author's translation.

17 Blažević 2011, p. 16. Manuscript version, the author's translation.

18 Indeed, when the need arose to create a smaller, touring version of the show, the first to go was the dramaturgy room.

19 Harding and Rosenthal 2011, p. 3.

Chapter 7

1 Mermikides and Smart 2010, p. 28.

2 McConachie 2008, p. 3.

3 LeDoux 1999, p. 25.

4 Surprise and disgust are also sometimes included.

5 Blair 2006, p. 176.

6 Blair 2006, p. 176.

7 LeDoux 1999, p. 19.

8 LeDoux 1999, p. 19.

9 LeDoux 1999, p. 63.

10 Lutterbie 2006, p. 149.

11 Claxton 2006, p. 63.

12 Claxton 2006, p. 66.

13 Eckersall 2011, p. 88.

14 Email exchange with the author in connection with *Women in Devising Symposium*, Kingston University Drama Department, 18 March 2012.

15 Thompson 2011, p. 141.

16 Meyerhold cited in Callery 2001, p. 71.

17 Öhman 2010, p. 710.

18 Öhman 2010, p. 711.

19 Rice and Radosavljević 2010, p. 91.

20 Evans 2001, p. 27.

21 Fischer and Manstead 2010, p. 456.

22 Fischer and Manstead 2010, p. 457.

23 Fischer and Manstead 2010, p. 460.

24 In Smart 2010, p. 172.

25 Claxton 2006, p. 65.

26 Lutterbie 2006, p. 153.

27 Lewis 2010, p. 743.

28 Paula Rego 1994.

Chapter 9

1 Campos and Shepherd-Barr 2006, p. 245.

2 Van Kerkhoven 2009, p. 10.

3 I follow Shepherd-Barr in using the term 'play' here, although 'performance' would probably be more appropriate given the range of work encompassed under this title.

4 Shepherd-Barr 2006, p. 199.

5 Shepherd-Barr 2006, p. 201.

6 Ronconi cited in Shepherd-Barr 2006, p. 200.

7 Turner and Behrndt 2008, p. 25.

8 Other companies and practitioners that might be added to the list are Curious (with their *Autobiology* project), the Clod Ensemble (particularly with their *Performing Medicine* project), Analogue (with *2401 Objects* (2009)), David Rosenberg (with *Ether Frolics* (2005) and *Electric Hotel* (2011)) and Third Angel (with *9 Billion Miles from Home* (2007) among others). It is unclear whether Shepherd-Barr would classify all of these as 'alternative science plays', though this may become apparent in her forthcoming special issues of *Interdisciplinary Science Reviews*, co-edited with Bartleet (2013 and 2014).

9 For Fuchs, 'each substantial change in the way character is represented on stage and major shift in the relationship of character to other elements of dramatic construction of theatrical presentation – constitutes ... the manifestation of a change in the larger culture concerning the perception of self and the relations of self and world' (Fuchs 1996, p. 8).

10   Mamet 1998, pp. 1–11.

11   The narrative principles of the Aristotelian dramatic tradition are also explicated in Edgar 2009 and McKee 1999, among others.

12   Dyson 2009, p. 4.

13   Fielding 2010, p. 8.

14   The more technically correct term for this is haematopoietic stem cell transplant; particularly as recent technologies allow these stem cells to be harvested from the donor's blood rather than from the bone marrow. We use the term BMT to avoid confusion with more controversial (fetal) stem cell technologies and for simplicity.

15   For more detailed information on this particular disease and form of treatment, including survival rates, see Stein and Forman, and Fielding and Goldstone (both 2008).

16   Shepherd-Barr 2006, p. 200.

17   Ede 2010, p. 137.

18   Sheets-Johnstone 2009, p. 300.

19   Quoted in Ede 2010, p. 150.

20   This can be heard at chimeranetwork.org/hidden-music (Accessed: 9 July 2013).

21   See Hunt and Hermann (2011) for a comprehensive introduction to the practice of data-sonification.

22   Abnormally low level of white blood cells called neutrophils (involved in immunity), which, in this case, is an effect of both the disease itself and the treatment.

23   Mermikides 2010.

24   Another 'dramatic' quality that has been attributed to the track is a sense of 'conflict'. In a related project led by P. Solomon Lennox at the University of Exeter, the two participating MA students articulated this as 'a sense of dilemma' and a 'binary opposition'. This was expressed in their physical improvisations created in response to various aspects of the track and its biographical basis. The results can be viewed at http://www.youtube.com/watch?v=X0Jp7ob9Xp8&feature=youtu.be (Accessed: 9 July 2013).

25 More commonly, six rather than five markers are tested. There is some variation in this depending on the exact circumstances of the prospective recipient and whether the potential donor is related or not.

26 Two recent publications attest to Cage's significance to sound, performance and artistic practice more generally (Larson 2012 and Haskins 2012). Nyman (1999) deals with his sound-based practice, but is insightful to the performance practitioner too.

27 Leukaemias are malfunctions of haematopoiesis, the process by which haematopoietic stem cells (HSC) in the bone marrow mature into the different blood cells we find in the blood. These malfunctions (caused by random genetic mutation) result in a proliferation of immature (and therefore useless) white blood cells. HSCs are also the cells which are transplanted in the case of BMT. Donor cells take root in the recipient's bone marrow, which has been ablated by aggressive chemo and radiotherapy, essentially 're-booting' their haematopoietic system. An odd result of this is that the recipient is a 'chimera' with two DNA systems co-existing in the body – and in Milton's case, with female blood within a male body.

28 Ede 2010, p. 150, also alluded to in Meynell and Skinner 2005, p. 79.

29 Mauro 2001.

30 This extract of *Cell Monologue* can be viewed at http://chimeranetwork. org/bloodlines (Accessed: 9 July 2013).

31 Mauro 2011.

32 Lehmann 2006, p. 85.

33 This argument runs parallel to the long-standing belief among some narrative theorists that story structure mirrors patterns of psychological development – see Bettelheim (1975) and Campbell (1968) in particular.

34 Lehmann 2006, p. 27.

35 Shepherd-Barr 2006, p. 216.

36 This is the argument of Edwards whose *Artscience* sees art-science interdisciplinarity as one of the key catalysts for innovation in the post-Google era.

37 Ede 2010, p. 147.

38 Shepherd-Barr 2006, p. 211.

Chapter 10

1 Turner and Behrndt 2008, p. 3.

2 Turner and Behrndt 2008, p. 3.

3 Van Kerkhoven 2009, p. 11.

4 Etchells 2009, p. 76.

5 Muecke 2004, p. 16.

6 Eckersall 2006, p. 292.

7 Etchells 2009, p. 72.

8 Etchells 1997, p. 204.

9 Berndt and Berndt 1989, p. 4.

10 Morphy 2008, p. 109.

11 Sorensen 2009.

12 Myers 2005, p. 10.

13 Marrugeku Programme Notes, 2009.

14 Gordon 1997, p. 8.

15 Gordon 1997, p. xiv.

16 Gordon 1997, p. 8.

17 Gordon 1997, p. 22.

18 Marrugeku 2006.

19 Gordon 1997, p. 22

20 Moffatt 1999, p. 65.

21 Summerhayes 2007, p. 15.

22 Durand 1999, p. 104.

23 Moffatt, 1999.

24 Durand 1999, p. 105.

25 Summerhayes 2007, 124–5

Chapter 11

1. 'Les ballets C de la B in 15 minutes'. http://m.lesballetscdela.be/en/news/142 (Accessed: 08 Jan 2014.)
2. Alain Platel, interview with Lou Cope, Ghent, 24 March 2006.
3. Nienke Reehoorst, choreographic assistant to Sidi Larbi Cherkaoui and Damien Jalet on *Babel (words)*, on which I was dramaturg.
4. I immediately registered concern about this, as had others, but Koen was clear that he wanted to perform, so the job became about trying to make this work.
5. I'm always aware of when *'you'* becomes *'we'*. I'm careful about it, but eventually it does happen. It is *his* show that *we* are making.
6. Designed by Wim van de Capelle, the décor was influenced by the eerie and silent images of photographer Gregory Crewdson. Koen wanted to capture both the stillness and the enormousness of these moments, and we made a link between the way they were always about 'the moment just after something important had happened' – just like *Au-delà*.

Chapter 12

1. Assmann 2000, p. 46.
2. Assmann 2000, p. 72.
3. Assmann 2000, p. 76.
4. Radosavljević 2009, p. 50.
5. Marianne Van Kerkhoven 1994a, p. 144.
6. Cools, programme note, 2005b, (no page numbering).
7. The central role of the witness function in ritual theatre practices but also for instance in the court deserves a full-length discussion on its own. Part of my own artistic research with Canadian choreographer Lin Snelling focuses on this. See also our website: www.rewritingdistance.com
8. Barba 1991, p. 68.
9. Murakami 2005, p. 376.
10. Van Kerkhoven 1997, pp. 20–1, author's translation from French.

11 One of my recent dialogues of the ongoing series of *body:language talks*, commissioned and published by Sadler's Wells was with the British theatre director and puppeteer Sue Buckmaster about the use and potential of puppets in contemporary performance practices. Through her I discovered *Puppet, An Essay on Uncanny life* by Kenneth Gross, to which this refers.

12 The second part of this chapter was originally commissioned by the German choreographer Stephanie Thiersch as a research document for her project *Deconstructing the best of us* and was part of a short lecture for the Globalize Cologne Festival 2012 with its theme *Remembering Tomorrow*.

13 Not by coincidence, grief and mourning have been a major theme in several of the dance productions I accompanied as a dramaturg. For a more extensive version of this topic, see the article *Giving a Voice to Mourning* (Guy Cools 2011).

14 Van Kerkhoven 1994b, p. 9, author's translation from Dutch.

15 Stalpaert 2009, p. 124.

16 Cools 2005a.

Chapter 13

1 Taylor 2004, p. 19.

2 Hodge and Smith, Wrights & Sites, 2012.

3 Thiarai 2011, p. 16.

4 This is not a term we used unproblematically. Radosavljević has drawn on Nancy to discuss the ways in which a porous or 'relational' dramaturgy produces an 'inoperative community' ('being-in-common' as opposed to 'common being') (Radosavljević 2013, p. 188), and my discussion of the works' negotiation towards community is indebted to these ideas. However, in this chapter, I also use the word 'community' to refer to a provisional, imaginary whole, rather like the mapping of a city, with all the problems and advantages that this implies (this is close to Benedict Anderson's conception of the 'imagined community'(Anderson 1983)). When used in this sense, I have placed this term within parentheses to indicate this problematic.

5 Turner and Radosavljević 2012.

6 Another term that must be qualified, with the acknowledgement that the freedom implied by 'public space' is usually compromised by private, commercial or other regulatory interests.

7 This is a generalization, and does not account for other factors that might contribute to the strength or weakness of the structure.

8 Bhagwat 2009, p. 299.

9 Anon 1980, p. 92.

10 Anon 1980, p. 91.

11 The metaphor conceived in terms of rocks and water leads to this assumption, though clearly disparate grains could pass through a porous structure.

12 Bhagwat 2009, p. 299.

13 Winnicott 1960.

14 See Pearson 1997, pp. 95–6.

15 Wrights & Sites 1997.

16 Aristotle, cited in Crick 1983, p. 5.

17 Wrights & Sites 2003, 2006.

18 We were indebted to John Hall, then Head of Dartington College of Arts, for drawing our attention to our use of the imperative tense. Subsequently we sought to use a combination of tenses ('What if you ...?' 'The city might be imagined as ...' 'Sometimes we have ...') to avoid implications of a directive approach.

19 This could also suggest the intrinsic porosity of the play text, which exists to be re-interpreted on every occasion. Some texts invite reinvention and some resist it, but all possess this quality to some degree. However, the staging of the play text does not usually retain this degree of porosity as the voids are 'cemented' by performance. Ironically, one might consider many play texts to be 'porous' in rehearsal, but less so in performance. However, the interpretative contribution of the audience means that some degree of porosity is always present.

20 LIGNA 2008.

21 LIGNA 2012.

22 Darby 2012.

23 Wrights & Sites 2007.

24 Wrights & Sites 2010.

25 Wrights & Sites 2010.

26 Bauman 2012.

27 Winnicott 1960.

28 Turner 2004, p. 387.

29 Occupy Exeter used the 'embrace' both literally and performatively when they offered hugs to public sector workers entering the Royal Devon and Exeter Hospital as a protest against reductions in public sector pensions. This 'peaceful activism' was a performative 'embrace' of the public sector, as well as a literal 'embrace' of individual workers, and was directed at raising awareness among both workers and hospital visitors.

30 For instance, though taking place within a purpose-built installation rather than on the street, Shunt's *The Architects* (2013), played an explicit game of entrapment, where the audience was divided, herded into dark spaces and subjected to eerie and threatening, if humorous, communication via a TV screen. The fact that the audience was indeed trapped, with no obvious route out of the space except back down a dark corridor and through a maze, could either enhance the experience of the game or inhibit it, depending on how the individual felt about their position.

31 Bauman 2012, p. ix.

32 Theatrum Mundi/Global Street 2013.

33 Turner and Hodge 2012, p. 117.

34 Dave Beech (2008, p. 3) distinguishes between the 'collaborative' and the 'participatory' making a similar distinction to mine between 'limestone' and 'sandstone' porosity (though 'collaborative' work may go further than either in terms of shared authorship).

35 Boym 2008, p. 6.

Chapter 14

1 Bennett 1990, p. 204.

2 Schechter 1995, p. 32.

3 *Mr. Puntila and His Man Matti (Herr Puntila und sein Knecht Matti)* by Bertolt Brecht, written in 1940.

4 Schechter 1985, p. 34.

5 Fortier 2002, p. 134–5.

6 'Disturbing the Gaze' is a phrase used by Elizabeth Wright in her book *Postmodern Brecht: A Re-Presentation* (1989) describing the tendency the audience has to impose their own gaze on the stage happenings, transferring their own fantasies onto the characters, creating empathy and making the images on stage seem natural. According to Wright, that is exactly what Brecht wants to stop (Wright 1989, pp. 55–6).

7 Interview participant, interview with Pedro Ilgenfritz, Wellington, 6 March 2010.

8 Interview participant, interview with Pedro Ilgenfritz, Dunedin, 28 March 2010.

9 Interview participant, interview with Pedro Ilgenfritz, Florianopolis: Brazil, 20 July 2010.

10 Interview participant, interview with Pedro Ilgenfritz, Auckland, 14 August 2010.

11 Bennett 1990, p. 213.

Chapter 15

1 Mulvey 1975, pp. 6–18.

2 Phelan 1993.

3 Key recent publications include, in particular, Fensham 2009; Read 2008; Kennedy 2009; and Bleeker 2008.

4 Fischer-Lichte 2008. In particular, see Chapter 5, 'The Emergence of Meaning', pp. 138–59.

5 Fischer-Lichte 2008, p. 17.

6 See Bourriaud (2002) and Bersani (2010).

7 Barba 1991, pp. 68–73.

8 See Rancière 2009, p. 8.

9   Rancière 2009, p. 14, original emphasis.

10 Rancière 2009, p. 17.

11 Lehmann 2006, p. 185.

Afterword

1   Van Kerkhoven 1994, p. 8.

Contributors

Koen Augustijnen has been working closely with *les ballets C de la B* since 1991, initially as a dancer, since 1997 as one of the company's house choreographers. His choreography *Bâche* (2004) brought him an international breakthrough, followed by *IMPORT/EXPORT* (2006), *Ashes* (2009) and *Au-delà* (2012). In addition to his work with *les ballets C de la B*, he often joins forces with theatre companies, such as Toneelgroep Amsterdam (Ivo van Hove) and Tg STAN to name but a few. Since 2013 he has been working freelance, and directed a dance solo in Australia for Dalisa Pigram of the Marrugeku Company, titled *Gudirr Gudirr*. His most recent work is *Badke*, for ten Palestinian dancers, produced by the Royal Flemish Theatre and *les ballets C de la B*.

Ada Denise Bautista studied Theater Arts at the University of the Philippine's Dulaang UP and obtained a Masters at Sorbonne Paris 3. She did stage management, set paintings, billboard and mask design, acting (for Anton Juan, Tony Mabesa, Alexander Cortez, Ogie Juliano), and was Philippine production manager for the Royal Shakespeare Company's tour of *Henry V*. She worked mainly as assistant director for movies (*Noriega*, *Brokedown Palace*, *13 Days*, *Whipped Cream*, *Général Leclerc* and *L'Empire du Tigre*.) She moved to Paris for Ecole Supérieure des Etudes Cinématographique. Currently she is working as assistant editor for TF1 and makes DVD coverage of stage plays. (*L'Illusion Comique* by Corneille, *Roaming monde*, *Cinéma and Jojo le Récidiviste*, both plays by Joseph Danan).

Melanie Beddie is a graduate of Sydney University and VCA. She was a co-founder of the $5 Theatre Co. and is artistic director of the independent theatre company The Branch. She works as an actor, dramaturg and director. She has directed at the MTC, Playbox, Hothouse,

La Mama, Theatreworks and in numerous other venues across Australia. As a dramaturg she co-founded *The Dramaturgies Project*. In 2004 she received a Dramaturgy Fellowship from the Australia Council. In 2009 she received the Gloria Fellowship from NIDA. Melanie is currently a lecturer in theatre at the VCA School of Performing Arts (Theatre), and is completing a PhD at Latrobe University.

Peter M. Boenisch is professor of European Theatre at the University of Kent, where he was, with Paul Allain and Patrice Pavis, one of the founding directors of the European Theatre Research Network (ETRN). His research explores the aesthetics and politics of contemporary theatre performance, drawing on critical philosophy by Slavoj Žižek and Jacques Rancière. His recent essays discuss works by theatre directors Thomas Ostermeier, Michael Thalheimer, Frank Castorf, Jan Fabre, Volker Lösch, Rimini Protokoll, William Forsythe and others. With Lourdes Orozco, he co-edited the essay collection *Border Collections – Contemporary Flemish Theatre* (2010).

Guy Cools is a dance dramaturg and associate professor for Dance Studies for the Research Institute Arts in Society of the Fontys School of Fine and Performing Arts in Tilburg, Netherlands. Having previously worked as a dance critic, curator and policy maker for dance in Flanders, he now works as a production dramaturg in Europe and Canada. He also developed a series of workshops that aim to support artists and choreographers in their creative process.

Lou Cope is a dramaturg, mentor, writer and teacher based in both Belgium and the United Kingdom. Her previous work includes being dramaturg to Sidi Larbi Cherkaoui and Damien Jalet on the award-winning *Babel (words)* designed by Antony Gormley; to Lisi Estaras of *les ballets C de la B* on *Soup*; to Fleur Darkin and the Darkin Ensemble; and to Phoenix Dance Theatre. She teaches process and dramaturgy on a number of theatre and dance courses across Europe, and also works as a workshop leader, mentor and coach. Her previous publications include: 'Looking inward, outward, backward & forward with Alain

Platel': for *Contemporary Theatre Review* (2010); 'Mapping the Multiple' – a chapter in *Making Contemporary Theatre* published by Manchester University Press (2010), and 'Reflections on Collaborative Process' for the Belgian journal *A Prior* (2009).

Joseph Danan is a senior professor at the Department of Theatre Arts at the Sorbonne Nouvelle University – Paris 3 (Institut d'Etudes théâtrales). He is also a playwright and a dramaturg. He has written numerous plays, as well as novels and poetry. Among his most recent publications are: *Qu'est-ce que la dramaturgie?*, *L'Atelier d'écriture théâtrale* (co-written with Jean-Pierre Sarrazac), *Entre théâtre et performance: la question du texte*, and three children's plays (*Les Aventures d'Auren, le petit serial killer, Jojo le récidiviste, A la poursuite de l'oiseau du sommeil*), all published by Actes Sud. Some of his plays and books have been translated into Spanish, Portuguese and German.

Dramaturgs' Network was co-founded by Hanna Slättne and Katalin Trencsényi in 2001 to share ideas, knowledge, resources and skills in current dramaturgical practices in the United Kingdom. The d'n aims to provide support for theatre-makers functioning in the role of dramaturg or literary manager, and educational professionals involved in dramaturgical practice. The Dramaturgs' Network explores dramaturgy through information, debate and practice. To find out more, please visit: www.dramaturgy.co.uk, alternatively, you can find the d'n on Facebook or Twitter (@dramaturgs_net).

Peter Eckersall is professor of Theatre Studies at The Graduate Centre, The City University of New York. His research interests include Japanese theatre, experimental performance and dramaturgy. His publications include *Theorising the Angura Space: avant-garde performance and politics in Japan 1960–2000* (Brill Academic, 2006), Kawamura Takeshi's *Nippon Wars and Other Plays* (Seagull Books, 2011) and *Theatre and Performance in the Asia-Pacific: Regional Modernities in the Global Era* (co-authored with Denise Varney, Barbara Hatley and Chris Hudson, Palgrave, 2013). He is visiting fellow at the International Research

Centre Interweaving Performance Cultures at the Freie Universität. He is the resident dramaturg for the performance group Not Yet It's Difficult (NYID), whose performance and media works are widely known in Australia, Asia and Europe. Peter is a co-founder of *The Dramaturgies Project*.

Yolanda Ferrato is a director, dramaturg and theatre administrator working in Canada and the United Kingdom. She founded Intersection Theatre, Toronto, and is an artistic associate of the London Quebec Culture Festival. In the United Kingdom she produced original performances at the Edinburgh Fringe Festival and Southwark Playhouse, and worked with Theatre 503's literary department. She has worked on the UK premieres of several Canadian works including *The Ventriloquist* (director, Rosemary Branch Theatre), *Scorched* (assistant director/dramaturg, Dialogue Productions/Old Vic Tunnels) and *Porcupine* (translator, LQCF). In Canada she directed *S-27* (Intersection Theatre/Toronto Fringe) and has worked with Tarragon Theatre and Theatre Gargantua. Yolanda holds an MFA in Theatre Directing from the University of Essex, and a BFA in Acting from the University of Windsor. She has studied at the GITIS Institute, Moscow, with the Academy at The Stratford Festival of Canada, and participated in the Royal Court's Young Writers' Programme.

Pedro Ilgenfritz is a Brazilian actor, theatre director, dramaturg, lecturer and researcher based in Auckland, New Zealand; a graduate of Bachelor in Performing Arts/Acting (UDESC/Brazil) and Masters in Theatre Arts/Directing (Toi Whakaari & Victoria University of Wellington). His work is focused on a style that might be termed *the laughter of the body* – a consistent series of physical exercises, improvisations, mask-driven experiments, clowning, philosophical study and dramaturgical research that is close to the popular roots of theatre in comedy. Pedro is the director of *LAB: Theatre*, and together the company produced *Alfonsina* (2009), *One by One* (2011) and *Comic Interludes* (2012). His directing credits include *The Remedy Syndrome*

(Chapman Tripp Award nominee 2005) and *Harmonious Oddity* (Touch Compass Dance Trust, 2008). He is currently a lecturer at UNITEC – Performing and Screen Arts Department in Auckland, New Zealand.

Gad Kaynar is the outgoing Chair of the Theatre Arts Department, Tel Aviv University (2009–13), and initiator of Dramaturgical Studies at the Institutfür Theaterwissenschaft, LMU University in Munich, and Venice International University. His book publications include: *Another View: Israeli Drama Revisited*, with Prof Zahava Caspi (The Ben Gurion University Publication, 2013); *The Cameri Theatre of Tel-Aviv* (2008). Kaynar is the former dramaturg (1982–2005) of The Israeli National Theatre Habima, The Cameri Theatre of Tel Aviv, The Khan Theatre in Jerusalem, as well as of numerous festivals in the country; co-editor of the quarterly *Teatron*; a poet, actor, director and translator. For his Ibsen translations and research, he was appointed Knight First Class of the Royal Norwegian Order of Merit (2008).

Andrea Pelegri Kristić is an actor and translator, currently completing her PhD studies at the Pontificia Universidad Católica de Chile. In 2006, she co-funded the theatre company *Tiatro*, which has since won awards in various festivals in Chile (2006, 2008). She has published scholarly articles, and translated several plays and books on theatre and performance theory. She is currently part-time professor at Pontificia Universidad Católica de Chile.

Alan Lawrence is a composer. In recent years he has written mainly for concert performance but has worked in film, theatre and television both in Britain and in Australia. He has composed music for most of the major British television channels and for theatre companies ranging from The Old Vic to the Warehouse Theatre Croydon, among many others, and in Australia, for the Queensland Theatre Company. While music remains his primary preoccupation he enjoys writing and talking about theatre, for which he nurtures a deep affection both as contributor and student of the discipline.

Alex Mermikides is senior lecturer in Drama at Kingston University, where she teaches undergraduate and postgraduate courses in devising and performance writing. Her creative practice involves dramaturgy with devising companies (most recently with Lightwork Theatre) and performance writing (her work has been performed at Battersea Arts Centre, Lyric Hammersmith and on BBC Radio 4). Her research interests lie in contemporary performance practices and she has published on the subject of devising and is editor, with Jackie Smart, of *Devising in Process* (Palgrave Macmillan, 2010).

Paul Monaghan is a professional theatre maker, director and dramaturg. Until recently he was senior lecturer in Theatre, and head of Postgraduate Studies and Research, in the School of Performing Arts (Theatre), Victorian College of the Arts, University of Melbourne. Paul's teaching and research areas include dramaturgy and the dramaturgical intelligence, theatre making, directing, Greek tragedy in performance (in antiquity and in the modern world), space and light in theatre, and philosophy and theatrical practice. Paul is a co-founder of *The Dramaturgies Project* (http://www.dramaturgies.net), and co-convenor/co-editor of *Double Dialogues* (conference and journal: http://www.doubledialogues.com), an ongoing project linking academic discourse with arts practice.

Ana Pais holds a degree in Literature and an MA in Theatre Studies from the University of Lisbon. Between 2003 and 2004 she worked as a theatre critic for the Portuguese newspapers *Público, Expresso* and *Sol*. From 2005 to 2010 she was assistant professor at the Escola Superior de Teatro e Cinema, She is the author of the *Discourse of Complicité. Contemporary Dramaturgies* (Colibri, 2004). Currently she is completing her PhD on the performativity of affect in the theatre at the University of Lisbon. In the context of this programme, she was visiting scholar at NYU – Tisch School of the Arts in 2011–12.

Duška Radosavljević is a lecturer in Drama and Theatre Studies at the University of Kent. She has worked as dramaturg at Northern Stage

(2002–5), education practitioner at the Royal Shakespeare Company (2005–6) and, since 1998, as a theatre critic for *The Stage Newspaper*. She is the editor of *The Contemporary Ensemble: Interviews with Theatre-Makers* (Routledge, 2013) and the author of *Theatre-Making: Interplay Between Text and Performance in the 21st Century* (Palgrave Macmillan, 2013).

Jackie Smart is a principal lecturer in drama in the School of Performance and Screen Studies at Kingston University, where she teaches devising, acting and postmodern performance to undergraduate and postgraduate students. She currently holds the post of director of studies for dance and drama. She is the co-editor, with her colleague Alex Mermikides, of *Devising in Process* (Palgrave Macmillan, 2010), a book which documents and analyses the creative processes of eight professional devised projects from start to finish. She has published work on a range of companies including Gecko, Forced Entertainment and Random Dance, and has created devised productions in collaboration with composers, choreographers and film-makers.

Rachael Swain is a founding member and co-artistic director (with Dalisa Pigram) of Marrugeku. Rachael directs Marrugeku's productions, created in situ in remote Indigenous communities, including *Mimi* (1996), *Crying Baby* (2000), *Burning Daylight* (2006) and *Buru*, co-directed with Dalisa Pigram (2010). Rachael is also a founder and director of Stalker Theatre in Sydney; her large-scale dance, circus and multimedia productions have included *Blood Vessel* (1998), *Incognita*, co-directed with Koen Augustijnen (2003) and the Chinese Australian martial arts and dance theatre thriller *Shanghai Lady Killer* (2010), created together with Tony Ayres. Rachael has curated Stalker's trilogy of Dance Dramaturgy Laboratories in Sydney (2010–14). She is the dramaturg and creative producer for Marrugeku's *Gudirr Gudirr* (2013). She is the director of the company's Listening to Country Lab in Broome, as a key component of her Australian Research Council funding to further researching dramaturgy as Listening to Country at a time of global environmental change.

Cathy Turner is a senior lecturer at the University of Exeter. Her primary research areas are dramaturgy and site-specific performance. In 2013 she and Duška Radosavljević (University of Kent) led a research network on 'Porous Dramaturgy: "Togetherness and Community in the structure of the artwork"', in partnership with Shadow Casters (Croatia) and Tinderbox (N. Ireland), funded by AHRC. Previous publications include *Dramaturgy and Performance*, co-written with Synne K. Behrndt (Palgrave, 2008) and a co-edited issue of *Contemporary Theatre Review* (again with Behrndt), on the subject of 'new dramaturgies', in 2010. She is a founder-member of artists' collective Wrights & Sites whose work concerns place and space. Their work includes *A Mis-Guide to Anywhere* (2006) and *An Exeter Mis-Guide* (2003), as well as performances, curation/mentoring and more recently, public art works.

Carole-Anne Upton is dean of the School of Media and Performing Arts and professor of theatre at Middlesex University. Her research focuses on contemporary theatre practice, translation for performance, directing methodologies, performance and social justice, and theatre and ethics. Her recent work has examined documentary theatre, and performance and 'the real' in Northern Ireland. She has previously published on modern Irish drama, and postcolonial anglophone and francophone theatre in Africa and the Caribbean. She is founder and principal editor of *Performing Ethos: An international journal of ethics in theatre and performance*. She maintains a passion for directing and her recent practice includes a small-scale tour of *Jordan* by Moira Buffini with Anna Reynolds, and a production of her own translation of *The Blind* by Maurice Maeterlinck. She is currently working on international projects including the first English translation of Armand Gatti's *Maze* plays, set in Derry during the 1981 Hunger Strikes.

Index